T0128962

UNFLINCHING TRUST

A Canadian biography of struggle to trust

"God is working this unflinching
trust within me."
-Dave Stewart, October 26, 1942

MELODIE VERVLOET

WESTBOW
PRESS®
A DIVISION OF THOMAS NELSON
& ZONDERVAN

WestBow Press books may be ordered through booksellers or by contacting:

WestBow Press
A Division of Thomas Nelson & Zondervan
1663 Liberty Drive
Bloomington, IN 47403
www.westbowpress.com
844-714-3454

Scripture taken from the King James Version of the Bible.

ISBN: 978-1-6642-5775-7 (sc)
ISBN: 978-1-6642-5777-1 (hc)
ISBN: 978-1-6642-5776-4 (e)

Library of Congress Control Number: 2022903006

Print information available on the last page.

WestBow Press rev. date: 03/07/2022

DEDICATION

I would like to dedicate this book to
the people who have been impacted the most
by the lives of Dave and Melva Stewart –
their children
Donald Gordon Stewart, (along with his wife Dolores),
and
Ardith Darlene Seeley

ACKNOWLEDGEMENTS

I would like to acknowledge the following for their
stories and encouragement in putting
this book together:

The Descendants of:
Donald and Hazel Dye
Dave and Melva Stewart
Dick and Kay Bittle
Vince and Blanche Bittle
Ruel and Winnie Dye

Special Thanks to:

Mrs. Melva Brewster for lending me her father
Ruel's notes on his early years,
Hon. Preston Manning, for use of his father's sermon,
plus, several farmers, friends, and pastors
in the Langdon, Bowden, Innisfail, and Vulcan areas,
"Langdon Through the Years" History Book,
the Trail Historical Society, CJAT,
Prairie Bible Institute archives, Harvester Mission, and the
Calgary Prophetic Bible Institute website,
my parents, Don and Dolores Stewart, for the use of
Dave, Melva's, and Doris' diaries and letters, and my
Aunt Ardith for her history album and notes.

PROLOGUE

"I think you're the first one who's ever read her diaries," my mother said to me over the phone. I had asked to see my grandmother's diaries, with the desire to turn them into a story. It did not come as a surprise that I was the first, due to the tiny handwriting which I could not read without the aid of a magnifying glass.

As I read on, I became fascinated with all the details of life in the 1930s and 40s, including entries about Hitler, the war, and dust storms. However, what started as an interesting history lesson, unfolded into deep spiritual truths. I found the words shedding off layers of modern-day Christian thoughts in my mind and driving me to a depth of a Christian reality and brawniness I knew nothing about.

I wept. I repented of my selfishness. And I took up her hope. The hope that there is so much more in my future than this world. This world is temporal. Very temporal. There are much greater things to come. Whatever I must go through here is not worthy to be compared to the glory that will follow.

My grandparent's lives were short, but they were not lived in vain. They have touched my heart. And my prayer is, not mine only, but all who read these pages.

Caveat

The following story is based on Melva, Doris, and Dave's diaries, plus numerous letters, and various historical archives. I had to fill in some gaps, and a few names have been changed to protect identities. Most of the dialogue is dramatized.

CONTENTS

CHAPTER ONE

HEARTBREAK

July 1936, Langdon, Alberta

Melva's hands shook as she lifted the starched white envelope. *"Finally! Another letter from him!"* She and Earle had been writing back and forth for a year and a half, but lately the letters were further apart.

"All is okay," she thought, putting her fears to rest, *"He's writing again!"* She tore the envelope open.

Her eyes widened. "Earle and Linda request the honor of your presence at their wedding, to be held on October 11, in the year of our Lord, 1936." Her mouth dropped. Her breath came in loud heaves.

Gradually, she set the card down. She stared dumbfounded at the miniature roses embroidered on her dresser scarf. The hollow sound of wind blew through her open window. Her dainty curtains fluttered against her stack of borrowed theology books. A brown cloud approached. Another dust storm. She shut the window, grabbed her small journal, and read. Entry after entry mocked her. "March—I get *the* letter from Earle! . . . lonesome . . . I miss my Saturday night visitor . . . I got a letter from Earle! Tickled and surprised! Answered it right away! Earle is coming tonight! Waiting . . ." She wanted to rip them out, but that would destroy other entries she wanted to keep. She looked at her wrist and felt the glittering bracelet he had given her for Christmas two years ago. Its sparkle and beauty were like a beautiful bouquet on a coffin.

"Why didn't he tell me? Why did he allow our relationship to go so long when he loved someone else? Who is Linda? Where and when did they meet?" Numbness washed over her. She closed her eyes. *"No. No. This can't be true. He led me on. And the nerve of him to send me a wedding invitation!"* The familiar creak of the top stair sounded, and her younger sister rounded the corner into their room.

"What does Earle have to say this time?" Vera asked. Melva turned to face her sister. Vera threw herself on the bed. "I was delighted when I picked up the mail today to see he had written again." She tucked her hands behind her head and smiled at the ceiling, as if readying herself to soak in the details of Melva's romance. Melva wiped a tear off her cheek. Vera shot up. "Melva! What's the matter?" Melva threw the card at her and ran out.

After Grandpa said grace at supper that night, Melva's mother turned to her.

"Here, dear, eat something." She handed Melva a plate of penny buns. Melva sighed and shook her head. She stared at the ecru platter with silver trim, piled with her mother's favorite buns. Butter slid down the sides. She passed it to her older sister, Alice.

"I don't mean to downplay your pain," Alice said as she took one, "but there are other very nice men around. Men who love God and want to serve Him."

Melva felt her face flush, reluctant to discuss her pain in front of everyone.

"I could name a good number of young men I've seen buzzing around Melva downtown at the telephone office," a young man opposite said. "No, you don't have a thing to worry about, Melva, there's plenty of—"

"Ruel. That's quite enough. She doesn't need any more thoughts of romance," Melva's mother Hazel said as she dished a healthy helping of hot beef and gravy onto her plate. Around the supper table sat Melva's four sisters and one brother, along with her Uncle Ruel and Aunt Winnie, their three little girls, her grandparents, and her parents.

Donald, Melva's father, cleared his throat,

"It could always be worse."

Hazel's eyes shot to her husband, "Yes dear. You always say that."

"'cause it's good ol' Sam Thompson's motto and it's the truth. Think of poor Viola," he said, as he heaped mashed potatoes on his plate.

"I hardly think Viola's situation is worth comparing to your daughter's," Hazel said.

Alice set her hand on Melva's arm. "Given time, the pain will lessen. Would you like to go for a walk after supper?" Her older sister's soft touch and caring voice brought comfort to her heart.

"Yes, Alice. That would be nice."

Grandpa Verne looked at Ruel's eldest daughter. "Now, is my big seven-year-old granddaughter able to help Grandpa tomorrow?" The little girl's eyes widened; she bounced in her seat and knocked over her milk.

"Oh yes! Yes! What shall we do Grandpa?"

"Joyce, mind your manners," her mother Winnie said as she dabbed at the spilt milk with her napkin.

"We need more grasshopper poison. Want to come to Dalemead with me?" Grandpa asked.

Little Joyce looked at her father, Ruel. He nodded, causing Joyce to squeal in delight.

Grandma Melvia laughed and looked at Joyce. "It's good you visit us on weekends, so Grandpa can have a helper!"

After coming in from their walk, Melva ran upstairs and peered out her lace curtain to the farmyard below. The buzz of flies in the corner of her window caught her attention. *"I just cleaned the fly dirt out of the corners! It looks so terrible."* Her shoulders slumped. Along the rounded edge of the dresser lay a thin layer of dirt from the last dust storm. She wiped her finger through it. Across a corner of the room her sisters had hung a rope to use as a clothesline to dry their dresses, hoping the fine dust would not reach them. But their efforts were in vain. Everything was covered in a light layer of dust.

"Why did God allow Earle to leave me? It hurts so badly. And he never even gave me an explanation! Just a wedding invitation! The nerve! Why did he mail it? Why not just phone and tell me? Why does God allow such pain in my life? What am I supposed to do now? Why are there so many dust storms? Why did this window get dirty so fast? Everything is against me!"

A sharp knock sounded on the door the next morning. Melva's mother quickly flipped the bacon and eggs on the cookstove and set the flipper down. She wiped her hands on her starched apron.

"Come in, come in," she called as she limped with her cane to the front door.

"Good morning, Aunt Hazel. I stopped by to see if Melva wanted a ride to work this morning, since I'm headed to Langdon," the young man said as he stepped into the entryway.

"I'm sure she won't decline a ride from her cousin, and that will save Donald the trip. Thank you, Vince." Hazel said.

Hearing Vince's voice, Melva hurried down the stairs. She quickly slipped her last bobby pin into her wavy hair.

"Hi Vince!" Vera said as she stepped out of the dining room.

"And a good day to you!" he said as he tipped his hat.

Vera stood on her tippy toes and cupped her hand around Vince's ear. "Earle is getting married to someone else!"

"What?" Vince's eyes enlarged.

"It's true!" she whispered.

"Vera!" Melva said as she wrapped her shawl around her. She pursed her lips.

Vince held out his elbow, "Come Melva. Tell me all about it."

"Wait!" her mother said as she hobbled to the back kitchen and came out with a bundle of baking. "For your week at work. See you next weekend, Melva. Love you! Goodbye."

Melva hugged her mother. Vince held the screen door for her.

Rustler wagged his tail and jumped on Melva. She pushed him down. "No Rustler!"

"You know, Melva," Vince said as he slid into the driver's seat. "Don't pay no mind to Earle. I never did get along with him." He turned the key.

"You hardly knew him," Melva said, resting her purse on her lap.

"Yeah . . . but he wasted a lot of your time. Remember? He'd tell you he was coming and never show up. What kind of a boyfriend does that? Naw—he's not good enough for you."

Vince looked at her. "To tell you the truth, Melva, someday I'm going to marry a gal just like you. I've always admired you. You're kind, sweet, and very pretty. In fact, if we weren't cousins . . ."

"Oh Vince, stop," Melva said with a smile.

Vince laughed, "I knew I'd get you to smile again!" Melva stared out the window.

Minutes later they arrived on Main Street.

"Well, here we are. Think I'll run over to the café. Coming to prayer meeting tonight? It's at Smarts," he said. Melva nodded.

"See you then!" Vince's cheerful disposition lightened her burden. She stepped from the boardwalk, entered a small office, and set her purse on the counter. Mrs. Scott, her supervisor, looked up from behind the switchboard.

"Dear girl, do take over for me, will you? Mrs. Anderson's baby has pneumonia! I just have to grab my medical kit."

"Alright," Melva said as she peeled off her gloves.

"I'll be back in a couple of hours!" Mrs. Scott said as she pushed back the curtain to her living quarters. Melva stared at the line Earle used to phone her. *"I guess that one isn't calling here anymore."* She rested her head in her hands. *"This pain. How could I allow myself to love someone and now he is just gone? No explanation, nothing. Not even a goodbye."* She felt her eyes misting. *"How will I make it through today? Will I ever feel normal again? Earle is marrying someone else!"* A call came in, jolting her to the present.

"Hello, this is Melva. How may I direct your call?"

"Hi Melva. Bernie here. Is Mother in?"

"No, she went to Andersons to help with the baby."

"Okay, I need to know how much coal to drop off at home. I'll run over to Andersons."

Melva set the plug down. *"How can anyone think of coal at a time like this? No one cares that I am suffering. And I still must go to work and act like everything is fine. This just hurts too much. I am suffering all alone. Dear God, my heart is broken, and I can't fix it. I don't want to keep going. I can't keep going. No one knows how deep this hurts. If only Mrs. Scott could heal my broken heart like she heals sick people in the community."*

"Maybe I should ask for prayer tonight at prayer meeting," Melva thought as she shut the blind later that afternoon.

"Does anyone have prayer requests tonight?" Mr. Smart said as he scanned the crowded living room.

"Mrs. Anderson's baby has pneumonia," Mrs. Scott said. "And land sakes, if I didn't tell her not to take the baby out yet!" Mr. Smart looked at her, cleared his throat, and dipped his pen in the ink bottle and scribbled on his notepad. He looked up.

"Mrs. Ferguson is getting her tooth pulled next week," a young woman said.

"We should pray for Rob Williams. He smashed his car last week," a young man said. Melva looked at the decorated linoleum. She squeezed her toes in her black high heeled shoes and tightened her grip on her Bible.

"I have a sore toe, might have broken it," a young man named Jack said.

"I'm sorry to hear that, Jack," Mr. Smart said, "How did it happen?"

Jack grinned. "I kicked our cow." Snickers sounded throughout the room.

Melva's courage rose. "I . . . I have a request." All eyes turned to her.

"Yes?" Mr. Smart said as his glasses slid down his nose. He promptly pushed them up.

"I, I—" she glanced at her older sister.

"Melva's had several hard days. Pray for her to be inwardly healed," Alice said.

"Yes, the sickness of the heart is perhaps worse than the sickness of the body. Let us remember to pray for Melva," Mr. Smart said as scribbled on his pad.

The prayer meeting went longer than expected with many requests for jobs, the dust storms to stop, and for God's mercy because of political unrest and the poor economy. After the last prayer, Melva followed a group of young people to the kitchen where they gathered around a large granite-ware bread bowl full of popcorn.

"Can I walk you home tonight Melva?" a young man said as he turned from the bowl, his hand brimming with popcorn.

"Oh, Hunt. That's kind of you. Yes."

"It isn't far to Mrs. Scott's. Too bad," Hunt said. Melva glanced at her escort as they stepped out. His blue eyes sparkled in the moonlight.

"Yes." Her heels clicked on the boardwalk.

"I hope... you heal from whatever has caused you pain."

Melva cleared her throat and looked straight ahead. "How do people heal? It doesn't feel like I'll ever be myself again." She felt a lump in her throat.

Hunt glanced at her. "You're not meant to be yourself again. You're meant to grow. And growing can be painful, but the result is maturity. You're not a girl anymore, Melva. You're twenty-one. And whatever caused you pain, time will heal it."

He glanced at her. "Melva." He stopped and rubbed the back of his neck. "I was wondering. Would you be interested in going to the carnival in Calgary with me next weekend?"

Melva glanced at him. *"A carnival? How could I possibly laugh and have fun when it feels like I'm dying inside?"* "I appreciate the offer, Hunt, but ... no thanks."

Hunt's eyes enlarged, "You mean like—no?"

Melva nodded.

"Melva. Hunt." A young woman passed as she gave them a nod.

"Oh Rhonda! I was meaning to talk to you. Can I walk with you?"

Hunt asked as he caught up to her. Melva watched as they walked away, laughing and visiting. She sighed. "Men!"

Melva unlocked the front door of the tiny telephone office and entered the dimly lit room. Mrs. Scott had come back early to answer the phones. She sat reading by the switchboard.

Walking past the switchboard, Melva pushed through the curtain to the back, across the living room and into the tiny bedroom where she roomed during the week. She pulled back her curtains to watch the remaining people leave prayer meeting. She sighed as couples laughed together. *"Who can heal my heart? I only wanted to fall in love, get married, and stay near Daddy and Mother and Grandpa and Grandma, but my dreams are going in reverse. Dear God, please help me. Help me understand."*

She threw herself on her bed and sobbed.

When she awoke the next morning, she flipped open her Bible and turned to a familiar passage. "Fear thou not; for I am with thee: be not dismayed, for I am thy God: I will strengthen thee; yea, I will help thee; yea, I will uphold thee with the right hand of My righteousness."

CHAPTER TWO

ROB WILLIAMS

It was Sunday. A feeling of relief came over Melva. She always liked Sundays, a day of church and rest with family. The woody smell of spruce from the renovations surrounded her as she entered the church. It was located across the street from the phone office. She slid down the long bench with her sisters. Other families took their places, each on their own bench. Melva glanced at the wall. A few planks on either side were lighter where they tore out the tall bank teller desks. It felt strange to have church in the old Union Bank, but the Women's Institute had nicely renovated it for their purposes, and kindly let the fledging Baptist church use it. Recently, however, the Baptist church had purchased the Royal Bank, which was located right next to the telephone office, but the bank still owned it for a few more months. Hats of all sorts bobbed around her as more families filed in. Melva smiled as her mind wandered to Mrs. Whissen. A few years previously, she had worn her favorite hat to a UFA meeting. During it, the hosts' cat ate the stuffed bird perched among the hat's flowers, causing quite a disturbance.

Dick Bittle, Vince's older brother, walked to the pulpit.

"Good morning, ladies and gentlemen."

The congregation hushed. He stood straight as he spoke. Melva was proud of her cousin, Dick. He was taking courses in Calgary to become a teacher.

"This morning we have an evangelist from the Calgary Prophetic Bible Institute, Rev. Cyril Hutchinson. But before he comes, let us turn to page fifty-six and sing *Amazing Grace*." The familiar tune rang through the small building as everyone sang with gusto. Alice's fingers ran up and down the keyboard and as the last stanza ended, Mr. Hutchinson stood, straightened his suit jacket, and walked to the pulpit.

"Good morning. It is wonderful to be here in your lovely church in Langdon. Thank you for inviting me. My sermon today is called, 'A *Venture into the Unknown*.'"

Melva perked up. His melodic voice captivated her, and his topic sounded interesting.

"These are days of great adventures. When my father was a boy, the steam engine was a marvel and automobiles were unknown. When I was a boy, I lit an oil lamp to study. No radios. I didn't speak on a telephone until I was 14. Ventures! Yet, all ventures are not new or modern. A very old venture and its consequences are found in 2 Kings, chapter six to seven. Benhahad, King of Syria, invaded northern Israel and besieged the city of Samaria until the people were reduced to cannibalism. But at the gate were four leprous men.

"They said one to another, 'Why sit we here until we die? If we say, we will enter into the city, then the famine is in the city, and we shall die there. And if we sit still here, we die also. Now therefore come and let us fall into the host of the Syrians; if they save us alive, we shall live, and if they kill us, we shall but die.'"

Vera leaned over to Melva. "Grandma told me Grandpa gave her a vase for their engagement. After church I want to look in Grandma's drawer for it," she whispered. Melva furrowed her brow.

She glanced at her grandmother at the end of the bench. "How dare you suggest such a thing in church!" Melva said. Vera's lips drew in a tight line.

'And they rose up in the twilight, to go unto the camp of the Syrians, and when they were come to the uttermost part of the camp of Syria, behold, there was no man there. For the Lord had made the host of the Syrians to hear a noise of chariots, and a noise of horses, even the noise of a great host. They arose and fled and left their tents and when the lepers came to the uttermost part of the camp, they went into one tent, and did eat and drink, and carried thence silver and gold, and raiment.' The four lepers ventured out at a great risk . . . and found blessings. At the call of God, venture out, for why sit we here until we die?" The sermon continued for quite some time.

"You're just as curious to see it as I am," Vera whispered out of the corner of her mouth.

Melva sighed. "I'm trying to listen!" She glanced down the row. Grandpa Verne's head was bent over, and he quickly jerked it back. Asleep. Again.

Twenty minutes later, Mr. Hodgins, who oversaw the hymns, stood and took the pulpit as Rev. Hutchinson sat.

"Yes, why sit we here until we die?" Mr. Hodgins said. "One day, we are all going to die. And what have we done for the Lord? God knows we have worked hard enough. Worked the shirts off our backs to survive in Canada. Many of our ancestors were told of the great possibilities in Canada and cheap land, so we came here. And what did we find? A beautiful land, yes, perhaps the prettiest in the world. But the winters are unforgiving, and lately, the dust storms have been unrelenting. There's political unrest and great uncertainty. Amid this, make sure you fulfill the Lord's call for your life. Because one day you will die. And you never know when that will be. So why sit we here until we die? The fields are ripe for harvest. May God lay on each of you a burden for the lost around you. So, thank you, Cyril, for that thought-provoking message. Let us turn to page sixty-three and sing, '*Bringing in the Sheaves.*'"

Melva's mind drifted to the fact that even in Langdon many were unsaved. "*The fields are ripe. I need to do more, even here.*"

"Melva? Are you Melva Dye?" a young man said, as he hovered above her. His cedar-scented cologne filled the air.

She glanced up. Her sisters were standing and putting on their wraps. Her eyes widened as she stood.

"Oh, yes, and you ... are you Rob, Rob Williams?"

"Yes. May I take you home?" he asked. He wore a black vest over a white dress shirt with a bow tie. Rob seldom attended church, and

Melva only knew him as the newly hired local mechanic's assistant. She glanced at her line of sisters. They smiled back.

"Sure," she said.

"Let me help you with your shawl," Rob said as he helped her wrap it around her shoulders.

"Thank you."

"Seen my new car?" he asked as they walked out.

Melva shook her head. "No, but someone at prayer meeting mentioned you had smashed your car."

"Yeah, well, that was my old one. I like my new automobile better."

They approached a shiny black vehicle. "It's a 1936 five-window Chevy Coupe." He opened her door and she sat. The leathery smell of new upholstery filled the air.

"Very nice."

"Say Melva," he said as he started down the road. "Would you mind if . . . well . . . if we became . . . friends?" Melva felt her face flush. Rob was not the sort of guy she had considered. She looked out the window at a group of teenagers on the boardwalk who waved when Rob honked at them. A group of girls in front of the café giggled and pointed. Rob honked and waved.

"Umm, sure. I don't mind being friends," she said. Rob ran his fingers through his dark hair. He glanced at her, and his smile brought out a dimple.

"Great! Would you like to meet my parents before I take you home? They talk about you Dye sisters all the time, even though we don't know you gals very well. Andersons speak so highly of you all. Isn't one of your relatives part of the Cloverleaf Threshing Company? And your grandpa Verne, and dad, they're known all over the county for helping other farmers. Besides that, your grandpa owns land all over. You're some kind of rich, girl."

Melva raised her brow and cleared her throat. "Appears you know quite a bit about me." Rob chuckled. Melva continued, "I know about some of Grandpa's land, but I don't think even Grandma knows everything he owns."

Rob burst out laughing. "You don't say? The guys at the café say he owns land in Wisconsin, Texas, Nebraska, Oregon, Iowa, Alberta, Saskatchewan, and BC!"

Melva glanced over, "Really?"

Rob laughed again. "You mean you didn't know that? Ha! He's some kind of armchair general to boot!"

Melva shook her head. "Grandpa's no armchair general. He works hard. But some things we just don't talk about, two of which are money and"—she looked out the window and whispered—"baby Grace."

Rob raised his brow.

The shiny black hood glistened in the sun and the large silver fenders shook as the trees zipped by. Minutes later, they pulled into a farmyard. A young woman leaned on a rake, then walked up to Rob's door.

"Hey little bro, who's this?" she bent down and looked at Melva through his window.

"She's one of the Dye sisters. Now leave me be, would you? If you'd been in church, you could have met her whole family." Rob pushed his door open and walked past the girl.

"Well, how's that for an introduction!" she said, resting her hand on her hip. Rob opened Melva's door. "We'll only be a few minutes, then I'll take you home," he whispered. She nodded.

"Oh, Melva, this is my sister Addie. She prefers to stay home on Sundays."

"Ha! Look who's talking!" Addie yelled, "since when did you get religion, Rob? I'll tell you when! Since you heard the Dye sisters attended the Baptist church, that's when! And that was only last..."

"Addie!" Rob glared.

Melva faced Addie, "Umm … I'm pleased to meet you," she said. "Likewise."

An hour later, Melva entered the porch at her farmhouse and hung her shawl. The smell of fried chicken permeated the air.

Vern Junior jumped up from the dinner table and ran to the window.

"Wow, just look at that car! I heard about Rob's new car but didn't know it was that cool!"

"Vern, please sit," Father said. Melva stepped into the spacious dining room. All eyes turned to her. She approached her chair next to Alice. After she said her own grace, Grandpa cleared his throat.

"That was a very good sermon today, at least the part I remember," he said as he took a bite of chicken.

"Yes, Grandpa, I agree," said Alice. "We need to be more burdened for the souls around us. But with all that's happening in the world, we are all just thinking about ourselves."

"Amen to that," Hazel said as she passed the carrots.

"What did you learn from the sermon, Vera?" Grandpa asked.

Vera looked up from her plate. "Me? I . . . liked the part that we should venture out and not be afraid to do new things for God." She looked around the table.

"How was your week at work, Melva?" Mother asked her as she passed the chicken.

"I'm glad to be home, Mother. It was hard."

"Judging by how you got home, it looks like it ended right," Vern said with a sheepish grin. Donald furrowed his brow at his son.

"Melva, we got a letter from Viola this week," Grandmother said as she dished up the potatoes. "Feel free to read it; it's on my dresser." Vera glanced at Melva. Melva shook her head at her sister.

"Thank you, Grandma, I might just do that," she said.

"May I read it too, Grandma?" Vera asked.

"Of course."

"Alice, Clara, and Doris. I want you to do the dishes. Melva needs time to rest," Mother said.

After dinner, Melva headed down the dirt road. She was glad her mother told her sisters do the dishes. It was a chore that usually took two hours. Mother helped some, but having broken her hip years previous, and not having it set properly, she suffered daily with pain.

Melva wanted time to think, and it was almost impossible to find time for oneself in a large, busy household. She headed east along the irrigation canal. "*The last time I took this walk Earle was with me,*" she thought. She looked up. The road was flat and straight and stretched for miles. *"Is that how my life is going to be?"* The canal's gurgle caught her attention and she stopped to watch it shoot out of the small dam. *"Earle is getting married. To someone else! It feels like my best friend has turned into an enemy. I know he's not, but isn't that what an enemy is? Someone who breaks your heart? How will I ever forgive him? He hurt me, then walked away scot free! How long, how long must I endure this suffering? And now Rob. Does he think I'm his girlfriend now? I do not know what to do with that either!"*

Hours later Melva opened the screen door and glanced behind the thick dark curtain that framed the dining room. Some of the family sat around the table eating popcorn. Uncle Ruel sat by the radio with Aunt Winnie on the other side. Their three little girls sat quietly at the table doing a puzzle. Vern perched on the floor with his ear to the radio's large gooseneck speaker.

"Vern, please get out of the way," Vera said. "You're blocking the sound."

William Aberhart's voice pierced the still air. Melva slipped upstairs and entered her grandparents' living quarters. Normally, she and her siblings were not allowed in this part of the house. A beautiful lamp with roses painted on the globes adorned the dresser. Crystal vases and bowls containing fresh bouquets were scattered about on various dresser tops. Several white sheepskin rugs decorated the floor. Thick lace curtains hung over the windows and a white chenille bedspread adorned with little pink roses embellished the bed. Two oversized goose down pillows perched against the white iron headboard and the fragrance of sweet peas filled the room from the floral arrangement in the open window. An envelope lay between a china southern belle ornament and a pair of Sunday gloves on Grandma's dresser. *"No dust. Grandma must dust every day."* Gently, she pulled Aunt Viola's letter out of its envelope. It told of all the lighthearted antics of her children. *"She seems so happy. How could Aunt Viola be happy when she had gone through so much?"* Melva collapsed in Grandma's rocker and sighed.

Viola had married her Uncle Roger, who was her father Donald and Uncle Ruel's brother. Roger loved playing tricks and having fun. His antics were rehashed again and again by farmers at the café. Everyone loved Roger, everyone except Mr. Lacombe, who had farmed across from him. One day, Roger watched Mr. Lacombe dig fence holes. That night, Roger filled a hole with used tractor oil. After discovering it the next day, Mr. Lacombe dressed up and raced into town, telling everyone he had struck oil on his land. What a stir Uncle Roger had caused!

Sometime after this, Roger and his bride Viola moved away. Years later, they had six girls and Viola was expecting her seventh when, one morning, she woke up to discover Roger's lifeless body beside her. He was only 36. Viola moved back to Langdon with her children, and although Melva was only fourteen, she was old enough to help her aunt.

She would never forget the day Aunt Viola had her seventh baby. It was the saddest-happiest day Melva had ever experienced. Twin boys! But Roger was not there to hold her hand during labor, or whisper encouraging words. Dr. Salmon and the midwife, Mrs. Forgie, did that. The excitement of twins only exaggerated the sad, empty feelings her relatives experienced. "*Death. It had to be the greatest enemy. And the next was separation of relationships. Someone who had been close but now was gone, but still alive. Or was this worse?*" Melva sighed. "*I want to be like Aunt Viola. I want to get over this, this pain, this bitterness and be happy again. There must be life after pain. It must be possible to be happy after . . . death. Who is God and what is He like to allow all this?*" The window lace softly blew from the open window, exposing the clear blue sky. Melva looked out. A ring of rocks surrounded the base of the tall trees, framing Grandmother's beautiful flowers. It seemed miraculous that such beauty could exist in the same spot where, only a few months before, snow and ice lay, seemingly having succeeded in destroying all signs of life and beauty.

"Melva!" Vera whispered. Melva jumped.

"Vera!"

"She said I could read the letter, too." After reading her aunt's letter, Vera perked up.

"Let's look in Grandma's dresser drawer for the vase. Everyone else is listening to Mr. Aberhart."

Melva sighed. "Oh Vera."

"Come on, let's," she said.

They approached the tall dresser. A scrape of wood on wood sounded as Vera slid open the drawer. The drawer held knickknacks, which neither sister had seen.

"Melva, look!" Vera said as she gently lifted an ornate perfume bottle wrapped in silk. "This is it! Grandpa's engagement gift to Grandma!"

She held it up. Engraved on one side were the words, "Aug. 7. Melvia, 1884."

Gingerly, Vera removed the crystal stopper and took a deep breath. "Mmmm," she sighed. A hush permeated the room as the sisters stared in awe at the heirloom. Minutes later, they headed to their room. Melva sat on her bed.

"Grandpa bought Grandma so many pretty things over the years. The bottle was such a beautiful gift from one lover to another," she thought. She looked at her bracelet and twirled it around her wrist.

"Do you want this?" she asked her sister.

"Want it? You mean your bracelet? Of course I want it! It's so beautiful!"

"Doesn't mean a thing to me … anymore," Melva said.

CHAPTER THREE

BANK ROBBERY

The next morning, as Melva finished her toast and milk, a knock rang on the door. Grandpa Verne answered it. An unfamiliar voice sounded in the entryway, catching the family's attention. Grandpa entered the dining room with a lanky young man wearing overalls.

"As some of you know, I've hired Harold to help around here," Grandpa said. Harold nodded politely.

"Harold," Grandpa Verne began, "meet my family. This is my wife Melvia, my five granddaughters—Alice, Clara, Doris, Melva, and Vera and my grandson Vern, my son Donald, and his wife Hazel. Harold's eyes widened as he scanned the breakfast crowd.

"The family is small today," Grandpa Verne said. "Usually there are more of us." Harold's mouth dropped. Vera and Clara giggled.

"Have a seat, Harold," Hazel said.

Harold smiled. "Thank you, thank you very much. Smells delicious ma'am. I never turn down food, and it was a long drive from Nanton. Sure glad I was able to find work during these hard times." He pulled out the chair opposite Melva.

"After you eat," began Grandpa Verne, "I want you to take my granddaughter Melva to town. She works in the telephone office during the week."

Harold nodded. "Aha! It's good to finally put a face to the Langdon switchboard operator." Melva felt her face flush. Vera and Clara exchanged smiles. "And," Harold continued, "I'll drop my things off at my uncle's in town. He has agreed to let me room with him, in fact, he was the one who sent me the help wanted ad."

"I noticed in your father's hired help wanted ad that he owns a lot of land," Harold said as he opened the truck door for Melva after breakfast.

"It's not Daddy, it's Grandpa. He owns land and homes in the States and Canada."

Harold nodded. "Hmm."

Melva continued, "Grandpa has always made three things his priority. God first, family second, and by family, I mean grandchildren, uncles, aunts, and cousins. And third, land." Harold turned the steering wheel as they swung onto the dirt road.

"You're pretty lucky to have a grandfather with priorities like that. It sets the example for the whole family." Melva looked out the dusty window. She had never thought of herself as lucky. Lately, she had only felt sorry for herself.

Minutes later they pulled up to the Alberta Government Telephone office.

"Have a good week. See you next weekend," Harold said cheerfully. Melva smiled and stepped out of the truck. As she entered the office, she was met by Mrs. Scott's excited voice.

"Yes, constable, I am around tonight. Of course, I'll be at the switchboard with my assistant all day. We take turns working nights, too. Yes, you can reach me here. Melva Dye. I said her name is Melva Dye. You too! Goodbye." Mrs. Scott reconnected the plug to the board and turned to Melva. "Land sakes girl, have I got a story for you!" She grabbed her coffee cup.

"What? What is it Mrs. Scott?"

Mrs. Scott took a deep swallow of coffee and blurted, "The RCMP called from Calgary. They got tipped off that two men are planning to rob our Royal Bank in five days!"

"W-w-what?!" Melva shot her hand to her mouth, bumping Mrs. Scott's coffee pot. "Why, that's, that's just next door! I-I can hardly believe it!"

"I know! I know!" Mrs. Scott paced the small room, shaking her head, and wringing her hands. "What is this world coming to! I said *what* is this world coming to! I can't believe a body would be insane enough to rob a bank for money instead of earning it by good honest labor! And next door! If that don't beat all! They put our lives in jeopardy, because we can't leave our posts, in case the RCMP needs the telephone!"

Melva sat, stunned. "It could always be worse." She whispered the oft-quoted motto. "*It just got worse,*" she thought. The two women stared at each other.

"Melva! Wash and wax my living room floor, would you? I'll watch the switchboard."

Melva's mouth dropped open. "What in the world? Why?"

Mrs. Scott sighed. "Because in five days an RCMP officer is going to hide in my living room where he can watch the back boardwalk from my window, that's why. And I won't be having him see dust under my chesterfield! Come to think of it, when you're done washing the floor, let's turn the linoleum so the faded part is under the chesterfield."

Melva entered Mrs. Scott's living quarters and sighed. "*As if I didn't have enough in my life, and now this!*"

An hour later Melva put the wash bucket back in place. The sound of the front door opening caught her attention.

"Hi Mrs. Scott. Is Melva in?" a husky voice asked.

"In back. Melva?" Mrs. Scott yelled.

Melva entered the office.

"Hi Melva. Thought you might like this," Rob Williams said. He held a frosty bottle of orange crush and an ice cream cone.

"Oh, thank you! That is very kind of you," Melva said as she took the pop and ice cream. She glanced up at him. His eyes were fastened on her. She shifted.

"It'll do her good to have somethin' sweet in her life given what's going to happen in a few days," Mrs. Scott said as she turned to open the blind.

"What does she mean by that?" Rob whispered out of the corner of his mouth.

"I don't know if I should say," Melva whispered back.

"Melva, Melva! Wake up!" Mrs. Scott said from outside Melva's bedroom door.

Melva turned and stared at the door. "Mrs. Scott? What time is it?"

"Land sakes girl. It's six o'clock!"

"But my shift isn't until nine." Melva stood and wrapped her housecoat around her. She opened the bedroom door.

"Have you forgotten? It's the day the bank gets robbed! We must be up early! And whatever you do, keep the doors locked. Use the outhouse early so we won't have to leave. Be prepared to drop under the switchboard table at a moment's notice." Mrs. Scott stabbed a bobby pin into her tight bun.

"If I see those robbers, I'm tellin' ya, if I so much as see any suspicious characters enter the bank . . . why, I have a mind to give them a whippin' they'll never forget! No-good scoundrels! Low-down dirty rotters! The—"

Melva covered her yawn. "Alright, I'm up now. I'll get ready for work."

"Mark my words, girl. If I see them, I'll wring their necks tighter than my old wringer washer wrung my stockings last month! Wrung 'em so hard they came out eight feet long! Them two will regret the day they set foot in this here Langdon. Them two . . ."

"Mrs. Scott, did you have breakfast yet?" Melva asked.

"Breakfast? Who can think of food at a time like this?"

Melva glanced at the clock above the switchboard. Nine o'clock. She twisted the brass lid on the glass inkwell and studied the decorative bottle. The police had come. Two were hiding in the bank and one was crouching under Mrs. Scott's living room window.

Mrs. Scott mumbled as she dusted the switchboard. Suddenly, the policeman ran from the living room into the office. Melva blinked. He brandished his gun and was out the door in seconds. Mrs. Scott's feather duster froze in midair.

A few minutes later another officer burst in. "Mrs. Scott!" he yelled. "Come quick! Bring your first aid kit!"

Mrs. Scott's jaw dropped. She jumped up. "Watch the switchboard!" she yelled to Melva as she ran for her bag.

A phone line rang. "Hello? This is Melva. How may I direct your call?"

"Hi Melva. Mrs. Smart here. How is Mrs. Anderson's baby? I have some baking for her. I ordered extra yeast at the store because it was on sale. And the flour! Have you been here lately? The flour Mr. Smart brought in is whiter and it even appears to be sifted! It makes the nicest loaves. Salt was on sale and so we ordered twice what we normally do. I sure hope it sells. We haven't many eggs today, though. Does your Mother have more for me? I could sell them at a good price right now because of our low supply. Anyways, back to Mrs. Anderson, I know what it's like to have a mess of youngen's when one child is sick—well, it's all a body can do to keep up with all that needs a-doing. Is Mrs. Scott in? I want to talk to her."

"No, she's not in, but most likely she'll be back soon."

"Where is she?"

"She's at the bank. I'll tell her you called." The door burst open, and a police officer entered, carrying one end of a stretcher. A young man lay on the stretcher groaning loudly.

"Okay, easy now. Not so fast Thompson, not so fast," the police officer holding the front end of the stretcher said to his comrade, who was holding the other end. Melva dropped the line and her eyes widened as Mrs. Scott followed them into the room.

"Mrs. Scott?" Melva blurted. "You really meant what you said about dealing with the robbers! Did you—?"

The officer at the front of the stretcher walked by and Melva jumped to push back Mrs. Scott's heavy curtain. The group entered Mrs. Scott's living room.

"No, I didn't so much as lift a finger a-gin 'em," Mrs. Scott said abruptly. "They caught this here man, but his comrade escaped. He sped off in his car."

"Melva! Melva! What's going on?" Mrs. Smart's voice shouted at the other end of the receiver. Melva picked it up.

"Oh! Hi, Mrs. Smart. I'm sure Mrs. Scott will tell you all about it. Please call later. I must go. Goodbye." Melva set the plug back and took a deep breath.

A minute later Mrs. Scott returned from the living room. "You should have seen it! It was a holdup alright. He used two sawed off .22s! The police said, 'Stick em up!' and this here fellow dropped his guns and one of them went off. Shot clear through his leg. In the confusion his comrade took off. The police called me to do first aid and I bandaged him up. Now the police and the robber are waiting to be escorted to the Calgary police station, and then they will take the man to the hospital."

"You did first aid on the *criminal*?" Melva gasped. Mrs. Scott shrugged.

"The man needed me to. You know, Melva, at first, I was repulsed, but thinking it over, being kind to a robber isn't so bad after all. As I was cleaning his wound, I couldn't help thinking about his mother and how sad she would feel with her son's decisions. I feel sorry for him. And more importantly, I feel better myself. Being angry takes a lot of energy. For the last five days I've been so disturbed I couldn't concentrate on my job or eat much," Mrs. Scott said as she collapsed behind the switchboard. She hummed, then drank what was left of her cold coffee.

"Being angry takes a lot of energy." Melva walked to the narrow window that faced Main Street and peered through the thick blind slats. *"I want to feel better. For my sake, I am putting Earle behind me."* She sighed. *"But what if I never get over him?"* She mulled over the words, *"being angry takes a lot of energy."* "I *want* to feel better. I *must* put Earle behind me." She whispered, perhaps too loudly, *"But what if I can't?"*

"Hello Melva," Rob said as he stepped into the AGT building. "I told your parents I wanted to bring you home this weekend. Hope you don't mind."

"No, I don't mind. And thanks again for the ice cream and Orange Crush the other day," she said.

"Ah, weren't much. My pleasure. Say, didja have a good week at work?"

"I had an interesting week." The two left the office and headed for Rob's car.

"That's good. I prefer interesting weeks. That's why I took up mechanics. I get to work on all kinds of cool cars," Rob said. Melva slid into her seat. "Say, why don't you slide a little closer to me? The seat's a little more comfortable here near to the wheel." Melva looked at him and raised her brow. She slid a couple of inches toward him.

"Well, don't crowd me out!" he burst out laughing.

"I'm sorry, Rob, I just feel uncomfortable sitting too close."

"I get it. You want to get to know me first." He winked. Melva sighed.

As they pulled up to the farm minutes later, Rob leaned over.

"Goodbye, Melva. See you in church," he whispered.

"Goodbye! Thanks for the ride!" she said as she opened the door and jumped out. Melva watched as Rob revved his car and it disappeared in a cloud of dust and sped down the lane. She sighed as she entered the porch.

"Melva!"

"Clara!" Melva embraced her sister. "How was your week at the Rae's?"

"Great! It is so good to be home again, though. Cooking for all those hired hands and cleaning that farmhouse every day sure is a lot of work!"

"Mr. Dye, I'm telling you, I think the tractor needs a new oil pump," Harold said as he walked past Melva into the dining room.

"Oil pump? Can't possibly be. It's not that old," Grandpa said as he stirred embers in the fireplace.

"Harold is right. It needs to be replaced. I must have bought a lemon of a tractor at the auction," Donald said from the sink as he washed up.

"Honey! Careful not to spread those ashes over Hazel's clean carpet!" Grandma Melvia said as she got up from her rocker. "Melva," she said as she looked at her granddaughter, "come here dear and tell us about the attempted robbery. Mrs. Scott phoned and started to tell me about your adventure but someone else phoned and she had to answer that call."

"Wait for the popcorn!" Clara said from the kitchen. "The Rae's told me all about it! Donald Rae was getting a truck part from Winter's Garage when Mrs. Scott walked in and told him and those there about the attempted robbery." A few minutes later, Clara entered the room holding a bowl full to the brim. The strong smell of butter and hot popcorn filled the air. The door opened and Uncle Ruel and Aunt Winnie stepped in with their three giggling girls.

"News has spread all over town about the attempted bank robbery. We wanted to hear firsthand what happened," Ruel said as he took off his and Winnie's coat and hooked them on the hanger by the door. The clock above the fireplace chimed.

"Just enough time for her to tell the story before the news comes on," Alice said as she glanced at the clock.

"I'm so glad you're safe, Auntie Melva!" seven-year-old Joyce said as she bounced into the room and hugged her.

Melva looked around the room at her family. Everyone quieted and turned to her. After telling about the attempted robbery, she concluded with, "And so Mrs. Scott saved the life of a robber, instead of doing what she really wanted to do to him."

"Ain't that just like Mrs. Scott," Harold said as he shook his head and grinned. "I can't wait to tell the coffee crew at the café tomorrow!"

"Well, it gives a body a freeing feeling when one lets go of evil done by another, that's for sure," Hazel said as her knitting needles clicked.

Alice stood up, "It is wonderful that God protected you and Mrs. Scott and the others at the bank." She glanced at the mantle clock. "Well, it's time for the news to come on."

Clara leaned in. "Melva, I bought you something," she whispered.

"Come." The sisters excused themselves and ran upstairs to their room. Clara opened their bottom drawer and pulled out a little box. "I wanted to do something to encourage you. Here."

Melva took the box. "A box of rust-colored dye?" she said.

"Well," Clara began, "I couldn't afford a new dress for you, but I heard you tell Doris you wished your blue dress was a rusty orange, so I bought you dye."

"Oh Clara, this is so sweet of you! However did you afford it?"

Clara laughed. "I got my first paycheck from Rae's." Melva threw her arms around her sister and hugged her.

"Can I help you dye it tonight?"

"Yes, let's do it after supper."

"Mother!" Melva ran down the stairs holding her freshly dyed dress.

Hazel's eyes widened. "What happened?" The blue mixed with orange had turned her dress into a brown swirly mess.

"It could always be worse," her little brother Vern smirked as he walked past to the sink.

"Oh, Mother," Melva sat down and sighed.

"There, there now. You have another dress, have you not?" she asked.

"Yes, Mother, but I have to replace it soon and haven't money to buy another. I get paid twelve dollars from AGT this month, but I was hoping to save it for, for, Bible School."

"Hmm…" Hazel said.

"Oh, Mother. You know how much we girls want to attend the Calgary Prophetic Bible Institute. All the great guest speakers at church come from there."

Hazel leaned on her cane. "Yes, and gospel teams from the Bible school come out and they already teach you at young peoples. Isn't that good enough?"

"I want to know more, Mother. And so do Doris and Alice."

Just then her father walked in and set a tin bucket near the sink, frothy with milk. His eyes widened as he looked at the dress in Melva's hands. He scrubbed his hands vigorously.

"I can't say I'm fond of the styles these days." He winked as he dried his hands.

"Oh Donald, that was a mistake," Hazel stated. "And she hasn't the money for a new dress because she's saving for Bible school."

"Hmm …" Donald said.

Grandma appeared in the kitchen. "Hazel, where is Vern?" Hazel pointed with her chin to where Vern was drying his hands.

"Vernie-boy, I want you to weed my flowers again today, and this time, first remove all the rocks, then weed, then put the rocks back in place exactly as they were. Do you understand?"

Vern sighed and looked down, "Yes, Grandma."

Donald followed his wife and daughters into the dining room.

"I've already been thinking about Bible school for the girls, Hazel, and I've decided it would be a good thing for Alice, Doris, and Melva to attend. I get nervous with all the young men in town buzzing around my girls like a bunch of bees around flowers. If they wish to, they can go this fall. I've already contacted Mr. Aberhart and he does not charge for the Bible classes, only for the skills classes. They start in October to give the boys time for harvesting."

"Oh, Daddy!" Melva jumped up and hugged her father.

CHAPTER FOUR

CALGARY PROPHETIC
BIBLE INSTITUTE

October 1936

Accompanied by her sisters, Melva entered the boarding house in Calgary, tightly clutching the handles of her suitcase. A middle-aged woman greeted them.

"Hello ladies. If you give me your names, I'll show you to your rooms." Doris, Alice, and Melva followed her upstairs and down a long hall.

"This is your room, Melva. I have put you with Helen. You will meet her later. Doris and Alice, I have a room for you upstairs," she said as she ushered them into a small bedroom overlooking the street. "Cost for students is two dollars a week, some food included, but you must prepare it yourself in the kitchenette at the end of the hallway. There is a phone in the hall for your convenience as well." Melva glanced out the window to the busy street below. *I hope I can adjust to city living,* she thought. *"At least we will be home on weekends."*

The next day, Melva and her sisters stood on the sidewalk at eighth Avenue and looked up at six oak doors with triangular windowpanes. Melva's eyes moved to the tall, illuminated sign—"Calgary Prophetic

Bible Institute." She opened the massive door. Students wandered about, visiting. The sisters made their way down the hall and peered into some of the rooms. Some were offices, and one held an extensive library. A set of double doors opened to a large auditorium lined with benches. She had heard Mr. Aberhart talk about it on the radio, how it seated 1,200, and how the woodwork on the walls had been custom designed. She studied the beamed ceiling and decorative wall panels.

"Look! It's true! The pews have writing desks attached!" Alice whispered.

"This is more than I could have ever imagined," Melva whispered back. "Oh Doris, Alice, I am *so* excited!" Melva clasped her hands and giggled. Voices and footsteps sounded, and the sisters turned. A group of young people and a few older students filed in.

"Let's sit near the front," whispered Doris as she clung to Melva's arm.

In less than half an hour, the auditorium was full. Mr. Aberhart approached the pulpit and after a lengthy prayer, addressed the audience.

"Before I speak, I would like to set aside a few minutes for anyone to give their testimony. Does anyone have something burning on their heart they would like to say?" Immediately, several men and women stood to share what God had done in their lives, and how He had brought them to this Bible school. At a lull, a young man on the front bench stood. He had a husky build and brown wavy hair.

"Jesus means so much to me. Because of the depth of my sins, I believe I have more for which to thank the Lord than anyone here." He bowed his head and then looked up. He choked. Tears welled in his eyes, and in a deep, melodic voice he burst into song, "Oh how I love Him, how I adore Him! My breath, my sunshine, my all in all, the great Creator, became my Savior, and all God's fulness, dwelleth in Him." He sat.

"An amazing voice," Alice whispered to Melva. She nodded. Melva glanced around. There was not one dry eye around her.

"Thank you, young man. That was Dave Stewart, and what a testimony he has! I spoke with him, and he has agreed to share his testimony tomorrow during chapel," Mr. Aberhart said. Clearing his throat, he picked up a stack of papers and tapped them on the pulpit to line them up. No one stirred.

"Youth is not, in reality, a time of life," Mr. Aberhart began. "It is a state of the mind. It is not a matter of ripe cheeks, red lips, and supple knees. It is a temper of the will, a quality of the imagination, a vigor of the emotions. In short, it is the freshness of the fountain of life. The Calgary Prophetic Bible Institute appeals to the youthful and vigorous minds who believe that they should be trained to think, and who are not afraid of convictions that come from God's Word. The institute recognizes the need for men who will walk upright, think hard, feel for others, and talk with conviction. I believe each of you is this type. The world needs you. It needs you to be trained and equipped. An examination of our bulletin will reveal a splendid curriculum of courses."

Melva scanned the audience and the vast amounts of people. Excitement from deep within rose. *"This is where I need to be. I want to make a difference,"* she thought.

Later that day, a group of students headed out to hand out gospel tracts. Melva and her sisters joined them. Several people they talked with understood and committed their lives to Christ.

October 28, 1936

"Good afternoon, students. Please take a seat," Rev. Hutchison, a member of the Calgary Prophetic board, said the next day. A few latecomers filed into the back of the room. Melva took a deep breath in anticipation.

"Today, we will hear from two of our students," Rev. Hutchinson said. "To start with, Ed Keller, then Dave Stewart."

Alice leaned in to Melva. "Dave was the one who sang yesterday," she whispered. Melva nodded.

Ed Keller shared and after he finished, Dave Stewart came forward. He was stocky and wore dress pants and a white collared shirt with a tie.

"I can never remember our home when we didn't have family worship," he began, "very early in life I became acquainted with the fact that all have sinned and come short of the glory of God. Not realizing the great issues this involved, I was not concerned. I had a great respect for God, but little by little as I grew older, these things fell away. Many of my acquaintances were not religiously minded, and I gradually drifted, thinking religion was for old ladies and children. I was young and wanted excitement and did not think that being a Christian could give it to me. I had to learn by many a hard knock and bitter experience that God's way was best after all and afforded the greatest gain. I moved away from the influence of Christian parents and went wild."

Dave looked up and his expression bore a solemn far-off look.

CHAPTER FIVE

WILD

It was 1932, Moose Jaw, Saskatchewan. Dave arched his back to avoid the hand that reached to grab him. His legs felt like lead as every muscle exerted itself to its full extent to keep ahead. He scanned the familiar buildings as he dashed by. Where would he hide this time? Fingertips scratched his coat between his shoulder blades. Sweat poured from his face.

"I'll crack you!" yelled the Mountie. The words rushed past his ear, giving him an extra boost of adrenaline. From behind him, there sounded a yell and a scuffle. The relentless footsteps faded. He glanced over his shoulder. The policeman had given up and turned on one of his buddies. Out of breath, Dave turned down an alley. Twisting and turning through the maze of darkened streets, he stopped under a fire escape.

"Made it. Again." His heart pound as he leaned over and placed his hands on his knees to catch his breath.

"Dave!"

Dave jumped. "Mike! How'd you find me?"

"Oh, come on now bud. I know how to play your game. Your hiding spots are my second home!"

Dave gasped. "That was too close. I've gotta go."

"Go?" Mike asked with a chuckle. "You're the leader. You can't go."

"Got to. This is the fifth time. They catch me, I'm done. Don't want to spend the rest of my life in the slammer." Dave walked to the front of the building and peered around the corner.

Mike followed. "He grabbed Ben. I think he was content to catch one of us. Won't bother us no more."

Dave snorted. "Yeah, right. Ben'll spill the beans. Useless. Gutless softie. Told ya we shoulda ditched 'im long ago."

Mike rubbed the back of his neck. "Look, you can't leave. Your near arrests were in different provinces. They'll never connect the dots."

Dave stood to his full height and pressed his lips together tightly. He squinted.

"Have to." Shivering, he ran his fingers through his thick brown hair and wrapped his torn coat tighter. The buttons were long gone. A wave of shame washed over him. His mother had spent hours sewing that coat. Dave knew if she saw it now, she would eagerly take it and mend it. *"But it's unmendable. Like my heart,"* he thought.

Mike shoved his hands deep into his worn jeans. "But what about the dance tonight? The girls are looking forward to having some fun." Dave furrowed his brow and glared at his comrade.

Mike sighed, "What are ya going to drive?"

Dave's jaw tightened. "The pickup. I've decided to go far. Vancouver."

"But why? You didn't get caught! And you promised to split the loot!"

"Can't. Need the money for fuel. Look, Mike. I've been chased by the police five times, and three times I've been caught and narrowly escaped severe penalties! I'm done here. Give the gang my farewell." Dave sighed and jerked away from his friend's gaze and walked down the dimly lit street. He picked up his pace.

"Right!" Mike yelled behind him, "Wait till I tell old man Furmost you stole his truck! He'll be after ya in no time. If you leave, I'll tell! I'll tell about the horses and the other truck, I will!"

Dave shuddered and whipped around. "You trying to convince me to stay with your lame threats? Ha!" His face flushed as he considered all he had against him and the myriad of consequences. *"Gotta run.*

Far." He broke into a sprint. His mind flashed to when he first began to feel restless. It was those wild west stories he had read as a kid. They featured real men. Tough guys. Men who fearlessly conquered any obstacle despite the opposition. Heroes.

Drawing a deep breath and gripping the podium firmly, Dave steadied himself before continuing. He glanced around the room at the Bible school students. It was dead quiet. Wide eyes stared back at him. "I thought heroes didn't need crutches, and God was just a crutch, so I didn't want anything to do with Him. I made it to Vancouver and found a job trucking. I was there for about a year. Nearing Christmas, I had an inexplicable desire to go home, where I could have turkey dinner, be warm, and enjoy my family. Even though I had worked a year, I had nothing: no friends, no money, and no food. I knew that many hobos travel in railway cars, so I decided to give it a try. I no longer had a coat. Finding a freight train that was headed to Calgary, I snuck around it and examined the cars. They were either closed or full of cargo. I became desperate, so I came up with another option."

Dave glanced between two freight cars and scanned around him. *"I think I can make it."* He grabbed the steel ladder and hoisted himself up on a metal platform that tapered to the coupler. The pungent smell of grease and oil permeated the air. Minutes later, the whistle blew, and the train inched forward. A gust of wind swirled dust between the cars. Dave sat against the car. He grasped the bar tighter. A sudden jolt pushed him forward and back again, forcing his coatless back against the metal. The train creaked forward. Another deafening whistle sounded, and the train began to pick up speed. Dave looked down. Under the coupler the ground sped by, with the ties nothing but a black blur. He looked up to settle his dizziness. The train yard was behind him, and he was headed toward the mountains and home.

A few hours later, Dave looked at his hands. They were bright red.

The relentless wind and cold gnawed at him. They were ascending the Rockies. The temperature plummeted. Another hour passed. The intense sense of momentum pulled him forward. Forward. *"To where? To whom? Why must I be plunged into a future of hopelessness? Who is forcing me to go there?"* A sudden burst of cold and wind whirled between the cars, bringing with it a cloud of powdery snow. It filled his chest with what felt like ice. He breathed out, forming his own cloud. As hunger ripped at his stomach, an even heavier pain than cold and hunger gripped his heart. *"Loneliness. I don't want to go on. I've tried everything. I didn't know all the partying and freedom to do as I please would be this empty. I've hurt so many. I'm done. Suicide. It's the only way out."* Dave looked down at the blur as the ground whipped by. *"I need to end my misery. I'll jump beneath its wheels."* As he stared at the ground, contemplating his next move, the coupler came into focus. Its hook was curved at just the perfect angle to grasp and securely hold the tons of weight being pulled behind it. *"I will hold you fast."*

Dave looked up. A serene sense of God permeated him. It felt as if he was being upheld supernaturally in the arms of love. The majestic mountains sped past. "O God!" he cried. "If You care about me, save me! I'm freezing! I'm dying! If You save my life today, I'll spend the rest of my life in Your service!" His eyes widened, wondering what the repercussions were of what he just declared. He tilted his head, as if listening or waiting for something to happen. The rhythm of the train continued, and he still felt frozen and hungry. But a peace pervaded him. *"God is upholding me."* Dave looked at the sky. The air was so brittle that one wrong move might crack it. *"I will soon find out if God cares, only He can rescue me now."* Dave looked at his pitiful self. All that was left of him was a half-frozen coatless body. His boots were so worn the heels were almost as flat as the toes. *"Move. I must move to keep alive."* He looked at his fist and tried to move his hand. It didn't budge.

Hours later, the train's brakes screeched into the frosty air. Dave sat stiff against the car. *"Where am I? Am I still alive?"* He looked down. A layer of snow coated him. He looked at his hands, still clutching the steel bar. He could not feel them. The train came to a stop.

A man in dirty coveralls approached, "Son! Are you okay?" The stranger's eyes revealed shock. "Here, let me help you!" Slowly, the man tried to pry Dave's hands from the bar.

"Ahhh!" Dave yelled. The stranger took off his gloves and set his warm hands on Dave's. After a minute, he tried again. Dave yelled. He warmed Dave's hands again for a few minutes. Carefully, the man helped lift Dave to the ground.

"Can you walk?" he asked, wide eyed. Dave tried to stand and cried out as pain shot through every muscle in his body.

"N-n-no."

"Lean on me. I'll be your crutch. Let's get you something to eat."

"W-who-who are you, and w-where am I?" Dave whispered, barely able to make his mouth move.

"I'm just a brakey for the CPR, and you're in Calgary," he said. Dave leaned his weight on the man.

"Oww!" Dave cried out. "I-I can't walk." The stranger held him up.

"It's okay. Take your time."

Dave groaned as he forced his legs to move. The two entered the station and a blast of heat from a wood stove hit them. The man took Dave near the snapping fire and sat him on a bench.

"Thank you, thank you." Dave's eyes misted over. *"How am I not dead? I should have frozen, but God saved my life."*

After half an hour, the stranger took him into the crowded station restaurant and ordered coffee and a bowl of soup. "Here. You stay and eat. I'll be back." Dave shook as he attempted to fill the spoon with the steaming liquid. *"I haven't tasted anything this good since . . . since I was a boy,"* he thought, as he took a sip.

The stranger returned and sat down opposite him. "I don't know who you are or where you're headed but you are more than lucky to be alive. It's minus forty-five degrees Celsius out there. I'd say someone had to be watchin' over ya." He glanced at the ceiling. "Anyhow, you'll be needin' this." He handed Dave a sheepskin coat. Dave felt a tear slide down his cheek.

"Thank you. Thank you . . . God . . . and you . . . for saving my life."

It was two days later. The new sheepskin coat covered Dave's body but everything else about him was worn and faded. He had lost weight. Although he was short, he had always been husky, but now, his once-muscular chest was sunken. Did he really want to do this? He stood on the sidewalk just down from his childhood home. It was Christmas Eve. After hopping another train, he had made it to Moose Jaw, and had walked from the train station. The neighbours' homes still looked the same. The same fence that had lined the street for years, even the same faded and peeling red and green Christmas lights the neighbors brought out every December 1. The same streetlamps with the same cracked bulb cover where he had practiced with his slingshot. The snow crunched under every step of his worn soles. His home came into view. The veranda still stood strong out front. The veranda he had peddled his tricycle on, and where he would spy on neighbors as they worked in their yards. *"I've failed miserably. Not only am I a dismal loser, but I've caused a lot of pain for my mother. Who do I think I am to just go home when I am in need? Do I really think they'll accept me with all the pain I've caused them? I will never be one of them. I am no longer an innocent young lad. I'm a hardened criminal who has delved into all kinds of sin. I should be in jail. Things will never be the same because I am not the same."* The thoughts pierced his heart as he stepped closer. *"I'm a failure, the talk of every prayer meeting in this area, no doubt. I'm not the hero I've always wanted to be. I'm the villain, the one to be avoided at all costs lest I taint unsuspecting and naïve children."* Dave stopped. *"I can't go—"*

"Arthur David! Is that really you?"

Dave whipped around. "Mother!?"

"Oh! David! David!" The groceries she held crashed to the frozen ground. Suddenly, he was surrounded. Surrounded by the wool-coated arms of his mother. Dave stared dumbfounded at the orange that rolled past and the half-opened egg carton that oozed smashed eggs. He forced his eyes to look at his mother's face and behind her black-rimmed glasses, lines creased around her dark eyes. Looking deeper, a warmth shone from them he hadn't noticed when he was at home. A mysterious joy radiated from them like when it rains, and the sun is still shining.

"Mother!" His voice cracked.

"Oh Dave! How we've missed you! Home has not been the same

without you, my Dave, my Dave!" She buried her face in his sheepskin coat.

Guilt pulsed through Dave. He choked. "I'm so…s-s-sorry Mother." A tear rolled down his cheek.

"Dave's back?" screamed a boyish voice from the side of the house.

"Melvin!" Dave yelled. Instantly, his brother embraced him.

"Come, Dave! Come see what Jewel and I made! It's a snow fort! Father helped us! I was just waiting and waiting for you to come home so I could show you!" The lad looked up at him with a smile and sparkling eyes.

"Now, now, Melvin. Dave's tired from his travels and is no doubt hungry. You can show him later," his mother said as she released Dave from her embrace. It was that voice. That same soft motherly voice he had heard all his growing up years. The innocent carefree life he had lived until he ran away came back to him. His heart softened, he wanted that feeling again. If only he could back up and be who he was ten years ago, but all he felt was guilt and shame.

Minutes later, Dave sat in the living room surrounded by his family. "So, I spent the last year in Vancouver and trucked, and that's about it." Dave ended his story as he looked at his family members. The fire cracked and snapped behind the screen door of the fireplace and cast its dancing shadows on the oval rug.

"Oh Dave! This Christmas is going to be extra special with you here," his mother said as she wiped a tear.

His father leaned in, "Son, the thing we are all wondering is how you are doing spiritually. Have you come back to the Lord?"

Dave glanced at one face after another. "Well, on my way to Calgary I told God I would turn over a new leaf. So, I guess that's one reason why I came home. I want to get straightened out and settle down. My life, as it is, isn't working."

His father's lips drew into a tight line. "I see. Well, we are more than happy to have you back, son."

Dave straightened as he spoke. All eyes in the auditorium were glued on him. He continued, "So, because I actually hadn't made a commitment to Christ, but just had a desire to turn over a new leaf, I fell back into sin. It was then that my sister Kay mentioned an evangelistic meeting that was to be held on the evening of February 11, 1934. I wanted to make things right with God for real this time, and that propelled me, yet—"

Dave felt a battle in his mind. He partly wanted to go to the meeting, and partly didn't. But his desire to prove to his family that he could be good overrode his uneasiness about religious gatherings. *"Besides,"* he thought, *"the meeting is in the theatre I frequented, and I've never been convicted in it before."*

Dave and his sister Kay approached the theatre. People crowded in, smiling and greeting each other. Dave glanced at a group of women. They were to one side in the lobby, dressed sharply and whispering amongst themselves. One wore a trim dress suit, and her red high-heeled shoes matched her lipstick. Her hair was artfully arranged around her fashionable hat. She turned and stared at him. She tipped her chin up. He looked down at his clothes. *"Unfit. I don't belong, even in my own habitat. Oh right. This is a religious meeting. They belong, I do not. I've been too bad."* The woman turned back to her friends and a burst of whispers and giggles erupted.

"Never mind them," Kay said as she urged him on. He turned to her and smiled. Her bobbed curly hair bounced as she talked, much like her bubbly personality. *"How is it possible she always has a smile?"* he thought. An usher directed them to the center of the theater. They sat. Gold trim framed the vaulted ceiling and decorative cupids holding golden ribbons adorned the walls. Great round lights hung from the embellished ceiling. The theatre was abuzz with quiet chatter. *"All that's missing is the smell of popcorn,"* he thought as he watched the people stream in. The auditorium hushed as a plain-dressed man walked on the stage in front of the plush dark curtain.

"Every single person in this room will be dead in less than one hundred years. In fact, most of us, if not all, will be dead by the year

2014. That's eighty years from now. And not one of us is good enough to enter heaven." The man's voice boomed across the hats that sloped in front of Dave. A quietness as loud as death permeated the air. The man held up his Bible. "*This* is absolute truth!" he yelled. "And it says it is appointed unto man once to die and after death, the judgment. It also says there is no one righteous, no, not one. You there!" He pointed to someone in the front row. "Do you think you're good enough to enter heaven?" The unsuspecting man shook his head. "You there!" The preacher yelled as he pointed to a woman. "None of your good works is good enough to merit your salvation. You all!" He waved his hand over the audience. "You've been helping those in need during this difficult time, feeding the poor, giving necessities to the hobos, but it's not good enough! How can we escape our certain damnation? Christ, that's how! He took the punishment for our sins. How he suffered as He took our filthy sins upon Himself so we could claim His pure righteousness—imputed righteousness. Oh, the depth of His suffering to free us from eternal torment!" The preacher raised his hands to the ceiling and began to weep. "How unimaginable His heartbreaking pain!" Never had Dave seen a preacher weep. His mouth dropped.

"Remember your commitment to serve Me if I saved your life on the train? I saved your life, but you have forgotten Me, Dave." Dave looked up. It was a still small voice. *"God?"*

"I plead with you, before it is too late, surrender! Surrender to God! *Now* is the acceptable time! *Now* is the day of salvation! Come forward, lost and weary soul. Find rest! Get saved, then go to a world that is dying and make disciples of all!" Dave felt his legs lift him. His sister looked up at him and smiled.

"Excuse me," he whispered to the man next to him. The man moved his legs to the side and Dave brushed past. As he made his way to the front, he felt every eye on him. He paused.

"Come son, come, for the scriptures say, 'To this man will I look, even to him that is poor and of a contrite spirit, and trembleth at my word.'"

Dave approached the front and knelt before the stage. Immediately, he felt someone beside him.

"I'm Mrs. Hall," an older woman whispered. "I know your mother."

A wave of guilt and shame engulfed him. *"How much does she know about me?"*

"Not good enough. I'm not good enough," he whispered to her as the preacher continued his appeal.

"You heard what he said—even the best of us are not good enough. All our righteousness is as filthy rags," she replied.

"But I've been bad. Real bad."

The woman's eyes enlarged. She cleared her throat and straightened. "But all have sinned and come short of the glory of God. Quit focusing on your sin. Look to the cross instead. Those sins you committed? Christ already paid for them—in full. Accept His forgiveness and forget what is behind. Surrender to Christ, then press forward, son. There's work for you to do." The words were a soothing ointment on a broken heart. Dave looked up at the preacher. He was still weeping. Others came and knelt. Dave hung his head. *"If I pray to accept Christ, I can no longer participate in worldly pleasure. My life will be boring and rigid with a list of do's and don'ts."* Dave perked up and sighed. *"But I've tried everything already. And no pleasure lasted. It came as a package deal tied to shame and guilt which gnaws at me daily."*

"I sense your battling, son. Pray it through, pray it through. The enemy of your soul doesn't want to lose control over you. He wants to destroy you," Mrs. Hall said. Dave glanced at her. He looked down. *"I've been too bad. No one here is as bad as I am. God will not forgive me. I've hurt Him, my family, and everyone I've sinned against. I'm unforgivable."*

He looked at the ceiling as an immense weight bore down on his heart. "Father!" he cried. "Forgive me!" A lump formed in his throat. "I've sinned against heaven and before Thee! I believe in You!" A sudden light broke into his spirit. *"Whosoever believeth in Me shall not perish but have everlasting life."* Life! *That* is what he wanted all along. He had believed lies of how to obtain it. A feeling of freedom from condemnation and guilt washed over him. The heaviness lifted. He was clean! Christ had taken all his sin and shame. Gone! A deep joy bubbled up.

"I'm saved! I know I am! I'm clean! I'm free!" he shouted.

Mrs. Hall's eyes filled with tears. "Welcome, Dave, to your new life in the family of God."

As Dave left the auditorium, two emotions filled him. The first—joy, for the wonderful lightness he felt in his spirit, and the second—sorrow, for all those he had wronged. *"I will make reconciliation as much as I can, starting with Mr. Furmost. I will return his truck."*

Later, Dave stepped into the porch behind his sister. The smell of freshly baked cookies filled the air and he breathed deeply. He walked through the thick dark curtains into the parlor. His father's Bible lay open on the fern stand. For the first time in a long while, it was a welcome sight. A quilt lay scrunched on the chair. The padding of his mother's slippers sounded behind him.

"Dave!"

"Mother, I've surrendered to God. I'm saved!"

"Praise be!" she said, rushing to embrace him. The smell of her perfume wafted around him like a heavenly aroma. His father walked in.

"Oh Dave. We are so happy," he said. "Tell us what happened." Kay entered.

"Let's have tea and cookies while you talk," his mother said.

Dave began. "The evangelist spoke on the cross of Christ, and as he preached, he wept. I've never seen any man weep while he preached. It's like he really cared. It's like the gospel seed that he planted was watered by his tears, and right there, on the spot, it bore fruit in my heart. I knelt and took Christ as my Savior!"

"Perhaps, my son," Dave's father said, "it was the seeds your mother planted years ago in your heart that his tears watered." Dave glanced at his father and then his mother.

"I think you're right, Father."

Dave stopped for a moment, fighting back tears. "And that is how

I found Christ. I will be forever grateful that God saw my wretched condition and saved me. After I found Christ, I devoted some time to return items I had stolen and make things right with those I wronged. My Uncle A. L. Stewart became one of my spiritual mentors, and from 1935 to 36 I attended Millar Memorial Bible Institute in Saskatchewan, and now, I am attending here. My goal is to win as many souls as possible to Christ before He returns or before I die."

Before Dave left the platform, Rev. Hutchinson gripped his hand warmly and thanked him for his testimony. As Dave took his seat, the students stood and applauded.

Minutes later, the young people filed out of the auditorium. Ed and Dave stood by the door and greeted each one.

"Hi," Dave said as Melva approached.

She looked at her shoes. "Hello," she said with a smile. She slowly brought her eyes to his. An awkward few seconds passed. "Thank you for sharing. I really appreciated your testimony."

"God is good," he replied. Melva nodded.

"Melva, hurry. Daddy's here to take us for lunch!" Doris' voice rang through the lobby. Melva glanced at her sister and back at Dave. His warm smile sent shivers up her spine. She approached her sister.

"What's with you?" Doris asked as she stared at Melva's face.

Melva felt her face blush. "I-I don't know."

CHAPTER SIX

CHOICES

October, 1936

It was the weekend. Melva stared blankly at the switchboard that had been such a part of her life before Bible school. Now, it was dull, merely a way to make money. She sipped her tea. *"How I long to learn more spiritual truths and hear more testimonies from others. Nothing compares to the rich fellowship I had with other like-minded young people,"* she thought. As the morning wore on, Melva's thoughts continually shot back to Bible school and all she had learned.

As Melva ate her noonday sandwich, the office door jingled. Dave stepped in. Melva's eyes enlarged.

"Good morning, Miss Melva," he said with a twinkle in his eye. He held his jacket over his shoulder. His normally clean-cut wavy hair was a casual jumble. His sleeves were rolled up, exposing his thick upper arms, and his hands were dirty.

She stood. "Why, hello Dave." She smiled. "What are you doing here?"

"Your roommate Helen told me where you live and work. And seeing as Langdon is only an hour from the Bible school if the roads are good, I decided to check out the place."

A warmth spread over Melva's face, and she smiled shyly.

"But," he continued, "my car conveniently got a flat a mile out of Langdon, so I had to walk here to get another tire from Winter's Garage."

"Oh, I'm so sorry."

He smiled warmly at her. A call came through. "Excuse me," Melva said, as she connected the lines.

"Say, is there a sink where I can wash?"

Melva nodded. "Yes, I will take you to it. It's in the back, by the door," Melva said as she pushed the curtain back.

"Larry Dodge and I are preaching in Strathmore and wondered if you and your sisters would sing at the meeting. Helen said you Dye sisters like to sing and play the piano."

"Yes, I do. I mean . . . we do . . . love to sing . . . a-a-and we accept your invitation, I'm sure my sisters would agree." A few minutes later, the two re-entered the office.

"Thank you. It will add a lot to the meeting. Since the war a few years ago, and now with all the dust storms and political upheaval, people are more interested in spiritual things than ever. Right now, we have a window of opportunity. We must tell them about God. We must tell them either before the next national tragedy, so they have Someone to cling to or before the nation prospers and they think they have no need of Him. We must tell them about heaven and hell. Eternity—it is a reality, and heaven's more glorious than we could ever imagine! Far above the dimension we live in! No more sadness, pain, death. We must tell others! We must spread—"

The door burst open, and Rob entered. His eyes enlarged as he glanced from Melva to Dave.

"Hi. I'm Dave." Dave held out his hand.

Rob shook it. "Rob." He turned to Melva. "This is for you." He handed her a frosty bottle of Pepsi-Cola.

"Thank you, Rob," she said.

"Where is Mrs. Scott, Melva? I hurt my finger," Rob said. Melva peered over the desk. "Oh dear. It looks bad. She's putting tar on a leak on the roof."

"Thanks, I'll go out back to talk to her." Rob's eyes riveted on Dave as he turned and left. An awkward few seconds passed.

"Well, I should go back to my car. I have my work cut out for me," Dave said.

"Do you need help?" Melva asked.

"Naw, after I get a tire from the garage, I'll be fine."

"All right. Bye," she said.

After he left, she skipped to the narrow window and peered out the windowpanes. He walked north down the boardwalk. Dirt pasted to his boots and the cuff of his jeans. Her heart pounded and she smiled.

"Mrs. Scott wrapped it for me. Says it's sprained," Rob said as he came up behind her from Mrs. Scott's living room minutes later. He looked out the window then glanced at her. "Who's that guy?"

"From Bible school."

"Oh. Can I drive you home tonight?"

Melva thought for a few seconds. "Dick is walking me home. It's only four miles."

Rob squinted. "The guy who wants to be a schoolteacher?"

"He's my cousin."

Melva shivered as she sat by the switchboard. She walked to the woodstove and threw in another log. The fire engulfed the dry wood. She rubbed her hands vigorously. For a second, her mind wandered to the log. "*It's being consumed, that I might have warmth and life.*" Slowly, she stood, deep in thought. The jingle of the door sounded, and a middle-aged man entered.

"Why hello, Mr. Williams. How are you?"

"Miss," Mr. Williams choked, "I had to rush Rob into the hospital yesterday. It's his hand. Mighty swollen. They don't know what's wrong." He pushed his hat back and wiped his brow. "My son," he said as he collapsed into the chair in the corner. His large bald forehead creased, and his usually firm jaw quaked.

"Oh Mr. Williams, I'm so sorry to hear that."

"Miss, I know he is mighty fond of you. Could you write him a note that I could take to him?" He paced the small office and faced Melva. "Anything, anything to cheer him up. You're his main source of joy." The phone rang and Melva connected the lines.

"Yes, of course Mr. Williams, I can write him a note." She opened her purse and took out a pad of paper. Dipping her pen in ink, she wrote. Minutes later, she handed it to him.

"Thank you, thank you, Melva. I know this will encourage him." He neatly folded it and tucked it in his wallet. Melva leaned back in her chair and sighed. *"I'm his main source of joy?"* The phrase stuck and she turned it over and over in her mind.

Monday morning, Melva and her sisters went back to college. The week went by in a blur. Whether it was attending classes or street witnessing, Melva found joy in being among the exuberant students.

The next weekend found Melva back in the phone office. She was connecting a call when Dick approached the counter and leaned over. "I'm visiting Rob tonight in the hospital. Wanna come?"

Melva straightened. "Sure. Have you heard how he's doing?"

"I heard they had to operate on his hand," Dick stated.

Melva's shoulders slumped. "Really? That's too bad."

"Yes. I think his father is worried about him. Well, I'll pick you up after supper. See you later!" Dick said as he left.

A few hours later, Dick pulled up and opened the car door. Melva collapsed in the seat.

"What's the matter?" he said as they drove off.

Melva buried her face in her hands. "Oh Dick. I don't know what to do with Rob!"

Dick raised his brow. "What do you mean?"

"I do like him, but when I'm with him, I feel I lose my testimony." She glanced at her cousin and wiped a tear.

He looked straight ahead. "Hmmm…"

"What am I supposed to do with him? I want to be a good testimony, so I'm friendly, but—"

Dick chuckled under his breath and cleared his throat. "Sweet Melva, I'm afraid you have to learn to say no."

Melva stared at the chrome knob on the glove compartment. "Well, it's not like he's bad. He's friendly, and I treat him like a brother."

Dick glanced at her. "Yes, but godly guys see him hanging around you and assume you enjoy his company. Think that might scare the right one away?"

After stopping at the nurse's station in the Calgary General Hospital, they walked down the spotless hall and tapped on Rob's door.

"Come in," a weak voice said.

"Rob, how are you?" Dick said as he pulled back the tan bed curtain. Rob squirmed into the sitting position.

"Relieved. I think my hand is finally on the mend. Melva! You came!" he exclaimed as a smile beamed across his face. Dick glanced at her. Melva approached Rob's bed.

"I'm so sorry Rob, for all you've been through." She glanced at the oversize bandaging that clung to his hand and partway up his arm. She shivered. The iron bed squeaked as he shifted. The walls were bleached white, along with his starched bedspread.

"Had to have surgery, some kind of infection. No need to worry about me though. I'll be outta here in no time. My boss needs me back, and Dad needs me on the farm, and I'm hoping I can work soon. One loses his appreciation for work until one can't do it anymore." The room fell silent for a few seconds.

"Melva," Rob said as he gazed into her eyes, "thank you for the note. And thank you for coming. It means a lot." Melva nodded and glanced at Dick.

"Hey, what about me? Doesn't it mean a lot that *I* came?" Dick laughed.

"Yes," Rob said, "because you brought Melva. Thanks."

"It's nice to see you again too, Rob, and I'm glad you're on the mend," Melva said.

After discussing farming, and a variety of subjects for the next hour or so, the two left.

"See what I mean?" Melva said as they headed back to Langdon.

Dick nodded. "I have a situation in my life too. I got a call to teach in Ferintosh."

Melva's eyes enlarged, "But Dick, that's what you've always wanted! A teaching position!"

He reached over and patted her hand. "Yes, but . . . that means I have to leave Langdon . . . and Kay."

"Kay? Kay Street? Oh Dick. I didn't know!"

Dick stared straight ahead with a dreamy look. "I'm so glad your sister Clara invited her to the Dye reunion. But keep it under your hat for now."

"Oh Dick, she is a very nice girl, Clara will be delighted! Melva's eyes teared. "But you're leaving us! We are all really going to miss you."

Dick sighed. "Yes, I always thought I'd get a full-time teaching position in Langdon. But life has thrown me a curve ball. Melva. It's tough, but we must learn to adjust."

A cool breeze blew across the wooden planks of the boardwalk and Melva wrapped her shawl tighter as she closed the switchboard door. She made her way to the schoolhouse where her cousin Dick substituted.

"Melva!" he greeted as he turned from cleaning the chalkboard.

Melva looked down. "Hi, Dick."

"What's wrong? Is everything alright?" he asked. She shook her head.

"I really need to talk to you." The young man set the eraser on top of a cabinet and walked toward her, slapping chalk dust off his hands.

"How about you walk me home while we talk? Mother will no

doubt have fresh cookies out." Dick said. A distant dog barked, and children laughed on the swing set. A couple of boys played catch on the baseball field.

"What's the problem?" he asked.

Melva sighed. "I miss Earle. Ever since he dumped me, I feel this ache in my heart." Her shoulders sank. "And I don't know what to do with Rob … and to add to my confusion, there are some really neat Christian guys at the school."

Dick shook his head as he chuckled. "It's a problem most girls would love. Melva, what I would say to you if you were my daughter—guard your heart. Do not trade common sense for anything. Be patient and ask advice from the older generation. They are quiet, and don't like to interfere, but they discern much more than we, and have a lot more years of experience behind them. Listen to them, Melva."

Melva sighed. "You're right, Dick. That gives me a lot to think about. Thanks." Dick straightened his trench coat.

"Anytime you wish for advice, I will be available."

"Thanks, Dick."

"Anything for a cousin," he said.

The alarm sounded and Helen shot out her hand and hit it. Melva sat up. "Morning *already?*" She wrapped the blanket around her and shivered. She had forgotten she was back in Calgary at the boarding house.

"We have an early morning class today, don't you remember?" Helen said as she stood. She swooped down and grabbed an envelope under the door. "Look, Melva. A letter for you!"

Melva's eyes widened, and she took the letter and ripped it open.

"It's from Dave!" she shouted.

"Well, I'll be!" Helen grinned.

Melva scanned it. "Looks like it's mostly about theology. I asked him a few questions last week."

CHAPTER SEVEN

SWITCHBOARD LIFE

Sept. 28, 1937

Melva's father had picked up his three daughters from the Bible school on Friday afternoon and after a good rest and a happy family breakfast, Melva was ready to work on Saturday at AGT.

"Thank you for the ride, Harold," Melva said as she slipped out of the truck in front of the office in Langdon.

"No thanks needed! As your grandpa's hired hand, I just do what I'm told!" he laughed. "Have a good day!"

Melva entered the office, hung her coat, and added a few logs to the wood heater. Except for the crackling fire, the office was silent. She stared at the switchboard. *"I have to spend all day behind these wires. I'm tired of being stuck here."*

Melva idly leafed through a book. The phone rang. R1203. *"Hmmm, wonder who that is,"* she thought. "This is Melva. How may I direct your call? Oh! Hi Dave! ... No, you didn't disturb me at all. Just reading . . . It's called, *The Restraining Hand.* You know Dave, I'm beginning to realize that God is above all that's happening in our lives, and in the world, and, believe it or not, His restraining hand is on evil. If it wasn't, life would be a lot worse. It gives me comfort that He is in control of my life, too." Melva and Dave continued their conversation for quite some time.

After Dave hung up, Melva once again paged through her book. Rob entered and leaned on the counter, "Melva, how about a double date tonight?" he said. His eyes sparkled.

Melva tilted her head, "I-I don't know. What's up?"

"Mr. Hotchkins is speaking in Calgary at the Nazarene Church tonight. Harold's driving in with Gladys and asked if I wanted to bring someone."

"It is very kind of you to think of me, Rob. I would love to hear Mr. Hotchkins. Yes, I do believe I will accept your invitation."

Rob returned her smile. "Personally, it's not my first choice for a place to go on a date, but I know how much you like these religious gatherings. You, Harold, and Gladys are all the same." Rob grinned. "Kind of cold out for autumn, so dress warm! See ya round five-thirty."

Melva parted the blinds. "Mrs. Scott. Look! It's snowing!"

"I'm not surprised, this is Alberta, after all. Not unusual for snow during harvest," Mrs. Scott stated, as she joined Melva at the window. "Lousy roads tonight, I'll tell you that much."

Melva sipped her soup later at the table with Mrs. Scott. A rap sounded on the back door.

"Come in, come in," Mrs. Scott yelled.

Rob stepped in. His natty suit and tie complimented his neatly combed hair.

"Hi Mrs. Scott, Melva. Despite the weather, Harold thinks we can make it. I wouldn't want to take my car, but Harold, well, he's just Harold," Rob laughed.

"Hi Rob. Just finishing up. I'm coming," Melva said.

"Young people today!" Mrs. Scott muttered, shaking her head. "How many times do you need to get stuck before you learn what a little snow does to the roads?" She cleared the table. "Dress warm and wear lots of layers. Don't want you freezing to death, and remember what to do in an emerg—"

"Mrs. Scott, we'll be fine, just fine," Rob cut in. Melva took his arm with her gloved hand and smiled. Minutes later, they slipped into Harold's car.

"Here's hot potatoes to keep everyone warm!" Harold announced, handing them around. Gladys giggled from the front seat.

They had only travelled a few minutes when Harold slowed. "This road is terrible! Look at the snow and slush!"

"At least we're still moving," Rob said. "Keep going."

An hour later, Harold pulled up beside the Nazarene Church. "Made it," he sighed.

Rob checked his watch. "Yeah, and only thirty minutes late." He opened Melva's door.

One-and-a-half hours later, they left the church and spent nearly ten minutes clearing snow and ice from the car. "What a great message," exclaimed Gladys. "Did you like it, Melva?"

"I sure did! He's a good speaker. I'm glad we came."

"Too bad it's still snowing," Harold said, settling in behind the wheel.

"We made it here, so hopefully we can make it back, I mean it's snowed a lot in the last one-and-a-half hours," Rob said, helping Melva into the car.

She shivered as she sat on the cold upholstery. Harold turned in his seat. "Say, I'm hungry. How about the Carlton? Just up the street."

After enjoying a leisurely meal, the group headed out. "How's the time?" Gladys asked as she snuggled into her scarf.

"Ten forty-five," Rob said.

"Wow, I didn't know it was *that* late!" Harold replied. "We were having too much fun!"

As they left the city, the car swerved and spurted a jet of steam. Resisting the urge to pull over, Harold exclaimed, "Now what? Something wrong?"

"Sure hope not," said Rob, wiping condensation from his window. "Probably the cold or maybe the bumpy road. Hey! Maybe it's this old wreck of yours! Let's keep going." Harold grinned and shrugged. After thirty minutes, the engine clanked, sputtered, and slowed. Harold pumped the gas pedal, but after another clang and knock, he pulled over.

"We're stranded," he sighed, leaning his head on the steering wheel. "Come on, Rob. Let's see what we can do." Snow quickly accumulated on the front window while the two men used Harold's flashlight to examine the engine. Harold poked his head into the car. "I'm going to walk to the closest farm and see if I can get help." Melva tightened her collar and pushed her hands deeper in her wool coat.

"Yeah, you go and I'll keep trying here," Rob said. "I'll need your flashlight, Harold."

"You scared, Melva?" Gladys asked after Harold disappeared into the dark.

Melva sniffed. "Well, sort of. You?"

"Let's sing," Gladys said.

A few minutes later, Rob slid in the back seat next to Melva. "Nothin' out there I can do. I'm freezing! My hands—can't stop shaking!"

"I'm cold too," Gladys added. "Let me sit beside you, Melva."

The three sat together and as Melva and Gladys continued singing, Melva's mind wandered. *"Another scrape . . . what a mess this is!"* The back seat was so small Rob squished Melva into Gladys, breathing so close to her she shivered. It was dark, the damp smell from his coat was almost overpowering, especially in that he had his arm over her shoulder. She looked away. *"This is so awkward,"* she thought.

Rob flicked on the flashlight. "Melva, I want you to have this," he said, taking off his watch.

"Oh Rob. I couldn't take your watch!" The gold oval face and fine gold hands flickered in the flashlight's gleam. "I shouldn't—I-I-I can't—"

"Please." Rob slid it over her hand. "For good luck. Say, do you know why Langdon is called the good luck town, other than the horseshoe shaped railroad turnabout?"

"No, why?" Gladys asked, oblivious to Melva's embarrassment.

Rob cleared his throat. "Because between 1883 and 1908—that's twenty-five years—there wasn't one death! Not even one! Everyone was so healthy, they had a shoot a guy just to start the cemetery."

"Oh Rob." Gladys groaned.

Two hours later, Harold arrived with a horse team. He opened the driver's door and asked, "Everyone alright?"

"You kidding? I've been pinned against Rob for two hours!" Melva thought.

"Fine," Gladys said. "Except I'm chilled, have a sore throat, and a headache. But I'll live. Glad you're back. You OK?"

Rob helped Harold hitch the team to the car. "This'll work fine!" Harold said, flicking the reins over the horses' backs.

As Langdon's main street came into view hours later, Melva heaved a great sigh of relief.

"We're here!" Harold announced. "Three in the morning is better than not arriving at all!"

"Hope my parents don't kill me!" Gladys said, coughing. "Never been this late before."

Minutes later Melva hurried to her room behind the telephone office. Shaking, she set Rob's watch on the dresser before pulling on her long nightgown and curling into bed. *"So awkward sitting close to him for so long! Oh my!"* Although she wanted to enjoy his presence, it didn't seem right . . . something held her back . . . something she could not put her finger on.

Still shivering, she burrowed deeper under the blanket. The room was warm, but the bedding, to someone who had been outside in a storm for so long, felt cold. A scuffling sound in the other room told her Mrs. Scott was adding wood to the fire. *"Shouldn't have gone,"* she thought. *"Could've been lots more dangerous!"* Too wound up to sleep, she couldn't resist a giggle. It was cute watching Harold and Gladys. Warmer now and even more awake, she got up for a drink. Harold and Gladys, yes, quite a pair. She grabbed her journal and after writing about Rev. Hotchkins' message, and about the stressful evening, she concluded with, "Oh well, praise God anyway!"

Melva peered out the office window. Rob entered the café across the street. *"I must return his watch. I just don't feel comfortable with it."*

"Mrs. Scott, I have to step out for a few minutes. Be right back."

"Sure," Mrs. Scott replied. Melva found Rob on a tall stool sipping a soda pop.

"Hi Rob," she said, trying to steady her nerves. "I don't feel right about keeping your watch, but thanks anyway." She gently put it on the counter in front of him and was halfway to door before he could stand and blurt, "But, but why? I want you to have it!"

The warm weather in the fall of 1937 helped farmers gather their crops and kept Hazel's kitchen warmer than was comfortable. She, Melva, Alice, and Clara were sweating through doing dishes with their mother when a knock sounded on the door. "Come in! Come in!" Hazel shouted. Melva, up to her elbows in soap suds, slipped a glistening plate into the rinse water as Vince stepped into the kitchen.

"Vince! Just in time to help!" Clara laughed, flicking a tea towel at him.

"Mercy me, Clara! That's no way to—" Grandma started.

"Aw, that's OK, Grandma Melvia," Vince cut in. "I should help. After all, Clara helped Dick find a wife." The women froze and turned to him. Vera's mouth dropped.

"I declare!" Grandma stated as her eyes enlarged. "You serious? You can't be!"

"Now that's it's out, I'm allowed to tell," Vince grinned as his eyes met Melva's.

Clara squealed, "Kay? Kay Street?"

"Yes. Ever since you invited her to the family reunion, Dick's had his eye on her. No wedding date has been set yet."

Alice reached to set the plates into the cupboard. "Congratulations to Dick. He's found a genuinely nice girl," she said. The rest agreed and broke into excited chatter.

"Ladies!" Vince spoke above the excitement. "I came to take all of you to prayer meeting. It's at Andersons' tonight." Hazel eyed her daughters.

"Only Doris and Melva, Vince. Clara and Vera must finish plucking feathers from the geese for tomorrow's supper.

"These roads sure are mucky!" Vince complained minutes later as they pulled onto the dirt road heading west. The car slithered sideways a few feet.

Doris' eyes widened. "We're not going to make it, Vince. Turn around. Please."

"Ah, nonsense! You worry too much," Vince laughed. He jerked the wheel to force the car back to the middle, but it continued sliding until it lurched against the tall grass. Vince glanced ruefully at his passengers. Doris' lips straightened in a thin line. Memories of her trip to Calgary with Rob shot through Melva's mind.

"Don't worry, ladies, everything's under control. I came prepared. Got a shovel in the trunk." After removing the wet clay from the wheels and between the spokes, Vince piled grass and sticks in front of the rear wheels and stepped back in the car, his boots and lower pant legs splattered with thick mud.

"Life's full of detours, ladies, and we need to adjust." A grin flashed across his face as he revved the engine. The tires gripped the grass and sticks and by carefully accelerating, they were on their way, more cautiously this time.

"Vince! W-w-where are you going?" gasped Doris. "We're off the road! Vince—"

"What's it look like? I'm driving through the pasture. Andersons live just over there."

"Yeah, I know where Andersons live, b-but people just, just don't drive through fields!" Doris squawked.

"This people does. Ha-ha. Like I said, life's full of detours. Adjust and have fun while we're at it!" He accelerated more forcefully, and the car hit a succession of pasture bumps, jolting them from their seats.

Minutes later, they pulled into Anderson's yard. "See, Doris? We arrived and had fun doin' it."

"Oh, Vince! You are simply impossible!" Doris said as she and Melva pushed past him.

Weeks flew by for Melva as she attended Bible school all week and did switchboard duties every weekend. She and her sisters, along with the students at Calgary Prophetic, held many evangelistic meetings in small communities, singing, preaching, and handing out tracts.

CHAPTER EIGHT

CONFLICTS

"It's your lunch hour, wanna go for a drive?" Rob asked as he leaned on the counter.

"Sure!" Melva said. "Oh, and Rob. Let me introduce you to Shirley. She's new here. Mrs. Scott just brought her in this morning."

"Nice to meet you," Rob said.

The new girl smiled. "You too."

"Will you be alright on your own for forty-five minutes?" Melva asked as she put on her coat.

"Of course," Shirley replied. "I'll manage. Thanks."

As they approached the car, Rob turned to her. "I want you to drive."

"Rob, you know I don't prefer to drive, especially not your fancy cars."

"Yes, but my hand . . . it hurts when I turn corners. Come on, try it. See what it's like."

Melva slowly opened the door and climbed in. She drove down the street.

"Very nice, Rob. It drives smooth."

"Melva, your sisters were talking about Dave yesterday. Remember? I met him in the office a while back. Who is he?"

Melva glanced at Rob as she turned the corner. "I told you already. He's a student from Calgary Prophetic, studying to become a pastor and an evangelist. He also preaches a lot."

After a few seconds of silence, she continued, "He's a nice guy, Rob."

Rob's eyes narrowed. "I thought *we* were a thing."

Melva sighed. "You're a nice guy too, Rob, but I-I don't want to get serious with anyone right now."

"Stop at the post office, would you?" Rob said. Melva pulled over to the boardwalk and stopped. She looked at him. Rob faced forward and straightened. His jaw tightened.

"Now turn the car around and go back to work."

"Alright. But can I at least get my mail while we're here?"

Rob sighed, pushed his hat back, and wiped his forehead. "Yeah, yeah, okay."

Minutes later, Melva got out of the car at the telephone office.

"Goodbye," Rob said, staring straight ahead.

"Goodbye," she replied, getting out. Rob got out and slipped behind the steering wheel. He slammed the door and drove off.

"That was a fast forty-five minutes," Shirley commented, as Melva entered.

"Yes, sure was," Melva said as she sat. "And plenty long enough, believe me!"

All the next day Melva answered calls. Trucks and tractors, some pulling wagons, rolled by the AGT office. As the sun set, Clara called.

"Hi Melva. Too busy to talk?"

"No," replied Melva. "Go ahead. Getting ready to close for the day. What's up?"

"Just found out I'm cooking for the Rae's threshing crew next week. The ninth."

"And?" Melva asked.

"They are bringing the food to the old, haunted house at the edge of their land. Mr. Rae examined the stove, and says it's usable, but I don't want to be alone! Everyone else is busy, even Doris is babysitting. Could you please get the day off and be with me?"

"I don't know, but I'll ask."

"Thank you, thank you," Clara said. "I'll wait to hear from you. See ya!"

A few days later Melva walked with Alice down the dirt road toward the haunted house.

"I'm glad you decided to come with me to help Clara. I don't blame her for not wanting to be by herself," Melva said.

Alice nodded. "Oh Melva, it's not really haunted, it just looks creepy. Anyways, I'm just glad I got permission to take Mary," Alice said as she looked at the toddler in the stroller. "Say, what's with you and Rob? I heard he was mad at you."

Melva shrugged. "He was mad at me. He asked about Dave. But yesterday he took me to Chestermere, just for a drive. He's not upset at me anymore." Alice looked at her sister from the corner of her eye. "What do you think of him?"

"Just a friend. Why?"

"Hmm, just wondering. I'd sure be careful, Melva. He's not a Christian. Dave is a much better guy."

The abandoned house stood tall and often, as they walked along the irrigation ditch, they saw it silhouetted in the distance.

"Imagine, Mr. Rae bringing food to the haunted house for Clara to cook!" Melva said.

"If the stove's still usable, why not?" Alice stated.

As Melva and Alice approached, Clara came to a window, which was missing its glass.

"Clara, how did you get here?" Melva asked.

"Donald Rae dropped me off with the food. I'm so glad you both could come! It's scary in here and look what I have to cook today!" Melva and Alice entered. The long table groaned with the weight of several large roasts in roasters, a gunny sack of potatoes, a pile of carrots, a heavy bucket of lard, a tin of sugar, a sack of flour, and ten jars of canned saskatoons.

"Oh Clara!" Melva said. "So much!"

"I'm waiting for the oven to get hot enough to put the roasts in, then I'll peel potatoes, and make the pies. As she untied the potato sack, she turned to Melva, "Mother told me Rob was mad at you. How is he now?"

"He took me for a drive to Chestermere. He's not mad at me anymore. Did you bring extra aprons?" Melva said.

"Yes, behind the potatoes. He's a handsome enough guy, but do you really like him? Alice and I are concerned about you and him," Clara said as she checked the oven temperature.

Melva tied on the apron. "I don't know what to think, Clara. I don't know. I mean, I just—don't know what to do with him. But I am praying the Lord to keep me."

"I'd be really cautious if I were you," Clara said.

As little Mary played with her doll in the stroller, Alice looked up from peeling potatoes. "Maybe you ought to go with Aunt Ruth to Carseland. They are having an all-night prayer meeting this Friday. They are mostly praying for the street meetings being held in Calgary, but you could ask prayer for an unspoken request."

The next day Melva was back at the switchboard when Rob stepped in.

"Hi Melva, how's your day been so far?" he asked, leaning on the counter.

"Fine," she said.

"Mind if I hang around and visit a while?"

"Sure, that's fine." Melva took call after call, visiting as best she could.

"Hello, Melva speaking. How may I direct your call? Oh! Oh, hi Dave!" Melva said with a smile.

The door slammed hard, and Rob was gone.

Oct. 31, 1937

Melva connected a call as Mrs. Scott entered with Shirley.

"I brought Shirley in to help you for a while, then she is going to help me with my canning. Anyways, if I could skip one day a year, it would be today! How I hate Halloween!" Mrs. Scott said as she slammed her keys on the counter. Shirley smirked.

Melva turned to Mrs. Scott. "What happened? Did some prankster already do something?"

"The outhouse. Someone tipped it over last night," Mrs. Scott said.

"Maybe it's the same person who steals milk from your back porch," Melva commented.

Mrs. Scott shook her head. "I told the milkman to put the milk bottles closer to the door, and they haven't disappeared since. But never mind about that, Bernie can set the outhouse upright when he gets home from work tonight." As Mrs. Scott entered her private quarters, Shirley turned to Melva.

"As for me, I don't really believe in all that Halloween stuff."

"What do you mean?"

"Witches and goblins. You know … freaky stuff." Just then a call rang and Melva connected the lines. After a few minutes of further explaining the switchboard to Shirley, Melva sipped her tea. Shirley looked at her. "What do *you* think of ghosts and goblins?"

"For the most part, I don't believe in that either."

"For the most part?" Shirley's brow knit in a confused expression.

"Well," Melva cleared her throat, "there is an invisible world, with good and evil. Tell me Shirley, do you know who Jesus Christ is?"

"Is? Don't you mean was?" She stretched. "Yes, I know who He was. A good man who lived long ago. People didn't like what He said and did so they killed Him." Melva opened her purse and unfolded a piece of paper. "This is a lecture written by Mr. Ernest Manning. He read it in one of our classes. It is called, *Why Did He Come? —He meaning* Jesus. Really interesting."

"Could you read it to me?" Shirley asked.

"Sure!" The phone rang and Melva connected the line. She turned back to the page.

"That Jesus Christ walked across the path of history is an irrefutable fact. Not only the sacred scriptures but the secular record confirms the impact He had and continues to have on human history. It has rightly been said of Him that all the armies that ever marched, all the navies that ever sailed, all the kings that ever reigned, all the parliaments that ever sat have not changed the course of history as much as He. When He was here, people debated two questions: who was He and why did He come? Christ was the greatest teacher who ever lived. But this isn't why He came to this earth. He didn't come to usher in a new social order, end war and violence, poverty and exploitation. First Timothy one fifteen says, 'Jesus Christ came into the world to save sinners of whom I am chief.' Our first parents, Adam and Eve, by their wrongful exercise of freedom, brought their glorious state to a disastrous end. They chose to disobey God. Their sin immediately alienated them. They died spiritually. The virus of sin infected their natures. No one can deliver himself from the guilt and condemnation. But there is good news. 'God so loved the world that He gave his only begotten son that whosoever believeth in Him should not perish but have everlasting life.' You may know about Christ as a historical figure. You may respect His teachings and try to follow His example; but if that is the extent of your relationship with Him, your sin problem that separates you from God remains unsolved. Your eternal salvation depends wholly on you knowing Christ as your personal Saviour." Melva set the paper down.

Shirley placed her hand on her mouth. "I didn't know *that*. If that's true, why didn't someone tell me? I thought I could get to heaven by being good. I'm much better than most." She glanced at Melva's sheet, holding it up to the light.

"Good by whose standards?" Melva asked. "If you broke even one of the Ten Commandments, you're not good enough. Here, read them." Melva handed her the small Bible she kept in her purse. Shirley took it and began to read. The girls talked for several more hours.

"I guess I'm not good enough. What do I do now?"

"First John chapter one, verse nine says, 'If we confess our sins, he is faithful and just to forgive us our sins, and to cleanse us from all unrighteousness.' And, Acts chapter sixteen verse thirty-one says, 'Believe on the Lord Jesus Christ, and thou shalt be saved.'" The door opened and Mrs. Scott entered with two plates of food, then quickly left.

"Supper already?" Shirley asked. The girls broke from their conversation as they ate. As they finished, Shirley asked, "Who can be saved?"

"Anyone," Melva started to say, but the door opened, and Grandpa Verne stepped in.

"I was driving down the alley to get a load of lumber when I saw someone had tipped your outhouse. I stood it up, but it needs to be better secured. I'll be over with some men to anchor it tonight."

"Thank you, Grandpa!" Melva gave him a hug.

It was after midnight. "We've talked for hours!" Shirley said. "I had no idea that's why Jesus came. I want to believe that what you are saying is true, but I need to think it through. Wow, I should have been home hours ago. Hope my parents aren't worried. Let's talk about this later. Bye!"

CHAPTER NINE

ROMANCE

Christmas break, 1937

Melva hovered over the woodstove and rubbed her hands.

"Don't think I'll ever get accustomed to these chilly Canadian winters," Mrs. Scott muttered as she wrapped her shawl tighter. The door burst open, followed by a blast of cold air.

"Mrs. Scott, I've not much to do today because my hand is still bandaged. Mind if I hang around here for a while?" Rob said.

"No, I don't mind at all," Mrs. Scott said. Rob glanced at Melva.

She smiled. "In that case, Rob, would you like some coffee?"

"Now you're talking! Sure would!" He slid a chair close to the switchboard.

The phone rang and Melva connected the lines. She arose and took a log.

Rob stepped in front of her and with his good hand, took the wood. Their eyes met. Melva went back to the switchboard and Rob put the wood in the stove.

"As long as I'm here, let me stoke the fire," he said. He sat down and lifted the newspaper.

Melva smiled. "But you have a hurt hand."

"I want to help you," he said with a smile. She walked to the window. A light dusting of snow fell, covering excited shoppers as they scurried from store to store.

"Twenty-two cars in town today!" Melva said.

"Wow. Everyone must be Christmas shopping at once!" Rob exclaimed as he joined her at the window. "Tell me," he whispered near her ear, "what would you like for Christmas?" Melva stepped back. Laughter sounded outside and the door burst open.

Donald and Hazel entered. "Daddy! Mother!" Melva hugged her parents.

"Oh Melva! Wait until you hear about the revival meeting in Strathmore!" her mother blurted.

"Ten young men got saved today," her father said.

"Oh, that's wonderful!" Melva squealed.

"It was. And the Christmas music was beautiful! It was like when you and the girls sang there. A real nice spirit among the people," Hazel added.

"No work for you today?" Donald said, glancing at Rob. Rob set down the paper and held up his bandaged hand. "I'm not feeling too well because of this. Still sore."

"Oh. Sorry to hear that," Donald replied.

Donald turned to his daughter, "Something else. I traded our old Chev for a 1933 Ford."

"Mr. Dye, you did? Can I see it?" Rob shot up and strode to the window. "Hey! Looks pretty nice, pretty nice, Mr. Dye!" The door opened and Vince rushed in.

"Uncle Donald," Vince began, "I was at the café and Vern told me you got a Ford. Can I look at it?"

Donald chuckled, "Sure, boys. I'll show you." They followed him out.

"Something else, Melva," her mother said. "Rob gave us a duck he shot and I'm going to cook it in the back kitchen for Christmas. The turkey I'll cook in the front kitchen. I was hoping you could pluck the feathers. Clara and Vera did it last time."

Melva woke to the sound of the wind whistling around the window. She sat up and glanced around. A light layer of dirt and snow covered the windowsills. Vera lay asleep beside her. Melva rested her foot on the gray-painted wood floor and squealed. "Yikes, that's cold!" Her foot shot under the covers again. The springs creaked and Vera bounced and groaned, pulling the quilt closer under her chin.

"Vera," Melva whispered. "The sill has dirt and snow on it! And on Christmas!"

Vera turned, "Oh. Merry Christmas." She rolled over and burrowed deeper under the covers. Melva sighed as she crawled out of bed, wrapping her housecoat tighter and stepping into her crocheted slippers. She headed downstairs, in hopes to warm by the fire. A fine layer of dust mixed with snow lay on most of the sills. Footsteps and the thump of a cane sounded and Melva turned.

"Land sakes! Just look at the dust! And on Christmas! Well, father told me earlier when he went to do chores that it's rare, but there is such a thing as a snow-and-dust storm. Just what we needed alongside of all the other dust storms of the thirties! Won't even let up for Christmas!" her mother brooded.

"Oh Mother, I'll help clean up," Melva said as she took the enamel basin and filled it with warm water from the stove's reservoir.

"Go get dressed and wake your sisters, will you? They can help clean and bake before everyone comes for dinner. We need four more pies at least. Daddy will make the ice cream. I'll cook the dressing you made last night, plus the birds. Hmm—potatoes! The girls can peel and Vern can stoke the fires," Hazel said as she busied herself in the kitchen.

Melva turned and dashed up the stairs. Within minutes, her sisters were up, and Vern came in from chores. The household rang with laughter as each worked to make the house presentable for guests. After Vern added four leaves to the dining room table, Clara decorated the center with evergreen boughs and red Christmas ornaments. One by one, relatives pulled up and by two o'clock, everyone was around the large dining room table. The table was filled with delicious food. The duck lay on a platter at one end, and the turkey at the other. In between lay cranberries, Jell-o salads, stuffing, mashed potatoes and gravy, peas, and steaming honey-ginger carrots. A pile of fresh white buns with butter melting on the tops sat in the middle. Grandpa Verne cleared his throat, and everyone looked at him.

"For these blessings, Lord, we give You thanks. Thank You for a good harvest, and the food You have given us. Thank You that the girls were able to get the dust cleaned before we eat and thank you for the many hands that prepared the food. Thank You for each life around this table. May we always give thanks and glory to You, as today we remember the baby in the manger. Amen." A chorus of amen's sounded, and a sudden burst of voices and laughter rang as various ones took platters and filled their plates.

A while later, Melva felt stuffed—a good, contented feeling. When everyone finished, they moved to the living room. Melva played Christmas carols on the piano and a chorus of voices followed her lead until Santa burst in, carrying a large wooden crate.

"Ho ho ho!" he chuckled.

"Mother! It's Dick! It has to be!" Vera laughed. Mother smiled and nodded. Santa passed out little cakes to everyone.

"Someone has been busy baking and it wasn't me," he said as his eyes sparkled behind his fluffy white beard.

Oohs and ahhs sounded throughout the room as presents were passed out from under the decorated spruce tree. Melva looked at her precious gifts—powder, perfume, silk hose, and money from her parents for a dress.

"Melva, I picked up the mail. These are for you," Clara whispered. Melva took the two envelopes and opened them. One was from Rob, the other from Dave. She blushed at the loving words each contained. Slowly, she closed Dave's, and felt the glitter on the front.

"Game of checkers?" Vince asked. Melva glanced up.

"Sure Vince, and I'll beat you too!" Melva said, feeling confident.

January 1, 1938

The wind swirled and plastered snow against the window. Melva turned from the window to the table where her extended family sat reminiscing, a New Year's Day tradition. She took a handful of popcorn and sat.

"Tell us more, Grandpa. Your thoughts about living in Iowa, and what moving here was like," Vince said.

"Well son, I think we tend to romanticize the old days the further we get from them," he chuckled. Hazel took a sip from her hot chocolate.

"I can't romanticize what it was like for me to move here," she said. "It was one thing to ride on that passenger train with Ruth, Muriel, and Ada, but travelling with two-year-old Alice and one-year-old Melva was quite another! I am still amazed how fast that train went."

Ruel grabbed another handful of popcorn and grinned. "'Member when Donald and Roger found out about how fast Dad's car could go?" All eyes turned to Donald. A sheepish grin spread across his face.

"Tell me about it," Harold, the hired man, said, "I haven't heard this story yet."

"Well," Donald began, "Even though Dad just bought a new 1913, seven passenger Lexington Touring car, he still took the horses to town."

"That's because I didn't quite trust cars yet," Verne said, "now a horse, that's flesh and bone. I know all about horses, but a car? Nothing but a pile of metal."

"So," Donald continued, "When Dad left for town in the horse and wagon, Roger and I would sneak in the barn and pull out the car. We would head straight west as fast as the gas pedal would let us. Found out it could go sixty miles per hour, we did! Then when we got home, we would each take a broom and sweep the car tracks over. Dad never knew."

Verne cleared his throat. "Never knew until I realized the tank was half empty, and then you boys got what was comin' to you." Various snickers were heard around the table.

Verne took a sip of hot chocolate. "Ahh, that Lexington. It had a carbide lights generator mounted on the running board for head lights and long brass rods to the front to hold the top in place. Pretty reliable it was."

"Back to the topic of riding in a train," Ruel said, "try riding in a train car with a bunch of thick-skulled cows and horses, like Donald and I had to do. At least Dad was with us to settle the animals when they acted up."

Grandma Melvia cut in, "Well, I miss the sweet taste of Iowa corn."

Verne sipped his coffee. "Yes, the corn there grows upwards of twelve feet, most likely because on average the summer temperature hovers around ninety degrees Fahrenheit, and it's humid."

"I'll never forget the day in February of 1916 when we stepped off of the train in Langdon," Uncle Lee, Dick and Vince's father, said. "We arrived in the middle of a chinook. I jumped out on the platform at the train station to get my first view of Langdon. The mountains looked so near I hurried to unload so I could hike over to them. When someone told me they were about one hundred miles away, I was speechless."

Verne laughed. "Yeah, they did look close. Melvia and I had been married twenty-eight years, we had nine children, and I wanted more land. Prices too high in Iowa. Trading my farm in Iowa for this here piece near Langdon is the best trade I ever made. Glad to have you all move up with us, grandchildren and all. Let's hope and pray God continues to enlarge us in Canada, even in this new year." Those around the table nodded.

January 19, 1938

Alice, Doris, and Melva left the Prophetic Bible Institute building as a cool wind swirled light snow around them. Melva tied her scarf around her neck.

"I don't like walking home this late," Doris said as she tucked her chin into her collar.

"Let's just hurry," Alice added. "Too bad the meeting went so late."

"What annual meeting ends early?" Melva mumbled through her

scarf. The girls strode down the sidewalk to the boarding house. A car appeared out of the darkness and slowed beside them.

"Someone we know?" Doris asked.

"Don't think so," Alice said. "Don't look. Keep going." The girls picked up their pace. The street was empty, and the car continued beside them.

"Hurry! Let's cross," Doris yelled. Just as they were about to cross, the car cut them off. Melva's heart pounded, and the sisters froze.

A large man appeared out of the driver's seat.

"Jump in. I'll give you girls a ride home." Fear washed over Melva.

"No thank you," Alice replied as she hastily led the way around the vehicle to the other sidewalk.

As the girls entered the boarding house, Melva spoke. "How strange. He froze when we crossed in front of him!"

Alice smiled, "He shall give His angels charge over thee, to keep thee in all thy ways."

The next morning, Melva phoned Dave.

"Dave, I need to talk to you. I was so frightened," she began. As Dave listened, he made a few consoling remarks then added, "If it's alright with you, how about we go for a drive? You need time to talk this through. After classes today? I'll wait for you in the entry of the Institute."

"That would be nice," Melva replied.

"Hello Melva." Dave approached her near the entry doors of the Institute. He looked at her with his charming smile. "So sorry about your scare." He opened the car door. "Praise God. He kept you safe."

"Yes," Melva said as Dave started the car. "It seemed like the man just froze as we hurried across the street."

"Maybe, he did. God definitely protected you girls." Dave turned into the traffic. "How about I take you to the Calgary Currie Barracks where we can just sit and talk?"

"Sure," Melva said.

Minutes later, they pulled up in front of the Currie Army Barracks.

A snow-covered hedge graced the front of the extra long building. Dave stopped the car. Melva fidgeted, clasping her hands on her lap.

"Melva," Dave started as he looked at her, clearing his throat. "I've been thinking a lot about you. I appreciate your love for the Lord and your cheerfulness, especially while you serve others. You really do have a servant's spirit."

Melva's face flushed. "Why, thank you. I've been thinking a lot about you and the testimony you gave at the Institute. It's amazing what happens when God enters a person's life."

Dave chuckled. "Yes. It is. It's miraculous." Melva looked out her window. A few children chased each other and laughed in the nearby snow-covered field.

"Melva," Dave spoke softly, "I was wondering if I could have permission to get to know you better. You know, become closer friends?" Melva's heart leapt and sank. *"My heart. Earle ... it's too soon ... What about Rob? Would I be two timing? Naw, he's just a chum."*

"Dave, I do admire you, and I would like to be your friend, but ..." Her words drifted off.

Dave ran his fingers through his thick hair. The light scent of his aftershave filled the car.

"But what?" he asked. "Something wrong?" Melva looked at her skirt. *"Dear Jesus, what do I say? I'm not over Earle . . . and I can't give Dave my whole heart yet . . . it's not fair to him . . . but he is the kind of man I've always wanted, much more so than Rob."*

"You're a godly man, Dave, and I do want to get to know you better," she whispered as she glanced at his face. The corner of his mouth turned up into a warm smile.

"Good then! Do you mind if I ask you about your family? I don't want to appear nosy, but I'd like to get to know you and your family better." Dave's eyes twinkled.

"Sure. Go ahead." Melva relaxed.

"First, I would love to hear your testimony," he said. "When were you saved?"

"When I was nineteen, I heard a man named Mr. Neighbour preach in Calgary. It was December 30, 1934. I knew I was a sinner, even though I grew up in a Christian home, so I repented and asked Jesus into my heart."

"Hmm," Dave said. "Same year *I* got saved! February 11."

An hour passed. Melva told him about her family, and how they had moved from Iowa. After a break in the conversation, Dave spoke.

"My main desire is to win souls for Christ. Melva, I tried what the world has to offer, but nothing satisfied. And now I'm left with the consequences. I battle regret every day, and I'm still trying to make things right with those I hurt. When I feel discouraged with the process, I think of the benefits of my past."

"Benefits?" interrupted Melva. "How is that possible? How can good come from what you did, how you lived?"

"Yes, benefits," Dave explained. "My negative past is ever-present to keep me humble. And because of what I went through, I can minister to the unsaved because I was there once. How I long to be in full time work for God. Melva, just think of all the lost souls we see every day. Just one breath away from eternity, yet their eternal destiny is hell. Forever torment. Oh, the depth of God's mercy to save us out of our lost estate!"

"Maybe Dave is too spiritual for me. What would he do if he knew I was friends with Rob? And I've never even asked Rob if he is saved. Alice doesn't think he is."

"What do you think, Melva?" Dave asked.

"Yes, I agree. And I would like to hear more about how God worked in your life, and about your family. Tell me about your sisters and brothers."

As Dave talked, Melva felt her tension and fear dissolve. He was so kind, with an inward maturity that was different from the other men she knew. The more he talked, the more Melva's heart softened to him.

It was almost midnight when Dave dropped her off at the boarding house. "It was lovely visiting with you, Melva. I hope you don't mind getting in late."

"I loved our conversation and had no idea it was this late! Thank you so much for taking me out, and for supper as well," Melva said, stepping out of the car. She glanced into his eyes and saw a soul on fire. A courageous warrior. Yet, a man who looked in love.

"Goodbye," she whispered, barely able to control her voice.

"Goodbye." His eyes reminded her of Vince—they had a loving yet mischievous twinkle to them.

Melva stared at the dark ceiling and rolled over. No sleep came. She sat up in bed. Helen slept soundly. Still restless, Melva lay down and stared at the dark wall. Unable to sleep, she slipped out of bed, turned on her desk lamp, and opened her Bible.

The next night, Melva put on her housecoat after supper, with the intention of going to bed early. Minutes later, she was called to the hall phone.

"Hi Melva, Dave here. What did you think of our visit last night?"

"Hi Dave. I enjoyed it. Gave me lots to think about."

"Yeah, me too. I've been thinking about what God wants me to do in the future. I want to go into full time Christian work; there are so many who need to hear the good news. I've also been thinking about you—I mean—us . . . together—ministering together in the future, and, and perhaps—"

The conversation continued late into the night. When Melva entered her room, Helen was already sleeping. Again, another restless night of tossing, turning, and staring at the dark ceiling. *"Dave is already talking serious with me . . . he's implying marriage, us, ministering together."* A picture of Earle floated into her mind—Earle across from her in the café . . . *"Melva, you're the only one for me. I'll never love another."* She wiped a tear away and knelt by her bed. *"Dear Lord, why do I struggle and have no peace? Please give me peace. Lord, I've never met anyone as godly as Dave, but my heart is not over Earle . . . I can't give Dave my whole heart right now . . . but I want to. I badly want to, but it wouldn't be fair to him to give him only half my heart. O Lord, I surrender to Your will. Heal my broken heart!"* She stared at the ceiling and sighed. "I will tell him tomorrow." She slipped back into bed.

January 23, 1938

Melva had barely shut off her alarm the next morning when the phone rang in the hall. She grabbed her housecoat and ran to answer.

"Hello Dave? Yes, seven-thirty tonight works. See you!" Melva sighed. *"Dear Lord, I don't want to hurt him. What should I do? What should I do? He's such a nice guy."*

All day during her classes Melva's thoughts turned again and again to Dave and what she should tell him.

That night at seven-thirty, Melva stood inside the Institute door waiting for Dave.

"Hello Melva. Like to walk?" Dave asked, "or would you rather we drove?"

"Walking's okay by me."

As they stepped outside, Melva looked at him and after a few moments of silence, turned to him.

"Dave, I haven't slept much the last couple of nights. You've given me so much to think about. It is rare to see a man so on fire for God, one totally yielded to Him and His will. I admire you, Dave." He glanced at her and smiled. The crunch of snow sounded beneath their footsteps.

"And I admire you," Dave said. "I've dreamed of a girl like you but didn't think one existed! Melva, you're just too good to be true."

"Oh Dave!" Melva stopped and touched his arm. "I-I don't want to hurt you Dave, but I-I-I feel God telling me we need to slow down. I think our relationship is moving too fast. I'm, I'm just not ready to get serious. I don't want to hurt you, but, but—" Melva turned her face away.

"Dear Melva," he smiled, "my life is surrendered to Christ, as is yours. If that is how you feel, so be it. I will slow down. It is the will of God."

They continued walking. The quietness felt painful. She glanced at Dave and felt an icy sting on her cheek as a tear trickled down. *"I thought he was going to disagree or at least argue. But he meekly submitted to what I said. I can't believe this man. Truly he is a man of God."* She looked at him again and even though he walked straight and confident, she knew she had hurt him. They continued around several blocks and their conversation turned to more lighthearted subjects. When they approached the boarding house, Dave asked, "Do you mind if I still phone?"

"No. That's fine. Please do."

"Thank you, and please forgive my hastiness in our relationship. It's just that you're so—so—attractive, in, in every way." Melva blushed. "I should have known a gal of your caliber would be a hard catch." He grinned, looking into her eyes.

Melva hastily entered the building and peered out the window, watching Dave slip into the night with his long wool coat trailing behind him. Her heart sank. She ran to her room and flinging herself across her bed, wept. Helen, immersed in her studies, spun from her desk and knelt beside Melva's bed.

"Melva! What's wrong? Melva!"

"Oh Helen. I feel like I've cut off his right arm," Melva sobbed.

CHAPTER TEN

STRUGGLES

January 25, 1938

Melva, Doris, and Alice walked briskly toward the Bible school. Faced with the chill of a typical Calgary winter morning, Melva turned up her collar and Alice tightened her hat ribbons. A car drove by and honked. Remembering their previous experience, Melva instinctively turned away.

"Look! It's Dave!" Alice exclaimed. Melva waved, along with her sisters, and Dave pulled over. "Far too cold to walk," he called. "Want a ride?" Melva, Doris, and Alice slipped in the back and Alice chatted cheerfully until they stopped at the Institute.

"You were sure quiet," Doris said with a grin as they took their seats in the auditorium.

"Didn't feel like visiting," Melva said.

January 30, 1938

Melva loosened her wool coat and scarf, looked around the Langdon Baptist Church and counted. Twenty-seven people. Pretty good for such cold weather, she thought. Vince shoved a couple more logs in the woodstove while a few children warmed their hands. The floorboards creaked when Mr. Smart took the pulpit.

"Good morning, ladies and gentlemen. Today, we have a special guest. A young evangelist is going to speak. Dave Stewart is from Moose Jaw and is a student at the Calgary Prophetic Bible Institute. Dave?"

Dave held his Bible and notes and strode to the pulpit. "Thank you for having me. My message today is from First Kings chapter eighteen, verse forty-five. 'And there was a great rain.'"

He scanned the audience, adjusted his Bible and papers on the pulpit, and began.

"It was a long and consuming drought. Leaves shriveled. Wells dried. Cattle bellowed. The nation was perishing. Seeing the conditions around him, Elijah prayed seven times on Mount Carmel. The text says a great rain came. Ye fearful saints, take fresh courage! Let us consider a few things about this prayer that brought about such a marvelous result. It was a humble prayer. The feeling of the soul often indicates the posture of the body. Elijah cast himself down upon the earth and then put his face between his knees. We only have a few years and then we stand before God. Yet we are so cold and proud. Where is Jesus in our lives? How little we seek Him. How little we seek to rescue the lost. Where is heaven? How little it thrills us.

"Elijah prayed a persistent prayer—seven times—before the blessing came. I'm sure he would have prayed a hundred times! An occasional prayer doesn't amount to much. Pray, pray, pray. One thousand times if necessary. Be prostrate, sob in earnest. Loved ones need to be saved. Is that not worth the struggle?

"Elijah's was a definite prayer. He could have prayed about fifty things. And look at us—we live in a commercial world and have too many glittering generalities in our prayers!"

Dave looked up with his arms stretched to heaven. A tear rolled down his cheek. "Oh, that we could be made to feel and know we are responsible for those over whom we have influence. The Lord will some day ask us about those in our care. The blood of their souls will be on us!

"As we continue to consider Elijah, notice his was a confident prayer. No *maybes* about it. He sent his servant up the mountain to check. Do we have the same positive expectancy? Do we *really* believe Jesus means what He says when He said, 'Ask and it shall be given you'? Away with our half-hearted prayers! They die ere they leave our lips! Jesus said, 'Let not that man think he shall receive anything from the Lord.'

"Do not insult God with your unbelief. Pray with the confidence of the mother who made a quilt for her soldier son. On it she embroidered, 'He arose and came back to his father.'"

Dave held up his Bible. "Oh dear people. How can we stagger and doubt with such a Bible, such promises! Ours is an ice-bound church! Let us *pray!*

"Elijah's was a successful prayer. He got what he wanted. Rain. Do our prayers bring success? Not rain for the land, but prayers for sinful, drought-stricken souls? Work hard for it, friends—climb the mountain—pray. The right kind of prayer will bring it. Pray in private. Pray in public. Pray now. Pray perpetually.

"When did it rain for Elijah? The same day. When will our prayers be answered? How long will we be without salvation? We cannot wait until tomorrow. It is rain *today* we want, that we must have!"

Dave looked up. Tears streamed down his face.

"*That* we will have, but only if we centre our passions, minds, and energies of our soul upon it."

After expounding on prayer for awhile longer, Dave closed his Bible and looked at the congregation.

"Prayer like vapors are rising from sea to sea. God's mercy is forming to pour out a blessing. Let us lift high our voices. Let us plead with the Holy Spirit to do a great work. Plead for the Lord God to come into His holy temple. Let us pray for souls to be saved."

Dave carefully picked up his Bible and sermon notes and left the podium.

A deep silence filled the church. Long moments passed until Mr. Smart slowly stood, wiped his brow, and dismissed the congregation.

At the door, Dave greeted each one.

"Great sermon, young man," an elderly farmer said, clasping Dave's hand. "You have much passion. Not many preachers can keep me from falling asleep, but you kept me awake the whole time! The whole time!"

"Some sermon," Grandpa Verne said as he took Dave's hand. "Keep it up."

"Got fire in ye bones, I can see that." The elderly Mr. Jackson approached Dave, leaning on his cane. "Thank you, thank you, Mr. Stewart."

Little Simon Nelson grinned as he looked up at Dave. "One day I want to be a preacher like you!"

"To be a preacher is a fine ambition. Just fine!" Dave said, tousling the boy's hair.

Widow Sarah approached, "Sonny, I would be a-burstin' with pride ifin you were *my* son. You're a handsome young man with lots of power in ye." She patted his arm. "Ye can't be much older than twenty-four! Your mama should be down right proud of ye!"

Dave chuckled. "Thank you, ma'am. God has done a great work in my heart."

Melva stepped forward. "Very good sermon, Dave."

Dave looked into her eyes with his warm tenderness and as she turned to leave, he said, "Melva. Thank you for slowing our relationship down. The Lord is using it to deepen my walk with Him."

Melva smiled. "I know He is, I can tell." She looked at him and for a moment, their eyes locked.

February 6, 1938

"Hello, this is Melva. How may I direct your call?" She connected the line and took another sip of tea. The door burst open. A burly man wearing a thick fur coat approached.

"Uncle Ruel! So good to see you," Melva said.

"Likewise. Come see my new car. Bought it yesterday."

"Sure, sure. Let me grab my coat. Mrs. Scott, will you watch the switchboard?"

"Oh, Uncle Ruel! It's, it's beautiful!" Melva walked around the sleek black car and peered into the window.

"It's a 1937 Terraplane Hudson. Winnie and the girls fit in it just fine. Like it?"

"Yes, yes, I do! Congratulations!"

"After work I can give you ride if you'd like."

"Yeah! That would be fun. Sure!"

"Say Melva, did you hear that Dave is sick?" Ruel said.

"Really? So that's what Doris and Alice were whispering about. I guess they didn't want to tell me. No, I didn't. How bad?"

Ruel shrugged. "Don't know. Just overheard your sisters talking last night. He's been in bed sick for a few days. Well, see you later!"

Back in the office, Melva dropped into her chair and rested her chin in her hand. *Did I do the right thing? I care a lot about Dave. I want to see him, to bring him something, to visit him . . . but I can't, I just can't! But he'll think I hate him if I don't see him!*

"Together, forever, Melva. You and I . . ." Earle's smiled at her over the hot chocolate he held in his hands. She smiled, with a thrill coursing to her fingertips. She clutched her hot chocolate and giggled.

"Earle and Linda request the honor of your presence at their wedding . . ." Melva pushed back her chair abruptly. *"How could you? How could you just stop loving me?"*

She bit her lip and wiped a tear.

Mrs. Scott walked in and glanced at her. "Melva? You alright?"

Melva walked to the window. "Oh, Mrs. Scott . . . I-I don't know . . . I don't know."

February 7, 1938

Wind and snow swirled around the office window. A bundled man and a woman entered the office. Melva looked up. "Daddy! Aunt Winnie?" Donald stood by the door shaking and Winnie held baby Keith.

"Brand new car and plumb froze up. I had to pull Ruel's car to Bittles'. By the time we got there, Winnie and baby Keith were well nigh freezing! I guess a new car is no guarantee that it will be more reliable than an old one."

"Oh dear," Melva said. "Here, come Aunt Winnie. Take off your wraps and warm yourself by the fire." Melva jumped up and took the two-month-old baby.

"Thank you, Melva," Winnie said. "I was in the middle of shopping with the baby when the car froze. That's when I saw your father walk out of the garage and asked him to see if he knew what was wrong with it. Would you mind babysitting while I finish shopping? Won't be long."

Mrs. Scott entered the office, rubbing her hands with lotion. "Of course, we'll watch the baby—that's what neighbors are for," she said with a smile as she took little Keith from Melva. *"Aunt Winnie is so lucky to be happily married and settled,"* thought Melva as she watched Mrs. Scott bounce Keith on her lap. *"If only my life were not so complicated."*

February 14, 1938

"No classes today?" Rob asked as he entered the office.

Melva looked up. "Normally, I have classes on Monday, but not today."

"Good then! Happy Valentine's!" Rob reached across the counter and handed her a thick envelope.

"Thank you, Rob. Should I open it now?"

"Whenever you want. It's a Valentine's letter." He winked and Melva blushed as she tucked it under her purse.

"Say, your sisters said that Dave guy is pretty sick."

Melva sighed. "Yes."

"They told me about his pre-Bible school days. Quite the thief."

"It's called his testimony, Rob. Yes, he was a thief but now he's gotten right with God. That's what salvation does."

Rob sat on a chair beside Melva. "Still, a girl like you shouldn't be interested in an ex-criminal, should she?" He moved closer.

The phone rang and Melva connected the lines. She turned to Rob. "Neither should a girl like me be interested in a man who drinks and nearly does himself in, in a drunken brawl."

Rob jumped out of his chair. "W-W-What? How did you—"

"Mrs. Scott told me. She saw the whole thing from this window."

"Well," Rob cleared his throat. "Dave's no better than me."

"You're right. The only difference is that his sin is under the blood of Jesus."

March 11, 1938

Laughter and chatter rang through the spacious auditorium as students took their places. Doris leaned over to Melva. "I really like your new hat and suit. Looks so sharp on you."

Melva smiled at her sister. "Thanks. Wasn't it fun shopping yesterday? There are so many options in Calgary, especially since Daddy gave us all money." Doris nodded. Melva glanced around the room. Dave sat near the front in a row of other young men. *"I'm so glad he's feeling better. I need to talk to him."*

Rev. Cyril Hutchinson approached the pulpit. "My message today is called, 'The Hazard of Living for Jesus.' The centre of what I will say today is a little-used word, but a heroic one: *Hazard*. It means an enterprise that involves danger of risk or loss. We know very little about hazard in Canada. Early Christians knew it. To take the name of Jesus in pagan Rome was to risk your life. But let us make no mistake. We *do* live in hazardous days. Christianity is being confronted with opposition by all of hell's powers. Have you not sensed it? We live in a frightened world, so greatly changed from just ten years ago. This is the time of increasing political upheaval. This is also a time of spiritual lethargy. We have heard of young Christian Africans, full of joy and zeal. They encounter our western world and are bewildered by our lack of vitality, urgency, and joy. Our Christian world is sapped by worldliness, enamored by materialism, bound by selfish fear of losing some fancied security.

"We have lost our daring! We have forgotten how to exercise the hazard of living for Jesus!

"It will do us good to look at two men who did not forget. Paul and Barnabas. A pair of heroes! Time fails me to tell all the story of the glorious missionary journey they did not need to take, but they took the hazard! Later, Paul faced Diana of the Ephesians . . . and a riot over it. He faced the materialism of Corinth, the intellectualism of Athena, and the legislative authority of Rome. One little Jew with the courage of a lion! These men hazarded their lives for the Lord Jesus.

"And what of today? What do we do in hazardous days? Timidly retire? Our day calls for heroes! Jesus orders us to 'Quit you like men.' 'Quit' here means 'to make a man of. Occupy till I come.' Hard days make strong men. The north wind made the Vikings. The measure of our hazard reveals the vitality of our faith. The heart of faith is venture. In Hebrews, the great memorials begin with, 'By faith' and describe splendid risks. There is no true faith without venture. Merely to hug a creed and take no risk is no more faith than hugging a timetable is to take a journey.

"Shall we toy with Christianity or put our life into the business? You ought to have a purpose! Daniel purposed in his heart. What do *you* purpose? Young men and women, the supreme challenge is yours to a life of danger, risk, and hazard—and in eternity, glory hallelujah forevermore. Are you going to stay on the baby bottle or get into the battle? Be a victor or a vegetable? A conqueror or a cabbage? As for me, I want to be recorded as one who hazarded something for Jesus Christ— my life! He will not fail us. 'If God be for us, who can be against us?' We are more than conquerors through Him who loved us."

Closing his Bible, Rev. Hutchinson resumed his seat and after a few minutes of silence, Bill Laing dismissed the students. Melva peered around, looking for Dave. *"I was too hard on him. I miss him."* Melva made her way toward Dave. Just then, Rev. Hutchinson approached Dave, along with a group of students, all eagerly talking. Melva turned and left.

June 15, 1938

Melva opened the window in the small office to let in fresh air. A car rumbled down the street. *"Dave!"* He drove to the end and turned down the next street. After a few minutes he passed the office again. Melva sighed and Mrs. Scott looked at her.

"I saw Dave in town two days ago," Mrs. Scott said. "He spent well nigh an hour visiting the men at the garage. And, he bought a mess of grasshopper poison. Must be helpin' some farmer. Heard Mrs. Smart gave him a standing invitation to room and eat at their place when he's in town." Mrs. Scott peered at Melva over her glasses.

Melva nodded. "He just drove past, twice! And without stopping."

"Hmmm, eager to see you? Guess it's none of my business, girl, but it seems to me you've been avoiding him." Melva took a deep breath and bit her lip.

August 10, 1938

Clara pushed back the lace curtain in the dining room. "Vince is here!" she said as she jumped up and clapped her hands. "Oh Melva! I am so excited to be Kay's maid of honor! Melva studied her younger sister. Clara had matured so much. She was already twenty-one. Her pretty blond hair was wavy and stylish, and she wore a cotton floral print dress with short puffy sleeves. She clutched her purse and ran out. Melva followed.

"It's not every day I have the fortunate position of chauffeuring two young ladies to my brother's wedding," Vince said as he opened the car door for the sisters.

"Oh Vince," Clara laughed. "You sure look sharp!" Her eyes sparkled. "I love weddings!"

"Melva," Vince said, "Rob is waiting for you at the church."

"How's it feel to lose a brother?" Melva asked.

Vince laughed. "He's been gone over Kay since the 1934 Dye reunion. Maybe I'll get him back when their honeymoon's over." Minutes later, they pulled up to the church. "I'm proud to be his best man," Vince said, "and Clara, I'm glad you are the maid of honor. You deserve it." Clara blushed. Vince opened the door and as the sisters climbed out, Rob approached.

"Shall we?" he asked, offering his elbow to Melva. "You look beautiful, Melva." He wore a black suit, immaculate white shirt, and a tie with a gold bar. His dark hair was combed to the side and his aftershave smelled of pine. Melva placed her gloved hand in his elbow and the two made their way to the front of the church. Minutes later, Alice and Doris arrived, followed by the rest the family. Doris sat beside Melva and Rob. Alice went to the piano and began to play. After a few minutes, the pastor of the small church walked to the pulpit.

"Dearly beloved, we are gathered to witness the marriage of Kay Street and Dick Bittle."

Melva's mind drifted back to Earle. Minutes later, Kay's sweet voice rang through the building. "I, Kay, take thee, Dick, to be my wedded husband, for better, for worse, for richer, for poorer, to love and to cherish, till death do us part."

"Till death do us part? I've already experienced a tiny bit of what that would feel like. Earle's married and I'm broken and bleeding. He really didn't love me at all."

"...Friends, that is what love is. It suffers long and is kind. It keeps no record of wrongs," the preacher continued. *"I must get over Earle and release him."*

"Now, Melva and Doris will sing a duet." Melva stood with Doris and nodded to Alice at the piano.

After the singing, the pastor announced, "A lunch will be held outside directly following, and Mrs. Hazel Dye has agreed to host dinner later at their farm for anyone who wishes to stay."

As guests filed out, Rob whispered, "Melva, you're some kind of pretty!"

"The same line that Earle used," she remembered. *"The same line."*

"Have a few minutes to go to the café with me?"

Melva smiled. "Sorry Rob, I'm serving."

"Hey doll, you get close to me, and you'll become the served, not the server." Melva lifted her brow and walked away.

CHAPTER ELEVEN

TRIALS

August 20, 1938

Melva connected the lines and sighed. It was Saturday. She wished she could be at home, but Mrs. Scott had asked her to work. She picked up her needles to knit. The door opened. Rob strode in, clenched his fist, and slammed it on the counter. Soot smeared his shirt and cheek. "We nearly lost our barn!" He looked at her with a furrowed brow. "I don't know how it started but I aim to find out! If it were done on purpose—"

"Rob! Rob! W–what happened?"

"A fire! In our barn! Destroyed near half of it! The barn where Dad keeps his prize race horses! I'm going to pound the livin' daylights out of Sam Jacobson if he started it. His dad's horses are our competition and he's always been jealous. Father has the fastest horses in this here whole county!" Rob's lips narrowed and his jaw tightened. Melva watched him storm into the café. She took a deep breath and sat. *"I need to break off my relationship with him, but how?"*

Sept. 26, 1938

Melva relaxed in her chair and took a bite of her sandwich. She glanced at Mrs. Scott.

"That was a busy morning. Maybe this afternoon will be slower. I'm going to listen to the news for a few minutes," Mrs. Scott said as she walked to the back and clicked on the radio. Melva took another bite.

"Melva, listen!" Mrs. Scott shouted. "Hitler again!" Melva jumped and strode to the radio in the back. "With regards to the problem of the Sudeten Germans, my patience is at an end!" Hitler's voice rang out from the interpreter and through the crackle of the radio.

Melva's eyes widened. "What's that mean?" Mrs. Scott put her finger to her lips and continued listening. After a few minutes she turned off the radio and shook her head.

"I don't know, Melva. Sounds serious."

"I'm phoning Daddy," Melva said as she headed for the switchboard.

"Hi Daddy!" she exclaimed. "Did you hear Hitler's speech? Mrs. Scott says it sounds serious—what do we do now? . . . Oh! All right. You too. Goodbye."

"What'd he say?" Mrs. Scott asked.

"He said he's just going to keep harvesting. Wonder why he isn't concerned."

"Melva, I'm sure he is concerned. What I think he means is even during political upheaval, we need to do the next thing."

October 9, 1938

Melva made her way to the front of the auditorium at the Prophetic Bible Institute with her sisters.

"Let's sit here," Alice said. Excited chatter filled the packed room until Rev. Hutchinson introduced the speakers, Dave Stewart and Larry Dodge. The auditorium burst into applause.

"Wow. We're fortunate to even get a seat!" Doris whispered.

"Yeah," said Alice, "It's as crowded as it was in September when Dave spoke. He's really getting popular."

January 4, 1939

Dave had just finished speaking at the Langdon Baptist Church prayer meeting.

"I really appreciated getting to know each one of you, and the Langdon community," he said. "Would you remember us in your prayers? Larry Dodge and I are going to travel and preach all over Alberta, so I wanted to say goodbye and thank each of you for your prayers."

Minutes later, Melva stepped into the cold wind of an Alberta winter evening and wrapped a cozy scarf around her head as she walked to Mrs. Scott's car.

"Melva!" a familiar voice sounded.

"Melva!" Dave puffed as he ran up to her. "I wanted to say goodbye personally." Melva's eyes met his.

"Dave, God is really using you and Larry. May He continue to use you both to spread the gospel throughout Alberta."

Dave smiled. "Yes. I feel His presence. He's so real and so near." The wind flipped up his collar and Melva turned to open the car door.

"Melva, may I write?"

"Yes, yes, of course," she whispered. Dave stepped closer. "I…I… miss visiting you."

Melva sighed and nodded. Silence came between them for a few moments.

Dave cleared his throat. "It's such a privilege to tell others the good news that God laid on my heart, Melva. So many are getting saved. Did you know that at the December eleventh rally in Calgary more than one hundred were saved? Mr. Lowry from the Nazarene church spoke. God is moving, and I want to be a part of it."

Melva touched his arm with her gloved hand. "I know. You *are* a part of it, Dave. You are. May God go with you and Larry."

He set his hand over hers. "Goodbye." Melva felt a tear slip down her cheek.

"Goodbye." She turned and faced the car door. Dave opened it, and Melva slipped in. He disappeared into the night. Alone in the dark car,

Melva dried her eyes and sighed. Minutes later, Mrs. Scott, fussing about being late, got in and put the key in the ignition. She glanced at Melva.

"Well dear, want to tell me what's wrong?"

"Oh, Mrs. Scott," she blurted, "I don't know what to do. The one I loved loves me no more, and the one who likes me, I don't like, but the one I think would be best for me, I like him a lot, and he likes me a lot and-and-and I can't get close to him because my heart is still stuck on the one who loved me but hurt me and-and-and went and married someone else! It's so confusing! I just don't know what to do or where to turn or who to speak to!" Melva's voice faded as tears slipped down her cheeks.

Mrs. Scott cleared her throat. "You need to say no to some of that lovin' before you get yourself in trouble. You any good at saying no?"

"What do you mean?"

"Can't you just say no to thinking about that guy who hurt you, and can't you just say no to the guy you don't really like, and can't you just wait for the right timing with the guy you do?"

March 5, 1939

Melva sat at the dining room table with her arm around her grandmother. Hours earlier, her father had taken Grandpa Verne to the hospital.

"I hope he's alright," Grandma said, wringing her hands. "What would I do without my Verne?" She dabbed her eyes and sniffed.

"Here, Grandma. Have some tea," Alice said as she passed a pretty rose cup.

"Thank you, dear. At least it's Sunday, so you girls are all home and can be with me."

March 17, 1939

"How's your Grandpa?" Rob asked as Melva enjoyed her lunch break on the bench outside the office.

"About the same. They thought maybe it was a bad tooth, so they pulled it. Didn't help much."

"Too bad. Well, guess what! I just saw that brand new tractor that's in town! Wow. Your grandpa would sure love it. It has a radio, heater, and everything! Costs $2,402. Not bad for what you get! When he gets better, he should take a look at it."

June 20, 1939

Grandpa Verne still did not feel well, so the dentist pulled two more of his teeth. Bible school had ended for the year, and Melva worked full time at the office, with Shirley as her backup.

The office door opened, and a tall young man entered. "Hi Melva. Clara sent this for you." He set a plate of cookies on the counter.

"Thank you, Donald Rae! Oatmeal raisin! Mmm!" Melva took a deep breath of the sweet aroma.

"That sister of yours sure is diligent, that's for sure! Mother's been so happy since she came to work for us," Donald Rae said as he pushed back his hat and wiped his brow. "I needed a part in town, and she asked if I could deliver these to you." The bell tinkled as he left the office. Melva looked at the cookies. *"I think he likes Clara,"* Melva thought. *"She talks a lot about him."* She sighed and leaned back with a cookie, wondering what Dave was doing.

July 7, 1939

"Hello?" Melva said as she answered her home line.

"Melva," her mother said. "Vince is coming to get you. I'm calling everyone. Grandpa's unconscious." A numb sensation washed over Melva as she mechanically called Shirley to watch the switchboard. Before she could recover from the shock, Vince pulled up.

"Grandma says he hasn't much time left. The doctor is there and everything." Vince shook as he yanked at the steering wheel. "He felt poorly in the night and this morning your parents were by his bed. He must have thought it was Uncle Ruel and Aunt Winnie because he said, 'Joyce is a nice little girl,' then slipped into a coma." Melva's heart thumped. "*No, no. Please no, Grandpa.*"

When they arrived at the farm, the yard was full of familiar vehicles. Melva ran into the house. Upstairs, Dr. Salmon stood by the bedroom door, and moved to let Melva in. Grandpa and Grandma's bedroom was crowded. Grandpa's large body lay still, his breathing barely discernable. His thick arms lay on the covers—loving arms that had held her, powerful arms that had easily hoisted hundreds of feed sacks on the wagon, tireless arms that had provided for his family. Grandma shifted in her rocker to greet Melva. "We wanted everyone to see him one last time," she smiled through tears. "Thank you for coming Melva. Doctor Salmon says it won't be long."

"Grandpa. Grandpa?" Melva whispered, leaning over, desperate for a response. But his eyes remained closed. "*It feels like he's ignoring me, but he's not. He's, he's dying.*" His weathered face looked peaceful. "*I can't believe I'll never see you on the tractor again, or digging potatoes, or carving the turkey. You've always been here, part of the farm, but you're leaving us … you're leaving us … never to return.*" She stared at his face, burning it into her memory. She shook her head. "*I thought you would always be just Grandpa, always here for me, Grandpa,*" her thoughts continued to circle.

"Grandpa," she whispered, setting her hand on his arm. She kissed his forehead. "Goodbye, Grandpa." Tears slipped down her cheek.

"*It's that same pain. Someone leaving. Not a word or explanation or goodbye.*" Sniffing sounded all over the room; her sisters huddled in a corner, crying. Melva slipped into the hall and entered her bedroom. She took her small Bible and left. She ran through the trees that bordered the farmhouse and across the dirt road to the irrigation canal. "*I want to keep running. To run forever. Away . . . away from pain. If only I could outrun it and be free. Free from goodbyes and death and sorrow and . . . Earle!*"

She slowed her pace. "*And now Dave. It hurts too much to love. Perhaps I will never let myself love again.*" A soft wind bent the tall prairie grass as she sat on the edge of the irrigation canal. Minutes, then an hour, ticked by. Melva lay back in the grass, hands behind her head, watching tall clouds in the deep blue sky. "*I wonder where heaven is. Not the clouds' heaven, but the real heaven, where Grandpa is going. He'll meet baby Grace.*

The baby Grandma and he never talked about. She only lived a few months. She'll be happy to see her daddy."

Rustler barked. Chickadees and robins sang. The barn door creaked and Melva got up. Harold stood by the door, bucket in hand. Chore time. Usually, it was Grandpa, Daddy, and Harold laughing and talking as they worked around the farm; now, nothing more than the silence of the soft wind and its rustle through the grass. Melva sat back down.

"Melva. Melva? You asleep?"

She looked up, not knowing how long she had been there.

"Hi Dick," she managed to say, wiping away tears.

Dick held out his hand, helping her up. "Melva, he's gone."

"Oh Dick!" She burst into fresh tears and hugged him.

"It's alright, Melva," he whispered. "He's in a better place. He's not suffering anymore."

"Oh Dick! When did he die? I want to write it in my diary, so I'll never forget."

"I looked at the time when he stopped breathing. It was one-forty." Dick put his arm around her as they returned to the farmhouse to find Uncle Ruel at the bedside with his Bible. When he saw Dick and Melva, he opened his Bible.

"Concerning them which are asleep, that ye sorrow not, even as others which have no hope." After reading a passage, he suggested, "Let's sing. Grandpa is free, and we can rejoice with him." After the singing, he prayed.

Melva looked at Grandpa. *"He's gone. If only I would have known, I would have phoned him last night! Oh, that I would have said goodbye last night when he was conscious! I would have thanked him for all he did for us, providing for us, for bringing us to Canada. I would have told him how much I loved him!"* Melva dabbed at her cheeks and put her hand on Grandma's shoulder. They hugged and Melva felt comfort as they both wept.

"Now, honey," Grandma said gently. "We are wasting our tears. He's much happier now, and he hasn't died, really, but is alive with the Lord. Let's not weep."

"But Grandma, I can't imagine life without him!"

Melvia looked at her lifeless husband. "Nor can I," she whispered. Crying and sniffing burst out around the room.

"Let us pray," Ruel said gently. The room hushed. "Dear Father, comfort our hearts. And especially draw near to Grandma. Be her comfort in the following days. Help us all get through this. Amen."

The group trickled downstairs and several men gently covered Verne and carried his body to a vehicle.

"Grandma, do you want me to stay?" Melva asked as the relatives gathered in the dining room. She rested her hand on the elderly woman's shoulder.

"No, no dearie. I'll be alright. Alice and Doris said they would stay with me, so you go back to work." Melvia wiped a tear from her cheek. "And to think just yesterday Verne wanted to see Ruel and Winnie, so he headed to Bowden. But he turned around in Olds because the dirt roads were too wet," she whispered to herself.

Minutes later, as Vince pulled up to the phone office, Melva turned to him. "How will I make it through the rest of the day? How I am supposed to be friendly as I answer the lines, when I feel nothing but pain inside?"

Vince sighed. "You will make it through the same way you did when you found out about Earle. One second at a time. Remember? You made it through that painful time."

At the mention of Earle, a pang shot through her heart and Melva sighed. *"I didn't make it through. I'm not over him. If I was, I would be in another relationship, but I just can't love again."* She looked at Vince. So strong, so full of energy, so eager to meet the future head on.

July 10, 1939

The door creaked open and Melva set her purse and gloves on the counter. She stared at the rows of wires on the switchboard. Each represented someone's home. She stared at her family's . . . Grandpa . . . She would never hear his voice again. Everything was quiet.

"Melva?" Mrs. Scott said as she pushed back the curtain. She wore her housecoat and had curlers tucked under her kerchief.

"Hello, Mrs. Scott."

"I'm sorry about your grandpa, dear. I feel bad I had to call you in to work after the funeral. Shirley's been doing the nightshift for me, but she couldn't come in tonight, and I feel sick."

"That's alright. Wouldn't have slept much anyway."

Mrs. Scott wrapped her housecoat tighter about her. "How was the funeral?"

Melva looked up and sighed. "It was at Jacques' farm. Rev. Hutchinson gave a good message."

Mrs. Scott nodded. "Well, good night, dear. Coffee's hot if you want some." Mrs. Scott disappeared into her home and Melva, with nothing to do, rested her chin in her hands. *"Grandpa is in a much better place. Why am I so sad? Dave always talks about heaven and makes it seem so wonderful, so close."* She looked around the room. *"I wonder what it was like when Grandpa was growing up. Grandma has his letters from before they married. Maybe I'll ask to see them. Why does time have to age us? Why do the ones we love so much have to grow old and die? But I know God will help me keep living without him, one day at a time."*

July 18, 1939

"Going to hear Dave tonight? He's speaking in Vulcan," Alice asked Melva over the phone.

"I hadn't heard. You going?"

"Yes. I love his preaching. Want me to pick you up? Doris and Clara are coming, too."

"Okay, sure. But it's Tuesday. Hope it doesn't go late; I have to work early."

"Don't worry, I have to houseclean, and Clara works tomorrow. See you at six!"

Melva hung up as a pang of envy shot through her. *"Alice is older and more mature. Maybe Dave likes her now. Oh, what's it matter!"* she chided herself.

Later that night, the girls settled into the narrow pews in the church at Vulcan. Dave sat in the front row, but Melva resisted the urge to speak to him.

"Good evening, ladies and gentlemen," a tall man said. "Tonight, we have a special speaker. The evangelist Dave Stewart is here to share the gospel. I appreciate his wisdom and humility. He told me of his past life and how God gloriously saved him from his relentless downward spiral. He was headed straight for hell, but since God rescued him, Dave has made it his aim to rescue as many as possible from their fate. Let us hear what he has to say. Dave?"

Dave approached the pulpit and scanned the audience. He wore a dark suit and tie and his smile emanated compassion. *"He's strikingly handsome. What was I thinking, to push him away? This room has a lot of young ladies who would love a chance at him. No, I will not let my heart go there."*

"My message today is entitled, 'My God, My God'. You may recognize these four words from the crucifixion. How we strain to hear the dying words of any man. They are important. My God, My God— yes, the dying words of Christ. A small thing, like these four words, may indicate something great within. For instance, a cloud, as small as a man's hand—yet it can foretell a mighty storm. So it is with man, a sigh, a broken sentence—shows more than a long speech. Likewise with Christ—these four simple words reveal volumes because they were words of obedience. He was obedient unto death. He not only suffered what *we* should have suffered, He obeyed all that *we* should obey.

"When the great plan of salvation was proposed to Him in heaven, He agreed, for scripture tells us He came to do the will of God.

"In the temple we see Him, even as a lad, about His Father's business. What was His Father's business? Seldom do we think of that. Again, scripture tells us.

"He came to speak to sinners—'My meat is to do the will of him who sent me.'

"Part of His business was to die for sinners. One might think Christ would shrink from the cross, but not so. He drank the cup to the last dark drop. 'My God, My God.' Behold how fully He obeyed—even unto death. No man took His life from Him. He laid it down of Himself. Hallelujah, what a Savior. Is He yours?

"My God, My God! These four words are words of faith because they reveal the greatest faith in the world. Faith is believing God—not because we see it to be true or feel it to be true—but because God said it. Even in hell, Jesus believed the word of God, 'Thou wilt not leave my soul in hell.' He did not just feel it or see it, He believed it. Oh fearful ones, unbelieving ones, distrustful ones, can you also cling to this Savior in just such a way?

"Jesus suffered in all ranks —*as a prophet*: 'prophesy unto us', and as a king: 'they robed and bowed in mockery, saying hail, king of the Jews!'

"He suffered from the soldiers, from passersby, from a thief next to him: 'Many bulls have compassed me about', because He was willing, 'Blotting out the handwriting of ordinances that was against us, which was contrary to us, and took it out of the way, nailing it to His cross. And having spoiled principalities and powers, He made a shew of them openly, triumphing over them.' But nothing was so painful as suffering from His Father. 'My God, my God, why hast thou forsaken me?' This was His greatest suffering. Dear friends—all the nails and scourging never caused Him to cry out, but the minute He was forsaken—ah— *then* He cried out! *Then* He was without comfort, *then* He had no feeling of support, no smile from His Father, no kind looks, no loving words. He felt what sinners will feel when they hear God say, 'Depart from Me!'"

Tears slipped down Melva's cheek. *"'Depart from me.' Jesus felt the sting of those words too? And it was my sin that separated Him from His father. I caused His pain. 'So likewise shall My heavenly Father do also unto you, if ye from your hearts forgive not everyone his bother their trespasses.'"*

"To say *depart from me*," Dave continued, turning a page of his Bible, "is like a sailor casting the anchor to the depths of the ocean. 'My God, my God, why hast thou forsaken me?' His Father answered, 'To save Dave Stewart—put *your* name there—whosoever.' That is why. My dear, dear people! Look at your sin the way God does! He must punish it! But Jesus took your eternal punishment! Come to Him tonight."

After expounding on various scriptures for a while, Dave picked up his Bible and notes and returned to his seat. Several came forward and knelt. Dave approached a young man, who was bent by the altar. As the man wept, Dave put his hand on his shoulder and prayed. Most of the audience had left by the time Dave made it to the back to greet. Melva and her sisters had waited for him.

"Good to see you!" Dave said, taking Alice's hand.

"Wonderful message, Dave. I admire your boldness and courage."

"Anything good in me is from the Lord," he replied.

"Hello Melva," Dave said.

"Hi Dave. So good to see you again." *"Why did I say that? Sounds too friendly. But I meant it."*

"Good to see you, too," he said as their eyes met. "How are you doing, Melva? I am so sorry about your grandpa."

"I'm . . . alright . . . I guess. And you?"

Dave smiled. "I'm trying to apply a message Rev. Hutchinson preached. He talked about crucifying self. At the end he asked us students how much time we spent on ourselves. Do you remember that sermon?"

Melva smiled. "Yes, yes, I do. And two days later eighteen students were baptized. Who could forget that?"

"Not me," Dave whispered. "How are your parents doing?"

"Managing, thanks." Melva smiled. "Daddy and Harold milk eight cows, every morning and evening. Next week Daddy and Vern finish summer fallowing."

Dave smiled and nodded. "I could use a good dose of farming right now." He looked into her eyes. "Good to talk to you again, Melva."

Melva lip's quivered, and as she reached the front door, she hesitated a second, then left.

CHAPTER TWELVE

WAR

August 3, 1939

Melva picked up the receiver. "Hello. This is Melva. How may I direct your call?"

"Hi Melva. My name is Kenneth Watts. Last week my family moved to a farm east of Langdon. Was in the office a few days ago to talk to Mrs. Scott."

"Yes. I remember now. Welcome to Langdon."

"Thanks. I'm phoning to invite you to my birthday party next week. Thought it would be a good way to get to know you." Melva sighed quietly. She held the receiver away from her ear for a few seconds.

"Umm, ah, Kenneth? Can't make it. I work full-time next week. Thanks anyway." As she hung up, her shoulders sank. *"I said no! But how am I to know the right one? Dear God, I'm not ready! Why can't I just be friends with men? Why does it have to always get serious? Help me not to make a mistake."*

The phone rang. "Hello. This is Melva. How may I direct your call?"

"Is this Miss Melva Dye?"

"Yes. Speaking."

"My name is Martin Bowker. My wife and I are doing full-time ministry work at Wimborne Alliance. It's a little church about an hour east of Olds, if the roads are good. We got your name through the Calgary Prophetic Bible Institute and wondered if you and your sisters could come and sing on Friday, the eighteenth. They also told us your Aunt Ruth speaks and sings. We'd be delighted if she could make it as well."

Melva's eyes widened. She had heard of the Bowkers. "I'll ask my sisters and aunt and talk to my supervisor and see if I can get the time off. Let me take your number."

August 18, 1939

"Alice? Melva? Ready?" Melva's Aunt Ruth called from the farmhouse door. Alice and Melva entered the porch.

"What a beautiful day!" Melva exclaimed as they got in the car with Aunt Ruth. Dust swirled under the tires as they turned down the dirt road. After passing Irricana, the car thumped, and Aunt Ruth pulled over.

"A flat," she said. The sisters changed it and were soon on their way. After stopping in Linden for directions, they arrived in Wimborne with plenty of time before the service.

The small church stood on the east side of Wimborne. Its white front glistened in the setting sun. An arched window decorated either side of the double doors. Above stood the steeple. Melva adjusted her hat as the women made their way up the few front steps.

"Good evening! You must be the Dyes," a kind-looking woman said as soon as Melva stepped in. She shook the woman's hand.

"Yes."

"Please to meet you. I'm Mrs. Bowker, and my husband is sitting on the stage." Melva glanced at Mr. Bowker. His bald forehead shone, and his small eyes concentrated on the hymn book in his hand.

After a few quick introductions, the sisters settled down to appreciate the music. When called upon, they sang several hymns and after the sermon, Mrs. Bowker and her husband presented a final song. As they sang, she smiled up at her husband; the melody drifted across the room, touching Melva's heart. *"How beautiful to minister as a couple."* A wave of regret washed over her for turning Dave away. *"Why did I do that? This is all I really want! Dave. I'm so sorry."*

September 1, 1939

"Germany invaded Poland!" Mrs. Scott clicked off the radio and shook her head. "Nothing stable anymore, girl, just nothing is stable or certain but death, taxes, and the Word of God."

September 3, 1939

"Great Britain and France declared war today after a British ship sank near Ireland, the SS *Athenia*." Mrs. Scott clicked off the radio and threw her hands up.

"I'm not going to enjoy listening to the radio anymore, not until this horrific situation passes." Melva moved to the window and stared blankly across the street as leaves fluttered to the ground. The row of trees across the street by the old Union Bank had turned from green to a bright yellow. Normally, she delighted in their beauty, but today, they did not appear beautiful. *"The heavy feeling of war soaks into every part of daily life, like standing under a gray cloud with no escape. What am I supposed to do about world events? Why must we have another war?"*

Mrs. Scott sat by the switchboard and sipped her coffee.

"Well, honey, why stare out the window? We've work to do. I have to wash and wax the floors; you take over the switchboard." A little boy ran by the window chasing a ball. *"He has no idea what is happening to the world right now,"* Melva thought. Reaching for her purse, she pulled out a small Bible.

"For consider him that endured such contradiction of sinners against him, lest ye be wearied and faint in your minds." *"Wearied and faint in my mind."* She flipped through her Bible. '*In everything give thanks: for this is the will of God in Christ Jesus concerning you.' Hmm … that means me, right now, in the middle of war and uncertainty. It's always been bad. Why should things be any different in my life? Why do I always want to escape things that are uncomfortable? Jesus walked with all kinds of suffering, and yet remained calm."*

The door opened and a young man approached the counter. "Hi, Melva. Could you connect me with the Currie Army Barracks in Calgary? I'm signing up."

"Glen? You-you're going to war?"

"Yup. Canada needs men."

"But, but, Glen! *You?*"

Glen glanced at his old clothes. "I know I'm just a farmer's son but aren't I man enough?"

Melva smiled. "Yes, yes, of course, but—why can't things stay the same? Why can't you be here and farm with your dad and play hockey, and-and-and everything be, well—normal? Why can't . . ." Melva swallowed hard and collapsed into her chair, burying her face in her hands.

"Melva! Melva! It's okay. One day things will be the way we want them . . . in heaven . . . but now, well now . . . there's a war going on! Some of us need to fight. Some need to stay home. But we all need to do our part." He went around the counter and gently touched her shoulder. "We're going to win; we're going to win." A smile spread across his face. "And if you know you're on the winning side, it helps you get through all the stuff in the middle." Melva pulled a handkerchief from her purse and wiped her eyes.

"I'll connect you," she said, her voice shaking.

September 10, 1939

"Canada declares war on Germany." Melva flipped off the radio. She hadn't really meant to turn it on in the first place.

"Melva!" yelped Vince as he burst into the office. "Melva! On the way to town right now I saw Brander's field, it's ablaze! Huge flames! Call the neighbors! Hurry!"

Melva immediately started phoning all the farmers in the area.

Hours later, Vince entered the office. "We won." He collapsed on the chair in the corner and slumped forward. He took a heavy breath. "Phew! What a close call! The fire came within feet of Brander's barn." His clothes were black, and soot smeared across his face.

"Let me get you a drink." Melva hurried to the back and came out with a tall glass of cold pump water. Vince guzzled the drink, shook his head, and wiped his mouth on his sleeve.

"Wow, sure good. Thanks!" She refilled the glass and it disappeared just as quickly. Wiping his brow, he stretched mightily and took a deep breath. "Thanks, Melva," he said as he headed out.

Melva watched him go into the café. "*There's a war going on and we all must do our part.*" Glen's words echoed in her mind. "*Even by phoning the barracks for Glen or giving Vince a glass of cold water, I am doing my part.*"

October 12, 1939

"Get the back door, would you, Melva? I'll watch the lines," Mrs. Scott said. Melva opened the back door. Her mouth dropped and her heart did a double flip. "D-Dave?! W-what are you doing here?"

Dave chuckled. "Hello to you too, Melva."

A warmth spread across her face. "Forgive me! Please, um, I mean yes, yes. H-hello."

"Mrs. Scott called yesterday. She bought a new chesterfield and asked if I'd deliver it since she knew I was speaking in Strathmore." Melva spun around, but Mrs. Scott had quietly disappeared behind her curtain. Melva laughed. "*Oh, that woman!*"

"How nice. You sure surprised me. Won't you come in? You brought a what, a chesterfield?"

"You got it," said Dave. "Always glad to be of assistance."

Mrs. Scott came back into the room and without batting an eye said, "Hello, Dave. Please follow me and I'll show you where it goes."

"Thank you for lunch, Mrs. Scott. Really kind of you," Dave said, enjoying his second cup of coffee.

"Well, you delivered my new chesterfield, so it's the least I could do." She glanced at Melva. Melva smiled and took another sandwich.

"Terrible thing, war is," Mrs. Scott said. "Did you hear the news on the radio this morning?"

Dave looked up. "Yes. But what's worse is the invisible war in our minds, a war between good and evil. Far more serious. Jesus said, 'And fear not them which kill the body, but are not able to kill the soul: but rather fear him which is able to destroy both soul and body in hell.' We have to tell everyone of the judgment to come, that everyone will receive what they've done in the body, whether good or evil." Mrs. Scott stood and collected the few dishes. "In fact, I hope to spread the good news," Dave said as he pulled a letter out of his pocket. "I've signed up to be a war chaplain, wherever they need me."

"W-w-what? Really?" Melva's eyes widened. Dave handed her the letter.

> Mr. A. D. Stewart.
>
> I wish to acknowledge your offer of September 7 and advise you that the appointment of army chaplains is done from Reserve officers. However, your offer has been classified according to qualifications and as soon as we can use a person with your qualifications it will be considered.
>
> Yours truly,
> District Recruiting Office,
> Calgary, Alberta.

Melva re-folded the letter and handed it to Dave, not knowing if she should congratulate him or cry. *"Everyone is leaving because of the war. Nothing is the same. Why does this have to happen?"*

Mrs. Scott nodded. "Well, good for you, Dave. God knows the army needs counselors and preachers like you. Preachers who aren't afraid to speak the truth."

November 18, 1939

It was Saturday. The door opened and Melva looked up from where she connected the plug. Rob entered, dressed in a uniform pressed to perfection. Each seam was ironed crisply, the front pockets lay flat, and his wide leather belt shone. His black shoes glistened, and his cap was tilted perfectly.

"Did you hear? I'm off to war. Mrs. Scott is planning a going away party, so I came to speak to her about it and show her my uniform."

"Rob!" Mrs. Scott exclaimed as she entered from the back. "My, my! Just look at you! My, how *handsome* you are!"

"Yes, well, about the party—um, ah, I don't actually leave for six months. May 8."

"Fine, fine, Rob, but I wanted a party now. I know you are busy with your training and all."

January 5, 1940

"Coming to the dance tonight Melva?" Rob's voice boomed over the phone.

"Rob," a wry smile spread over Melva's face, "you know I don't dance."

"Why not? Everyone's coming, even a lot of Christians. Try it! Lots of fun. Food and drink. Plenty of guys and gals from all over. It's a respectable way to get close to each other, if you know what I mean."

"I *do* know what you mean, and no thanks. Before I was saved, I played the banjo or piano for dances. I *know* what happens there." Melva hung up. *"God be praised He gave me the strength to say no!"*

A few hours later, Melva buttoned her coat, made sure she had her scarf and gloves, and locked the office door. The moon peeked behind a murky cloud. Her evening stroll was interrupted as she caught the sound of children laughing and the rasp of skates on ice. Despite the crisp night air, she headed to the rink and saw a few girls practicing spins and twirls and two boys shooting pucks at an empty net. A young woman skated towards her. It was Alice Smart.

"Hi Alice."

"Hi Melva! Didn't go to the dance?"

"No, I don't dance."

"Well, why don't you come skating?"

"I think I'll just watch, thanks. Got lots to think about."

May 8, 1940

The Langdon train station platform was crowded with families huddled together and young people crying and hugging. Children skipped about, enjoying the beautiful spring morning. As Melva gently wound her way to trackside and the looming passenger train, she glanced at the large clock beside the station door—six-fifty. *"Wow, so many out this early."*

"Melva! Melva!" It was Rob in his army uniform, with three other young men.

"Hi Rob."

"Thanks for coming out to see us off. We'll be in Toronto in a few days."

Melva glanced over the excited crowd at the train. Men in uniform stared out the windows, others climbed aboard, and others delayed boarding as long as possible, encircled by friends and family.

"And by the way, thanks for coming to my going away party. Didn't know you played the banjo so well," Rob said with a smile.

Melva blushed. "Well, I'm not *that* great. I still can't get over there were about one hundred in attendance!"

"I have to admire the church and community for honoring me like that. Sure meant a lot."

"Yes, and they've held separate parties for all the men leaving," Melva said.

"Rob! Rob Williams?" Three young ladies rushed to hug him and when they left, Rob turned to Melva.

"Goodbye, Melva. Have to go. Got a war to fight…"

Melva's heart tugged within her. *"This might be the last time I see him."* He turned to board and Melva touched his arm. "Rob, wait." He paused as she handed him a salvation tract. "I'd be doing a disservice if I didn't give you this."

He looked at it. "Umm. Ah, well, thanks." It quickly disappeared into a pocket and without a backward glance, he was up the train steps and gone.

CHAPTER THIRTEEN

IN LOVE

July 22, 1940

The summer sped by with berry picking, canning, and work. Dave traveled and preached, sometimes alone, sometimes with Bible school teams.

"Hello. This is Melva. How may I direct your call? Oh! Hi Dave! Where are you?"

"Hi Melva. I'm in Ogden, southeast of Calgary. Tonight's my last itinerate meeting for a while. I called your Uncle Ruel, and he has work for me starting on the twenty-sixth."

Melva glanced at the calendar.

"Really? That's four days away. Where are you headed in the meantime?"

"That's why I'm phoning. Could you connect me with your parents? I'd like to stay at your farm. Think they'd mind?"

"Umm…" Melva said. "It shouldn't be a problem. Hang on and I'll connect you."

Melva slumped in her chair and sighed. *"Am I ready for him yet? For any man? Is he wanting to get serious or is he seeing someone else? Maybe Alice. He's visited her a few times in the last number of months."*

Dave moved his few belongings to the Dye home. To their surprise, churches in the area began to call and invite Dave to speak. His four evenings booked up, speaking at a different church each night. During the day, he helped on the farm, and Melva worked at the phone office.

July 25, 1940

On the morning of July 25, the family gathered for breakfast. After grace was said, Alice turned to Dave.

"How was your meeting last night in Union Jack County★ Dave?"

"Went well. About forty-eight came. Of course, I really covet prayer as I preach. I heard Mrs. Hugh's held an all-day prayer meeting on June 17. I am dependent on prayers like hers."

"Yes," Alice said, passing the scrambled eggs. "She no doubt prayed for you, as well as other evangelists, and the war. She's quite concerned."

Taking a second piece of toast and reaching for the strawberry jam, Dave looked at Melva. "Heard about all the corn you planted."

Melva smiled. "Yes, Daddy and I had extra seeds, so after we put in the garden, we planted more in the ditch."

Dave chuckled, "The ditch?"

Mr. Dye smiled, "You know what they say, 'waste not want not'. I figure if we have the space, we better utilize it. No telling what will happen with shortages during the war."

"Well, that is true," Dave said. "And speaking of utilizing space, thank you, Mrs. Dye, for hosting me these last few days. And Grandma Dye, for letting me sleep in your sewing room."

"Our pleasure. Anything to support the work of the Lord," Hazel said, putting down the coffee pot. "Toast? More oatmeal?"

"No, thanks. I am stuffed." Dave turned to Donald. "I also really appreciate getting work with your brother Ruel. Jobs are sure scarce."

"Yes, well, Dad originally sold that section west of Bowden to the

Kerr family, but, not being farm minded, and barely able to pay the taxes on the place, they moved back to Vancouver. It was only natural Ruel would want it, so he bought it from them. If it creates work for you, all the better. It's a good thing it has a large farmhouse and some outbuildings. When's your train leave?" Donald asked over his coffee.

"Tomorrow night at eight. I think I will have enough time to go to prayer meeting with you folks at six first. But about today, I've been asked to speak at the Bible study in the Langdon Baptist tonight.

"You're a busy man!" Donald said. "Are you prepared? Do you have time to fence with Vern, Harold, and I today? Or you could help the ladies pick peas."

Dave smiled, "My message for Bible study tonight is pretty much prepared. I can help fence."

After a full day of work, Dave came in to wash. Melva and Alice sat on the porch with their enamel bowls brimming with peas. Beside them stood six five-gallon buckets of unshelled peas.

"Like some help?" Dave asked.

"Sure," Alice replied. "Bet I'm faster than you!"

"Ha! Don't be so sure of yourself," Dave exclaimed, grabbing a big fistful of pods from a bucket. Dave slid his thumb over a pod, and the ping of peas sounded in his bowl.

"Melva," he began, "would you like to sing with me tonight?"

Melva's mouth dropped. A warmth enveloped her. She stared at her flowery apron and its dark pink binding.

"Yes, I can do that," she said. "What are you singing?"

"I'm speaking on Joshua chapter one, verses fifteen and sixteen, so I thought 'I'll Go Where You Want Me to Go' would be appropriate."

"Yes, I like that hymn."

"Could you play for us, Alice?"

"I would love to. I think it's in our old hymnal. I'll check."

"Great." Dave continued shelling. "Should we take the wagon or my car?"

"The car, Dave. We're picking up Clara and those brothers you talked to," Alice replied.

That evening, on the way to the Baptist church, Dave, Alice, and Melva picked up Clara, who was working at Rae's. Then they stopped at another farm for the brothers, Joe and Dale, Dave had met in Langdon days earlier. After parking at the church, Dave walked down Main Street, inviting everyone he saw to the meeting. By the time the service started, the little church was so packed, it was standing room only.

"And they answered Joshua, saying, 'All that thou commandest us we will do, and withersoever thou sendest us, we will go.'" Dave's clear voice penetrated the air. After expounding on the passage for half an hour, he nodded to Melva. She approached the podium, straightened her suit dress, and stood beside him. An awkward feeling came over her, as if it was too intimate to stand so close. She backed up a step and Alice began the prelude. Dave offered an open hymnal and Melva gripped her side of the book. His voice rang through the building so clearly that she thought it might be heard throughout all of Langdon.

It may not be on the mountain's height,
Or over the stormy sea;
It may not be at the battle's front,
My Lord will have need of me;

But if by a still, small voice He calls,
To paths that I do not know,
I'll answer, dear Lord, with my hand in Thine,
I'll go where You want me to go.

As they sang in harmony, Melva stole a sidelong glance at him. *"To paths I do not know. But I want to know! I don't want to be hurt again! How can I sing this?"*

Dave's melodic voice filled the church.

"I'll answer dear Lord, with my hand in Thine,
I'll go where You want me to go!'"

When Melva stepped down from the platform, she shivered and wrapped her shawl tightly around her shoulders. *"Did I really mean what I just sang? I know Dave did. Did he sense my apprehension?"*

"Now is the day of salvation." Dave's smooth voice started the invitation. "Is there anyone here who needs the Savior?" Several came forward, including the two brothers.

July 26, 1940

It was Dave's last day on the farm. The Dye family had grown to love him, and they all hated to see him leave. The whole family decided to attend prayer meeting at the church that night, to say goodbye.

"Here," Donald said as Dave slid into the car to head to the meeting. He held out a roll of money. "For your work. You did an exceptional job."

"Thank you, Mr. Dye!"

Prayer meeting ended. Several farmers surrounded Dave, eager to hear more of the gospel message. Melva stayed in her pew, watching and waiting. *"Dave leaves tonight. At least he'll not be too far away. Uncle Ruel and Aunt Winnie only live west of Bowden now. Why do I care? I've already decided that I'm not going to fall in love again."*

"You looked beautiful singing with Dave last night," Mrs. Scott whispered as she walked past. "Just beautiful."

Melva shook her head. "It's nothing like that. Really, Mrs. Scott." Mrs. Scott smiled and left the church. Seeing Dave so intent in visiting those around him, Melva and her family left.

An hour later, Dave broke from the group that surrounded him, "Hey! Hey! It's after 8:30! My train!"

"Heard the whistle half an hour ago. Didn't know you were headed out tonight," an elderly man said.

"We're so sorry," another man said. "It was our fault for keeping you."

Dave shook his head. "No, no, it's *my* fault. Wasn't paying attention." His face broke into a smile. "Besides, it's more important to visit with you guys."

"But what about your train?" another asked.

"I can always get another ticket."

Hours later, Dave, Melva, Vern, her sisters, and her father sat around the table at home. Her mother had gone to bed after prayer meeting because her hip had been bothering her. It was nearly midnight and Vera stood by the stovetop, making more popcorn.

"I'm mad at myself for missing the train," Dave grinned, "but glad I got hold of Ruel so he wouldn't wait for me."

"Were you able to purchase another ticket?" Alice asked as she took bowls out of the cupboard.

"The train station was open, so I did, but unfortunately the first available trip to Innisfail isn't until midnight on the third of August. Can you believe it?"

"Don't worry, Dave. We can use your help around here for another week, if you're alright with that," Donald said, sipping his hot chocolate. He stared at the empty chair at the head of the table where his father Verne always sat. After a minute of silence, he spoke. "I really miss Father. I still can't believe he's gone. He was always so strong. In fact, behind his back us boys called him, 'governor,' but we wouldn't dare call him that to his face."

Dave sighed. "I'm sorry. Must be hard. How's your mother handling it?"

Donald rubbed the back of his neck. "She's taking it with grace, and there's a new kindness about her."

Melva let her father's words sink in. *"Grace? What is that? Oh, to be said of me that there is a new kindness about me because of what I've been through!"*

July 29, 1940

Melva entered the dining room with a plate of scrambled eggs as Dave and her father visited. "The Langdon church board asked me to speak again at their prayer meeting tonight. It's so nice to see a church that has prayer meeting three times a week. It's needed, especially now, during this war," Dave said.

"Yes, and so are your timely messages," Donald said as he stood to pour himself more coffee. "Today we're hauling grain and picking up coal. Care to join?"

Minutes later, Dave zipped up his borrowed coveralls and left the house with Donald, Vern, and Harold. Melva drew back the dining room curtain and watched them make their way to the barn. *"He's so handsome. And it soaks right through to his soul. He's genuine and not pushy."*

The five sisters filled the bench later that night at prayer meeting.

"Hi Melva. Mind if we sit with you?"

"Oh. Hi, Inez. Hi Eileen. Sure." Inez was a pretty girl who Melva had befriended at the Prophetic Bible Institute. She lived on a farm near Arrowwood, southeast of Langdon. Eileen was an old school chum who lived in Langdon.

After the hymns were sung, Dave began to preach. *"He's so confident and strong,"* Melva thought. Glancing at Inez and Eileen, she noticed them soaking in every word. Eileen's lips pursed tightly, and her long eyelashes were motionless. *"I wonder if she likes him. I can't bear that thought, but neither can I bear the thought of loving again."*

When Dave finished, some came forward and knelt or stood at the front. Dave approached one young man and put his arm on his shoulder. Caught up in the moment, Inez and Melva's sisters watched with deep interest. Dave bowed his head and prayed with the man, then moved on to three young people kneeling in prayer. Melva strode out of the building. She walked to the north side and leaned against the wall, tears falling freely.

"Melva! Melva! What's wrong?" Inez approached cautiously a few minutes later.

"Oh Inez. All I can think about are the words Dave and I sang last week, 'I'll go where You want me to go.' It's like praying a promise of letting Jesus control every part of me, including my future."

"What's so bad about that?"

"Earle tore my heart in two. I'm afraid to love someone else, lest it happen again. I couldn't endure the pain."

"Oh Melva! You can't live your life afraid of pain. Nothing worthwhile comes easy. You must take risks. Sure, it's painful if our dreams fail for a season. But if they succeed, the joy is worth it!" Melva looked at Inez and wiped her tears. "In fact," Inez continued with a sparkle in her eye, "I am forever indebted to Dave." She sighed a long sign and looked upward with a dreamy look.

"Just as I thought, she's in love with him."

Inez giggled.

"Inez, w-what do you mean? Are you, are you seeing Dave?"

Inez grabbed her arm. "Oh Melva, I've kept my secret too long from you! Last year, Dave Stewart and Larry Dodge held weeklong meetings near Acme and a guy named George Robinson recommitted his life to the Lord. Dave taught him so much!" Inez clapped her hands and looked up.

"So?" Melva said.

"George signed up for classes at the Bible school, the same classes I take, and, and, last week he took me on a date! Oh Melva! If it wasn't for Dave!"

Melva pushed away from the church wall and peered into the semi-darkness. She took a deep breath.

Inez touched her arm. "Melva, so many are being saved under Dave's ministry, everywhere he goes. Too bad there's not a woman in his life."

Melva spun around. "Why are you telling me this?"

Inez put her arm around Melva. "Let's go in," she said. "I came out to tell you Eileen just accepted Christ. I think it would be nice if you would pray with her."

Melva propped the bedroom window open with a stick and wiped her forehead. "It's stifling," she said. She lay down next to Alice and stared at the ceiling until her eyes adjusted to the dark.

"What are you thinking about?" Alice asked. A gentle breeze slipped through the window, rustling the lace curtain against the dresser.

"Dave. He leaves for Uncle Ruel's in two days."

Vera perked up from her bed. "Yeah. If he doesn't miss his train again!" She giggled.

"Vera, do you think he did that on purpose?!"

"Well, Melva, *I* think he did. Can't you see he's in love with you?"

"He's not in love with me!" Melva shot back. "We're just, just friends."

"Whatever!" Vera laughed.

Melva turned to Alice. "Do *you* think he's in love with me?" she whispered.

"Melva! Melva. Melva. It's sort of obvious."

"W-what do you mean?"

"The way he looks at you. He longs for you. But I've noticed a sadness about him, like he really wants to get close to you. Maybe he's afraid of rejection or something."

"Dave? Afraid of rejection? I never thought of that." Melva sighed. She went to the window and pulled back the curtain. The moon shone softly, giving the trees grey shadows. "I've only been thinking about myself," she whispered.

August 2, 1940

The family sat around the breakfast table. Hazel set a platter of sausages in the middle and Vera added a large plate piled high with scrambled eggs. Melva kept her eyes down. *"Dear Lord, please help me not to even look at Dave. I don't want to hurt him,"* she prayed.

"Thank you for hosting me another week," Dave said, addressing Melva's father.

"And thank you for helping us. We sure got a lot more fencing done than I had anticipated," Donald said. After saying grace, he turned back to Dave. "So, tomorrow night you leave. Any plans for today?"

Dave cleared his throat. "Yes. Um. Ah, I-I was wondering if Melva would like to go to Bowness Park with me." All eyes turned to Melva. A warmth rushed across her face. She glanced at her mother.

"That's alright dear, you go ahead. I can finish canning peas with the girls."

Melva looked at Dave. His handsome smile warmed her.

"Sure," she said as she slipped eggs on her plate. *"Guess God didn't answer my prayer."*

After clearing the table and doing the dishes, Dave and Melva slipped into his car and headed to Langdon to pick up her mail before continuing to Calgary. Melva opened the two letters on her lap, both from Rob.

"Rob's been writing," she said, as she read them.

"Yeah, I see. How's he doing?"

"Okay so far but missing home and not wanting to kill anyone over there."

"Yes, that'd be hard. Hard to imagine for me—going from an everyday civilian to a soldier in battle. But I think it's a mentality we all, as Christians, need to adopt. This life is a spiritual war zone. But, so far, they haven't called me as a chaplain."

Dave and Melva continued to visit. Everything he said stroked a chord in her heart. It only seemed minutes before they arrived in Calgary.

"Why park here?" Melva asked, peering out the window. They were at the Currie Army Barracks.

"I thought it would be fun to take the streetcar to the park," Dave replied, opening her door. Melva stood and adjusted the ribbons that hung from the back of her hat. The sun beat down and Dave wiped his brow.

"How about we get some soda pop before we go on the streetcar?"

"Sure," Melva replied. "I'd like that. I like orange. You?"

As the two stood by a refreshment stand, Dave turned to Melva. "Out of orange pop. Care to share a ginger ale?"

As they rode the streetcar, Dave and Melva took turns sipping the ginger ale. The car clanked along and Melva's mind wandered. *"Why did Dave want to spend today with me? What will come out of this day?"* They soon arrived at Bowness Park. Tall trees graced the path along the river's bank. Birds twittered and flitted from branch to branch. Every now and then, flower beds adorned the edges of trees and bordered the river. They walked in silence. After a few minutes, Dave asked, "Care to sit for a bit?" He gestured toward a bench facing the water.

Melva looked down, "Sure. That would be nice."

"Melva," Dave began as they sat, "I'm booked to preach on a circuit around Innisfail while I'm living and working at your uncle's. I feel preaching is God's calling for me. And…" Dave peered across the river "… I want you to know that the Innisfail Baptist Church has asked me to be their pastor."

"Oh Dave! That's wonderful! When do you start?"

He paused. "My first Sunday to preach is August 18. I have agreed to volunteer my time, Melva. The week of the twentieth, I am to move into the home of one of the members, the Johnsons. They have agreed to hire me as farm help. And in my free time, I am going to prepare my sermons and go fishing on the Raven River with some of the guys. Melva, your Uncle Ruel told me the fish in that river are huge!" Melva smiled. Dave looked at her and cleared his throat.

"So, do you still want to be just friends, or, or, do you think our friendship could be, ah, I mean, something more?" he asked.

Melva inhaled slowly, not trusting herself to speak. She stared at the river as if diverting her thoughts to follow it, but Dave's voice in her mind gently tugged her back to shore—*"Do you think our friendship could be something more . . ."*

"Dave. Ah. Um. Well, I would like to have a deeper relationship with you, ahhh, but . . ."

"But what?" Dave whispered.

"Oh Dave! I don't know what to say." As quickly as tears sprang to her eyes, she wiped them with the back of her hand. She sniffed. "Dave, I've been hurt before and I'm . . . I'm, I'm scared."

Relief washed over her. *"There. I said it. Finally, it's out."*

"I'll give you all the time you need. I can wait."

"I don't need time, Dave. I need something else . . . something to help me make sense of what I went through."

"Melva. Remember Job?" Dave said gently. She nodded. "He never made sense of what *he* went through. But we know why. His story has given hope to millions for the better part of four thousand years. God knows what He's doing. He makes no mistakes. Who are we to contend with the Almighty, as God said to Job? We look at our situations short-sightedly; we are the here-and-now generation. But God sees everything from the eternal perspective."

Dave stretched his arms as if explaining a thought to a congregation. "But I want you to know I understand. I have many, many things in my life I sure wish weren't there as well. You've heard my testimony."

"Yes."

"God heals the broken-hearted," Dave said. "Why don't we pray right now that He will heal your heart?"

"Oh. Yes. I'd like that very much. Yes. Would you?"

As Dave prayed, a peace and calmness gently infused Melva's tired soul. She did not notice when he finished, but as they sat on the bench in silence, no words were necessary for many minutes.

"Dave, I'm ready."

"For what?" he asked.

"To start a deeper relationship with you."

Dave's eyes widened. "Already? Really? Well! But, I mean, Melva! T-t-thank you, thank you."

It was his turn to wipe his cheek with the back of his hand. Gently, as if touching a delicate porcelain vase, he put his hand on hers.

The next morning after breakfast, a light knock sounded at the farmhouse door.

"Hello? Anyone home?" a feminine voice called.

"Come in, Eileen!" Melva said as she walked to the door holding the dish she was drying.

"Yes, well, Clara invited me over for the day, and I wanted to talk to Dave."

"He's out in the barn." The stomping of footsteps sounded, and the women turned. Dave stood scraping the mud off his boots on a boot scraper.

"Dave! Thank you, thank you so much for preaching the gospel a few nights ago. My life has already taken on such new meaning," Eileen said.

"The gospel sure does that. Praise the Lord," Dave smiled.

Dave turned to Melva. "Let's go for a walk along the irrigation canal.

As they meandered along the canal, Dave said, "Melva, I see you as a woman of integrity. A woman with a kind and gentle spirit. A real servant, someone who loves God." He paused, as if collecting his thoughts. He glanced at her. "I must admit, um," he looked down and kicked a rock into the canal, "let me get to the point. I want you to know before I leave that . . . I'm in love with you. And have been. For a very long time."

Melva closed her eyes to blink out her tears. "Really?" She dabbed at her eyes with her handkerchief. "Then I have been hurting you all this time."

"It was of God. I needed to learn a few things."

They walked in silence.

"Dave?" she said as she stopped, "I, I love you, too."

"You do?" he asked. "Really?"

"Oh Dave. I've hidden my true feelings again and again. But after yesterday and your prayer, I determined to go where He wants me to go and do what He wants me to do."

"Then, then, will you marry me?" he asked. Melva's eyes enlarged, and her mouth dropped.

"Dave!" she exclaimed, bursting into laughter.

Dave chuckled. "I talked to your father a number of times and he approves. I-I need a supportive wife in ministry. Won't be easy. I'll never be rich and will probably drive second-hand cars, and, and, we might always be moving, but I gave my future to God. All I know for certain is that God's call on me is to preach the gospel. Probably never own a house. I know Rob could offer you more financially."

Melva looked into his soft brown eyes. A new love and respect for him filled her heart. "It's not Rob I love, nor houses, nor land ..."

She cupped his face with both hands and leaned closer. "It's you. Yes. I will marry you, Dave Stewart."

Dave breathed a deep sigh. He laughed. "Oh! Melva! Melva!" His strong arms enveloped her, and she felt her heart would explode and melt at the same time.

"Dave," she looked up at him. He gently wiped a tear from her cheek.

"I have so longed to hold you," he whispered. "You have no idea." He lifted her chin and slowly they shared their first kiss.

When they entered the farmyard, they were met by Eileen. "Melva! Dave! Are you two engaged?"

Melva and Dave exchanged glances and laughed as only those who know they belong together can.

"Why do you ask?" Dave said.

Eileen's face reddened. "I was watching you from the upstairs bedroom window!"

*Called Union Jack, now the Vulcan, Alberta area

CHAPTER FOURTEEN

SURPRISE

August 4, 1940

Relatives gathered around the table at the Dye's for Sunday afternoon tea.

"Regardless of his financial situation, we all love Dave," Hazel said as she poured tea for her sister-in-law, Dorothy, who was Dick and Vince Bittle's mother.

Dorothy took a sip. "Yes, he's stolen all our hearts," she agreed. "A poor man with good character is far better than a rich man without."

"For a preacher he sure knows how to work. Donald told me how fast he fixed fences," Dorothy's husband Lee said.

"And," Hazel spoke up, "Donald has analyzed Dave's character and has found him to be true to the core." Hazel smiled at Melva and tipped the tea pot above her gold-rimmed cup. "Won't you have more, dear?"

Melva shook her head. "No thanks, Mother."

Vera giggled, "She's lovesick Mother, and Dave only left a couple of hours ago! Surprised he didn't miss his train again!"

"Vera, hush!" Alice said.

"Want to know what I think?" Vince spoke, taking another cookie. "Like the preacher said in church today, 'What's meant to be is meant to be', and—" he smiled at Melva, "Dave's getting a top-notch gal and you're getting a top-notch guy."

Melva nodded. "I know I am."

"It's a relief for me that she chose Dave over Rob," Donald said as he entered the dining room, taking a bite out of an apple.

"Or Earle, for that matter," Dorothy added. Melva's brow raised. *"How did Aunt Dorothy know about Earle? I am totally healed from Earle. Thank You, Jesus."*

Donald continued, "I am very glad she's going to marry well. Sometimes I think it's a curse to have beautiful daughters, why with all the men..." Hazel cleared her throat and Donald left that thought dangling. Dorothy sipped her tea and peered over the rim of her cup. "So Melva," she asked, "when do you see him next?"

"I'm not sure, Aunt Dorothy. Maybe after our vacation in Banff. I'm so excited about going to Banff! I am looking forward to swimming in the Cave and Basin."

Dorothy smiled and nodded. "Have you set a wedding date?" she asked.

"Not yet. Now that he has completed his Bible training, at Millar and then the Prophetic, I imagine we'll get married when it's convenient for both of us. Perhaps near Christmas. Aunt Dorothy, he hasn't much money, and he uses everything so carefully. Most goes into his work as an evangelist."

"I respect him for that," Melva's Uncle Lee said.

August 5, 1940

Melva and her sisters, along with Dick and Kay, their baby Neil, and Vince, left for Banff shortly after six. They took two vehicles. It was a beautiful drive even though Bittles went into the ditch. On the way, they stopped at Johnson Canyon to go on a walk. They then shared a rented cabin near Banff. The next few days were filled with touring the Columbia Icefields, swimming at the Cave and Basin, picnicking, and dealing with a bear in camp. Dick, Kay, Vince, and Melva also enjoyed time together in a boat ride.

August 8, 1940, Banff

"This is our last day in Banff. Dick, could we please stop at the post office? Dave said he'd send a letter to me while we're here," Melva said.

"Sure," Dick said. Later, they pulled up beside the Banff Post Office. Melva jumped out and dashed in.

"Do I have any mail, please? General delivery. Melva Dye." The postmistress flipped through a stack of letters.

"Yes. Melva Dye?"

"Yes! That's me!"

"Here's one for you. From Innisfail."

"Thank you!"

Melva sat on a bench near the door and ripped it open.

"Dear Melva, here it is Sunday afternoon, the fourth, and I'm just writing the first letter. Somewhat uncertain just where exactly to mail it but trusting it will fall into your hands. Pardon me for writing so soon. I hope you are having an enjoyable time at Banff. I'm lonesome already. Shouldn't I be ashamed? The Lord was so good in failing to answer your prayer, you know, the one you said you prayed at the table regarding not looking my way? I can hardly believe it all yet. May His will be done; I am confident He will lead us. It was hard to get to sleep. I read the portion from the Bible where Jesus and His disciples were asked to the wedding, and this story added to my already full heart. Praying for you, my love, Dave."

Melva's heart flipped. Her and Dave. To become husband and wife. She giggled as she brought the letter to her chest and took a deep breath.

Evening, August 8, 1940

Melva set her luggage on her bed. They had just come home from Banff, and she began putting her things away. The phone rang and seconds later her mother called her to the phone from the bottom of the stairs. Melva ran down.

"Hello? Oh, Hi Dave, yes it was wonderful…and thank you for the letter. …What do you mean soon? Like how soon?" They continued their conversation for some time. After goodbye's were exchanged, Melva hung up and entered the living room where her parents and grandmother were.

"Mother, Daddy," she began, "Dave said he wanted to marry me soon, perhaps this fall."

"Yes, Melva," her mother said, "we should discuss the timing of your wedding."

"Yes Mother," Melva said as she sat. The creak of the rocking chair sounded as her grandmother rocked. She looked intently at her knitting as her needles clicked. *"Too fast. They're not going to let me go,"* Melva thought. Her father stopped pacing to look out the window.

"Dear, why don't you sit?" Hazel said. Donald shook his head and rubbed the back of his neck.

"It's too fast, right dear?" Hazel asked Donald as she stood and leaned on her cane. Donald ran his fingers through his hair, causing it to stand on end. Grandma Melvia looked at her son as she knit.

"Land sakes, Donald, say something. Don't leave the poor girl in torment."

"Daddy, Mother, it's alright," Melva broke in. "I'm alright with waiting, if you think the timing is wrong."

Hazel looked at her. "It's just that it's so fast, dear. He wants to marry you this fall? He only just proposed . . ."

Donald swung around from the window. "It's not the timing!" he blurted. Mouths dropped, eyes widened, and Grandma stopped knitting. He shook his head. "He's just like Father . . . *and me!* That's what I can't get over!"

Hazel's eyes widened, "W-what do you mean?"

"When we lived in Iowa, Father had an urge to go north, and west, to Canada. You remember don't you, Mother? Remember how what started as just a suggestion soon saw us moving thousands of miles with our big family, including in-laws and grandchildren? And livestock!"

Melvia set down her needles and smiled. She looked at the ceiling. "Yes son. I'll never forget it. It was shocking to uproot and leave everything familiar for a new country, but looking back, it is exactly what the good Lord wanted us to do. Verne had the dream of our family owning land and expanding in Canada."

Donald sighed and nodded, running his hand through his hair again. "It hasn't been easy. The war, grasshoppers, dust storms, losing Roger—but somehow, the good has always outweighed the bad. We're making it, Hazel. We're making it. Father was right. God has expanded us. It took courage, and then, after the courage wore off, it took endurance. Plain and simple endurance." The ticking of the clock sounded through the room. After a few speechless moments, Donald approached his daughter.

"Your mother and grandmother love Dave, and they have been waiting to hear my opinion." Again, it was silent for a minute. Donald looked at Melva. "You have my permission to marry this fall. Who am I to stop the will of God, or as Job says, 'who am I to contend with the Almighty?'" Melva jumped up and clapped her hands to her face. "Daddy!" She embraced him. "Thank you, thank you, thank you!"

"We're going to miss you, Melva, oh how we're going to miss you," he said as he pulled away and disappeared into the kitchen. Melva glanced at her mother and grandmother.

"Well, I never!" her grandmother said, tears coming to her eyes.

"My daughter, my daughter!" Hazel and Melva embraced.

"Oh, Mother!"

"Land sakes, Hazel! We should stop the tears. She's twenty-five after all, and that man she's marrying, why he's twenty-six! Plenty old enough to be responsible!"

Hazel turned to her mother-in-law, "Yes, I know Mother. But she's leaving. She's leaving us!"

August 9, 1940

The whistle of the wind greeted Melva the next morning as she got out of bed. The room looked cloudy, and her bed, blanket, and dresser all had a fine layer of dust. She flopped back onto the pillow and sighed. *"The whole house will need cleaning again! Dave! I must reread my letter!"* She jumped up and coughed. Then sneezed. She grabbed the letter she had received in Banff and read it again. After dressing, she blew dust off her desk, and dipped the pen into the ink bottle. *"I must reply and tell him how much I love him."*

August 10, 1940

Melva tossed and turned. She couldn't sleep. *"I am soon to be married!"* She glanced at her sisters. It was Saturday, and they had the day off. The Raes had invited the girls to go swimming in their swimming hole. *"I won't be able to swim if I'm tired from lack of sleep!"* Melva sat by her desk, wrapping her blanket around her. The grandfather clock in the hall softly ticked. It was a sound that had lulled her to sleep ever since she was little. *"Soon, I'm not going to hear that anymore. I'm not going to see or hear anything familiar anymore. I am to be married and share a room with my husband!"* She giggled. Noiselessly, she crawled back into bed. Clara rolled over.

"If you can't sleep, go downstairs so I can . . . Mrs. Stewart," Clara murmured.

"Mrs. Stewart?" Melva laughed. "Sorry, Mrs. Rae, I'll leave you to sleep."

Clara jumped out of bed and whacked Melva with her pillow. "Mrs. Rae? Mrs. Rae?" She hit her again.

Melva laughed and hit her back. "Donald Rae likes you. Everyone can see it."

"He does not. I just work for his mother."

"Whatever," Melva laughed.

"Do you two have to be so loud?" Doris groaned as she sat up in bed.

"Let's hurry, remember? We are going swimming today at the Rae's!" Melva announced.

"In the morning?" Doris asked.

"Melva just wants to get to town to see if she has any more mail from Dave!" Clara said.

Hours later, Melva hummed to herself as she left the post office. Her sisters were waiting for her in the car. She ripped open another letter from Dave.

"Dear Melva, we are holding evangelistic meetings in the Eagle Creek School across from Uncle Ruel's, and they want me to preach Monday to Thursday. However, we need a pianist. Your kind aunt here suggested that we ask you to come up, and I think it's an excellent idea. Please try to come Monday the 12th, if possible. Aunt Winnie will be phoning you about it at nine thirty tomorrow, Sunday evening. May His will be done. We would all love to have you, and I'd be more delighted than anyone. Yours with love in Christ, Dave."

Melva held the letter to her chest and looked dreamily up. *"August 12? That's only two days away! to stay with Uncle Ruel and Aunt Winnie, playing the piano in the evenings for Dave's evangelistic services, how wonderful to spend more time with him!"*

Later that night, Melva knelt by her bed. "Dear Lord, please show me a verse to confirm that I should go help Dave this week." She sat on the edge of her bed and flipped open her Bible. Romans 15:32 jumped out at her. "That I may come unto you with joy by the will of God and may with you be refreshed."

August 11, 1940

"I must say I will miss you when you marry, girl!" Mrs. Scott said as she entered the office, later Sunday evening.

Melva rested her chin in her hand. "I'll miss answering the phones, too." Melva admitted as she glanced around the small room.

"You are getting such a fine young man. I'm so happy for you, but like I say, I sure will miss you when you get married. With all the young men who have come through these doors over the years because of you, I'm glad you settled for a man of the cloth. I'll be mighty lonesome, for sure, for sure. Mighty lonesome. Least I have Shirley." The phone rang.

"Hello. This is Melva. How may I direct your call?"

"Hi Melva. This is Aunt Winnie. How are you doing?"

"Oh, hi Aunt Winnie. Just fine!"

"Good! Say, Uncle Ruel, Dave, and I were wondering if you would come stay with us and play the piano at the meetings Dave is holding in the Eagle Creek School across from us. We would need you from Monday to Thursday, as Friday he preaches in Wimborne.

"Yes, he told me about the meetings. I would love to come, but may I phone Daddy first?"

"Absolutely. Let me know if that's okay, dear. And if so, I will book the bus for you."

Melva set the phone down and looked up at Mrs. Scott. Mrs. Scott peered over her glasses at her and turned to sort papers. "You have my permission to have those four days off," she said. Melva smiled as she realized Mrs. Scott had overheard. She quickly connected her home line.

Her mother gave her permission, and Winnie bought her a bus ticket for nine oclock Monday morning.

CHAPTER FIFTEEN

MARRIAGE

August 12, 1940

The alarm sounded, piercing the still morning air. *Six o'clock, Monday morning.* Melva's sisters would soon leave for work. She eased herself out of bed and Clara sat up.

"Melva! Today you leave us and we won't see you until Friday."

"Oh Clara, go back to sleep. You still have another hour to sleep." But Clara bounded out of bed, stirring the light layer of dust from a midnight dust storm. Her sisters coughed.

"Melva, I am going to find it hard this week without you." Clara said. Alice, Vera, and Doris awoke and surrounded Melva, their long nighties flowing behind them. Together, they formed a group hug.

"Oh please, girls, this is silly, I am only gone until Friday," Melva said. Her sisters broke out in laughter.

Minutes later, their Aunt Ruth entered, "You must hurry Melva if I'm driving you. I hate being late and we must be in Calgary. Your bus leaves at nine. I'm leaving here at precisely eight." The girls looked at their meticulous aunt. "Now come get your breakfast, Melva, I've made you toast and eggs," Aunt Ruth said. After getting changed, Melva went downstairs to eat breakfast. Her sisters joined her.

Almost an hour later, Melva sat on the hard bus seat, waiting. She clutched her handbag and adjusted her hat. Men and women, some with children, were hugging each other on the boardwalk, and some climbed into the bus. When the bus pulled out, Melva glanced at her watch. *"In only a short while I'll be with Dave!"* She closed her eyes and took a deep breath. As they left the city, Melva stared out the window. The bus was taking her away; it felt like a powerful force, directing the path of her future. But God had put Dave and her together. *"Very soon, I will not live near Langdon. I will live with the man that has captured my heart."* Melva giggled to herself. Every mile put more and more distance between her and her familiar life, and every mile brought her closer and closer to her beloved man.

"Melva?" a cheerful voice called. Melva stepped off the bus in Olds to be greeted by her aunt.

"Aunt Winnie!" Melva embraced her.

"So good to see you! And my, don't you look beautiful!" Aunt Winnie said. Melva's face flushed with pleasure. Winnie helped put the suitcase and packages into the trunk and half an hour later, they arrived at the farm. Trees lined the driveway and surrounded the farmhouse and barn.

"Dave's on the tractor in the south field," Winnie said with a smile as she grabbed Melva's suitcase. "Feel free to go greet him." Melva walked through the trees to the edge of the field. A tractor plowed. Within minutes, it stopped, and Dave jumped out and ran across the field.

"Melva! Melva!" He wrapped his arms around her and held her tight.

"It's so good to be together," he said as he kissed her. "You smell lovely!"

"Oh Dave, I love you!" she laughed. He picked her up and swung her in dizzying circles. Dave smiled and set her down. "You are beautiful. Oh my!"

Melva laughed. "Dave, you look like a real farmer!"

Dave smiled. "Just thankful for the work. Your uncle's a swell guy!"

"But Dave, do you trust him? You know what a tease he is, and us courting and all…"

"Ruel and I are good friends, Melva, he wouldn't play any tricks on us…I think." Dave wrapped her in his strong arms again, and she soaked in the warmth of another long embrace.

"I need about an hour to finish this field," Dave said. "How'd you like to go inside, and I'll catch up after I put the tractor away?"

Aunt Winnie took Melva upstairs. "This is your room for the week. It is the room I gave Dave, but he has offered to sleep outside in the bunkhouse. Ruel and I sleep downstairs with Keith, but the girls have these two bedrooms. I'm sure they'll be no bother to you. If they are, just let us know, and we'll keep them in line." Winnie smiled as she slid open the curtains.

"Thank you, Aunt Winnie. This is lovely," Melva said as she set down her suitcase. After Winnie left, Melva looked around the room. It held the sights and scents of a man; the leather-bound journal, the stack of theology books, the checkered shirts in the open closet, and the faint smell of cedar scented aftershave. She smiled as she took a deep breath.

"That was a very good meeting, Dave," Winnie said as she closed the schoolhouse door behind her that night. Ruel put his hat on, and Dave flipped his jacket collar up. A fierce dusty wind had started while they were in the service.

"It was the pianist," Dave said as he winked at Melva. Melva blushed.

"This dust! Thankfully, we just need to run across the road to get home," Winnie yelled over the howl. Minutes later, the group of four entered the farmhouse.

"There wasn't many out night, I hope more come tomorrow night," Dave commented as he hung up his coat. Winnie and Ruel headed to put their children to bed while Dave and Melva sat in the living room. Melva picked up her crocheting and Dave paced.

"Melva…" he began, "I've been thinking about when our wedding should be." Melva looked up from her needle.

"And?" she said.

"Just that. I've just been thinking about when it should be," he said. Melva smiled shyly. "Perhaps, since you are here until Friday, we could set a date before you go back home."

"That is a very good idea," Melva said, "That way I'd have some exciting news to tell my family when I get back."

August 13, 1940

"Melva," Winnie said the next morning after the men had left to work in the fields, "I just found out that the Prophetic Bible Institute heard that Dave is holding revival meetings in the Eagle Creek School in the evenings, and they think it would be wise to also hold VBS meetings for the children during the day there."

"That is a great idea!" Melva said as she sipped her tea.

"And wait until you hear the rest!" Winnie leaned in. "Bertha Montgomery was asked to teach, as well as your sister Alice!"

"Alice? Is coming here?" Melva's eyes brightened.

"Yes, today. She and Bertha are helping with the VBS which will run from this afternoon until Thursday afternoon. They were also asked to help teach VBS at Rocky Mountain House on Friday."

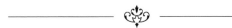

Bertha, Alice, and Melva, were among the teachers at the VBS meetings held that week. Everything went well, and many children accepted Christ.

August 15, 1940

Birds sang and hopped from branch to branch. Dave and Melva walked hand in hand along the edge of the field Dave had worked.

"Never thought I'd marry a pastor," Melva said, smiling up at him.

"And I never really considered who I'd marry. But you, Melva, exceed all my expectations. You know that verse that says, 'He is able to do exceedingly abundantly above all we could ask or think?' *That* is what God has done for me!" Melva squeezed his hand, delighting in the fact that she was alone with the man she would marry.

"He has done that for me as well," she whispered. Dave put his arm around her as they continued walking.

"I'm glad Ruel and Winnie went to Olds and I have the afternoon off," Dave said, "we really need to discuss some things."

Melva looked up at him. Dave cleared his throat.

"I've been thinking about when our wedding should be."

Melva burst out in laughter. "You told me that on Monday. Have you come up with a good day?" she asked.

Dave stopped walking and took both her hands in his. "Yes." He brought her hands to his lips and kissed them. Melva watched him with curious amusement. He took a deep breath. "Melva, having you here … well … it's hard for me to concentrate on preparing my messages and preaching … you … have stolen my heart." He looked up and his eyes scanned the horizon. "But being near you, it also gives me strength and courage … Melva, I don't want you to ever leave me again, it is just too hard on me."

Melva's eyes enlarged. "Dave, what in the world do you mean? I'm not planning on leaving you, or breaking up with you, if that's what you mean." Melva's mind raced to figure out the meaning of his words.

"Melva, Melva," he began again, drawing her to himself. He gently touched her cheek and kissed her, "Let's get married … tomorrow."

Melva's mouth dropped, and she took a step back. "T… t… tomorrow?"

"Tomorrow evening I preach in Wimborne, as you know, for Mr. Martin Bowker. I could phone and ask him to marry us after I preach. What do you think?"

Melva's heart raced as thoughts flooded her mind. "Please, Dave, I must have time to process this. May I let you know tonight after Alice and Bertha leave?"

"Of course, my dear."

Melva pulled away and looked across the field. Thoughts of her daddy, mother, grandmother, siblings, Mrs. Scott, the Bittles, and Uncle Ruel and Aunt Winnie filled her mind. What would everyone think of them? Would they be the talk of the farmers around the café in Langdon? Would theirs be called a shotgun wedding? But they were pure …

"Melva," Dave leaned in, "Are you okay?"

"Oh Dave!" she burst into tears. Dave brought her to himself in a tender embrace. As she felt his strong arms surround her, she laughed.

"Honestly! I don't know what to think!" she blurted.

"Goodbye, Melva, and see you next week! I suppose when we both get home the garden will be ready to start harvesting," Alice said as she gave her sister a hug and climbed into the drivers seat.

"Yes, I suppose it will be ready," Melva said with a smile. She glanced at Dave. He winked back.

After Alice and Bertha drove off, Dave turned to Melva, "Would you like to walk to Eagle Creek?"

"Sure." She replied.

Minutes later they headed across the field to the creek which bordered the southwest corner of Ruel's property. Dave had already used the creek to cool off in on a few hot days.

"Well, my dear, have you come to any conclusion over whether we should get married tomorrow night or not?" He squeezed her hand.

Melva hesitated. "Yes, Dave, I have. I would love to, but I am a bit afraid about what everybody would think and say about us."

"I understand Melva." Dave looked into her eyes with a tender understanding. It was that same look he had given her when she had told him to slow down in their relationship. It was quiet for a few minutes. As they reached the creek, they sat by the waters edge.

"Dave," Melva spoke at last, "Yes. I will marry you tomorrow night."

"Hello, this is Rev. Martin Bowker of the Wimborne Alliance Church. How may I help you?" A strong voice spoke over the phone.

Dave cleared his throat. "Yes, Hello Rev. Bowker. It's me, Dave Stewart … the reason I'm calling is … well, you know how you've got me scheduled to speak tomorrow night?"

"Why hello Dave. Good to hear from you. Yes, of course, is there a problem with that?"

"Well, um, it's just that, um … I know a couple that would like to get married after the service. Is it okay with you if I bring them along? And is it okay if you marry them?" A silence filled the air for a few seconds.

"I will marry them, but only if you are still going to do the preaching."

"Yes, yes, I will still preach! Thank you, thank you so much! And … see you tomorrow night. Goodbye," Dave said.

Rev. Bowker turned to his wife. "Honey, we need to purchase ice cream and cake for tomorrow night."

"Whatever for?" she asked.

"Dave's getting married."

"Mother?" Melva spoke over the phone.

"Oh, hello Melva! It's so wonderful to hear your voice! How are you? How were the services at Eagle Creek School? Did Alice and Bertha make it alright? Was anyone saved? I can't wait to hear all about it!"

Melva laughed. "Yes, mother, the services went well. There were a lot of children saved." Melva paused. "Um, Mother ..."

"Yes dear, what is it?"

"Um ... would it be possible for you and daddy and Grandmother and whoever else to come hear Dave preach at Wimborne Friday night at 7:30?"

Hazel remained silent for a few moments. "Well, I suppose so ... but daddy and Vern are in the middle of harvesting ..."

"Yes, I know, mother. I was also wondering if you could bring my white shoes and my wine dress with the teardrop brooch?"

"Well yes dear, if we can make it, I will ask your father."

Hazel slowly hung up the phone. Donald set the newspaper down. "What was that about?" he asked.

"It was Melva. She wants us all to come hear Dave preach tomorrow night at seven-thirty in Wimborne."

Donald lifted the paper back up. "Oh, come on now, Hazel, she knows we're in the middle of harvest."

"That's what troubles me. Donald, she asked for her white shoes." The paper rustled as Donald brought it down again.

"Tell everyone to be ready to leave for Wimborne tomorrow at five-thirty and let's pray it doesn't rain."

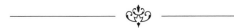

Late that night, Dave and Melva sat on the couch together. Dave cleared his throat.

"About tomorrow night," Dave said, "I tried to book a hotel room in Red Deer for our honeymoon, but the place I wanted was full, so I booked a room for Saturday night there instead, I hope that's alright with you."

"Oh Dave, Saturday night in a hotel is good enough for me. The important thing is that we're together, wherever that is."

"I hope you still think that after Friday night. I mean, we'll have to stay at the farmhouse for our wedding night." Melva smiled and looked down. Dave continued, "Like you mentioned earlier, I'm wondering about Ruel. He plays lots of tricks." Dave rubbed the back of his neck. "And I don't know about spending our first night in their home."

Melva burst into laughter. "Don't worry about Uncle Ruel, Dave. What could he possibly do? I am sure he knows not to take things too far, but ever since he was young, he was mischievous. Grandpa loved to tell the story about in Iowa when he built a new barn. Ruel was ten and he actually climbed right over it! Grandpa Verne spanked him behind the barn!"

Dave laughed. "I can see Ruel doing that. Always full of spunk. It's made him a good farmer. Say, about tomorrow evening, I'm speaking on Peter walking on the water. It was dark and stormy that night and the first thing Jesus said to His disciples was, 'Be of good cheer; it is I; be not afraid.' It's like Jesus lived above the storm, and in it, at the same time. He beckons us, 'Come,' like He said to Peter. Melva, our life together may not always be easy, but the invitation is the same, 'Come unto me all ye that labor and are heavy laden, and I will give you rest.' God will be with us through all the storms, Melva." She nodded and clasped his hand.

"How about I pray?" he said.

"Yes, I'd like that." Together they committed themselves and their marriage to God.

It was late when Melva slipped into bed. She stared at the ceiling. Her last night single. A surge of excitement shot through her. She giggled, then turned and tossed. Tomorrow was her wedding!

August 16, 1940

Melva glanced at the bedside clock. *"Already seven thirty? I hardly slept! How will I make it through the day! And to think no one back home knows I'm getting married today! Especially not Alice, there is no way of getting a hold of her!"* She put her hand on her forehead. *Oh, this dreadful headache! Must be from my excitement and laughing so hard with Uncle Ruel and Aunt Winnie last night!* She dressed quickly and went down the stairs.

"Good morning! How's our bride today?" Winnie asked, giving Melva a big hug. "Did you tell your parents?"

"I tried too, Aunt Winnie, but I just couldn't over the phone. I did tell mother to bring my white shoes. When I bought them this summer, I told her I was saving them for my wedding, so I know she'll figure it out."

Winnie burst into laughter. "Your as bad as your uncle! Always up to something!"

Melva smiled.

"Mr. Bowker guessed who is getting married tonight. He phoned Dave and told him he needs a marriage license, so I can take you and him into Olds this morning. I'm going in anyway. Maybe you'd like to buy a few things too?" Winnie said. Melva nodded. "Dave's out with Ruel," Winnie continued, "The hail adjuster's coming to look at our wheat."

"Here, have some tea, dear," Winnie said as she set a rose teacup on the table and filled it. Melva wrapped her fingers around the delicate rose-painted china. Warmth. Like the warmth in her heart.

An hour later Dave entered and swung Melva around and kissed her. "My dear Melva, today we become husband and wife," he whispered in her ear. Melva felt her face flush and she smiled.

"Dave, I am worried about everything today, although I do want to get married to you. But today?"

Dave's face broke into a wide smile. "Melva, there's a chorus I heard as I travelled Alberta preaching. No one knows who wrote it. I would like to dedicate it especially today for you, my dear bride. It goes like this, 'Cheer up ye saints of God, there's nothing to worry about, nothing to make you feel afraid, nothing to make you doubt. Remember Jesus never fails, so why not trust him and shout. You'll be sorry you worried at all tomorrow morning.'"

"Oh Dave!" Melva said as they both broke into laughter.

Hours later, Dave sat beside Melva in the back seat of Ruel's car with his arm around her. He leaned over and whispered in her ear, "Wimborne, here we come!" He kissed her cheek and Melva giggled and kissed him back.

"Hey, you two love birds!" Ruel said, peering into the rear-view mirror.

"Oh, you just shush, you big tease," said Winnie. "Leave them be."

"Sermon already to go?" Melva whispered in his ear. Dave patted her knee and murmured, "Always." Half an hour later they pulled into the small town of Wimborne. It was a small hamlet which had a few stores and a gas station. Dave headed east and turned left at the last street and pulled in the Wimborne Alliance Church parking lot. It was full of vehicles. Dave jumped out and opened Melva's door. As she stepped out, a squeal filled the air.

"Melva! Melva!" Vera embraced her.

"Is it true? Are you really getting married tonight? Oh Melva, I've missed you so much! Clara wiggles so much in bed and steals all the covers and …"

"I do not!" Clara said as she approached. She hugged Melva.

"Melva, are you seriously getting married tonight?"

"Yes." Melva smiled.

"Oh Melva!" both sisters said in unison as they formed a group hug. Doris approached and joined them.

"But Alice, does she know?" Doris asked. Melva shook her head.

"Here dear, is your white shoes and dress," Hazel said as she handed Melva a small leather suitcase. "I included some other items as well."

"Thank you, Mother, thank you, and thank you for coming, I knew you would understand." Hazel smiled and patted Melva's arm.

"Yes dear, daddy and I understand."

Melva's father held out his arm for Grandma as she slipped out of their car. Next to their car were the Bittles and others from Langdon. A thrill of excitement raced through Melva. She quickly headed to the church outhouse to change.

As Melva came out of the outhouse, her eyes scanned for her father. She approached him and embraced him.

"Now, now, no tears," he said clearing his throat. "Tonight you become Dave's wife, and I won't need to worry about you any longer!"

"Oh Daddy!" She kissed him on the cheek. The group made its way into the church and sat halfway up the aisle. Dave sat on the platform next to Rev. Martin Bowker. A pianist played hymns softly on the piano.

Thirty minutes later, as Dave ended his sermon, Mr. Bowker came behind him.

"Dave has asked me if I would marry him and Melva Dye. Melva?"

A wave of butterflies in her stomach accompanied Melva as her father escorted her to the front. Sniffs from their bench echoed in the high-ceilinged room. Dave's smile radiated joy as she approached the platform. He stepped forward and took her hand.

Rev. Martin Bowker cleared his throat. "Dearly beloved, we are gathered to witness the holy matrimony of Arthur David Stewart to Melva Talitha Dye, this sixteenth day of August, in the year of our Lord, nineteen hundred and forty." He picked up their wedding bulletin and read from the inside cover. "Thomas Campbell is quoted as saying, 'Can you keep the bee from ranging, or the ring dove's neck from changing? No, nor fettered love from dying, in the knot there's no untying.' Rev. Bowker cleared his throat. "Melva, repeat after me, "I Melva, take you, David …' Melva felt her heart pound as she repeated the oft-spoken vow. Seconds later, Rev. Bowker turned to Dave.

"Dave, repeat after me, I Dave, take you Melva …" As she felt his strong hands hold hers, she looked deep in his eyes. He was in love, in love with her, but behind that love simmered something in the spiritual realm that defied all explanation—a determination, a vigor, to carry out God's will, with her, as a team, no matter the obstacles. Melva looked at the ring Dave slipped on her finger. It was a thin band of white gold in the front, encased with three small diamonds. The back glistened with yellow gold.

"You may now kiss your bride." Dave gently rested his hands on Melva's face and slowly drew her to him. Cheers sounded as she gradually pulled away. Dick Bittle and Vince, along with Ruel whistled. She was a married woman now, determined to stand behind this unflinching man, whatever the cost.

As the happy couple exited the building, Rev. Bowker took the podium.

"Ladies and gentlemen, a light lunch will be provided in the parsonage next door."

The drive home was quiet with Ruel and Winnie chatting in the front seat and Melva comfortably scrunched up with Dave in the back. She kissed his cheek, not even noticing the beautiful moonlight streaming through the window. He winked at her. A half hour later, the car jerked to a stop. Ruel spun around. "Dave, do you mind stepping out? I think we have a flat. Winnie, hand him the flashlight from the glove compartment, please." Dave stepped out and immediately Ruel sped off. Melva's mouth dropped.

"W-what…" squeaked Melva.

"Ruel!" Winnie cried.

Ruel chuckled. "Had to do something, honey. You know me, and we're only a mile or two from home."

Minutes later, they pulled into the driveway. Ruel opened Winnie's door and then Melva's. She smiled at him and walked determinedly down the driveway.

"Melva! Hey, Melva! Where are you going?"

Without breaking pace, Melva half turned and laughed. "To join my husband!"

CHAPTER SIXTEEN

FOR BETTER OR FOR WORSE

August 17, 1940

Dave and Melva came downstairs the next day at noon. The others in the house had already come and gone for lunch.

"Well," Dave said as he looked around, "we can leave for Red Deer for our one-night honeymoon whenever you like, my dear. Then, we will come back here for a night or two, then we are to room at the Johnson's, where they have agreed to hire you as a maid, and me as a farm hand." Melva smiled.

"Would you like something to eat first?" Dave asked as he looked at a stack of pancakes left on the table.

"Sure." The two sat and ate. As they rose to leave, Melva surveyed the counters. Winnie had left, and dirty dishes were stacked near the sink, along with pots and pans. Dave raised his brow at the mess. Melva's eyes met his.

"Alright, let's," he said as if reading her thoughts.

Melva laughed, "How did you know what I was thinking?"

It was three-thirty in the afternoon when Dave and Melva finally finished cleaning the kitchen and pulled out of Ruel and Winnie's driveway to head to Red Deer.

August 18, 1940

As Dave and Melva entered the Innisfail Baptist Church, they were surrounded by friendly farmers and townspeople, all eager to welcome their new pastor and congratulate Dave and Melva on their recent marriage. Dave spoke, and his message was well received. At the end of his message, he leaned into the mic.

"Melva and I, and the Johnson family, would like to invite all who wish to share our wedding cake with us, to come to the Johnson home at seven tonight."

August 21, 1940

"Well, my dear. That wasn't much of a honeymoon with staying at your uncle's Friday night, then the hotel Saturday night, and preaching Sunday morning, and now moving to the Johnsons today. It feels a little too busy for newlyweds," Dave said as they pulled into the Johnsons' spacious farmyard. Melva looked at the large house.

"It was kind of them to host the church Sunday night in honor of our wedding. And I'm glad they hired me on as a maid and housecleaner. That'll fill my time and help us financially," she said.

"That and the money I make as a farmhand," added Dave. "I'm hoping we'll be able to save for a home—if that's God's will. Oh Melva, I am so excited about the circuit ride I've been assigned to in this area. Especially New Raven Church. It's tucked in a row of spruce trees just west of Spruce View. Lovely spot, great country people!"

"But Dave, I still don't know how you are going to farm full time, do a circuit ride, and pastor the Baptist Church!" Melva said.

Dave smiled and patted her hand. "I am trusting Mr. Johnson to let me get off an hour early each night so I can prepare sermons."

Dave and Melva took their few belongings and knocked on the door.

"Hello? Hello? Mrs. Johnson?" Dave called. A plump middle-aged woman appeared.

"My goodness me, you're here with your bride, Dave! Come on in and I'll show you to your room. And you're Melva? Congratulation's honey!" They embraced.

Mrs. Johnson led the two upstairs and down a long, wide hallway.

"Now, a bit about our family. My husband Harry senior and I have three children. Harry junior, he'll be working with Dave. And there's Barbara, she's nineteen and works at the hairdresser in Innisfail, and Dorothy. She married Stew two years ago. Perhaps you met them at Innisfail Baptist?"

"Not sure, ma'am," Melva said. "I met so many on Sunday it's hard to remember."

"That's all right, my dear. Dorothy comes here every few days to do her laundry. She likes my washing setup."

She opened a door. "This is the hired hand's bedroom. I hope it will be sufficient for you both." Melva peered in. A large bed stood against the wall in the middle of the room. To one side was a desk and chair, and to the other, a picture window overlooking the farmyard.

"It's a beautiful room, Mrs. Johnson. It will do fine," Dave said as they set their things at the foot of the bed.

"Harry will give Dave his orders and I will give my orders to Melva," she said. "Young lady, I hope you are not afraid of work. Today, I'd like you to clean the upstairs bedrooms, churn the butter, and start the ironing. It's piled on the ironing board downstairs in the laundry area. When that's done, I'll need help with supper."

"Yes ma'am."

"Put your things away then come downstairs, dear," Mrs. Johnson said as she left.

Melva sighed. "Looks like I've got my work cut out."

Dave embraced her. "Sorry if it's not what you expected, I mean … married life."

"No, no, it's not that. Before we were married, I'd work just as hard at home, and without pay." She slowly got up and put her things away. Near the bottom of her bag, she pulled out a neatly pressed apron. "I just love this apron you bought me in Red Deer. Thank you so much!" She held it in front of her and smiled. "And I think I'll wear this new calico dress on Sunday," she said as she peered into her bag. Dave and Melva changed into their work clothes and headed down the stairs.

"See you later!" Melva said as she kissed Dave.

Hours later, after a hard day's work, Melva checked her list and was pleased to see everything crossed off, except supper dishes. She had not seen Dave since he had gone out and he hadn't come in for supper. She filled the sink with hot soapy water and dishes, cringing at the tall stack of sticky plates and pots and the crusted pans teetering on the counter. An hour later, she wiped the counter. *"Good. I'm finished!"* The door opened and Dave stepped in. Drying her hands, she threw herself at him. "Dave! What? You're covered with dirt! Oh my!"

"Yeah, I sure need a bath before supper," he grinned, his teeth in stark contrast to his dirty face.

After his bath and supper, Dave took his plate to the sink and began to rinse it.

"Let me do that, dear. Why don't you go to bed?"

"Good idea. Worked hard today and I'm wiped. I had hoped to go fishing tonight, but—" He turned and trudged up the stairs. As Melva washed his plate, a clang and bang and clatter of pots and pans filled the farmyard. *"Must be dreaming. I've done too many dishes."* The racket increased.

"I'll get the door!" Mrs. Johnson said as she stepped into the kitchen. She headed for the porch and opened the door.

"Surprise!" a chorus of voices burst through the air. "Surprise! A shivaree! For Dave and Melva!" Mrs. Johnson turned and smiled at Melva.

"A shivaree?" Melva's mouth dropped. "H-how wonderful!"

"Please, come in," Mrs. Johnson said.

"I'll get Dave!" Melva said. A large group of young people poured into the house and when the newlyweds stepped into the living room minutes later, a wide stack of gifts was piled high on the floor. Melva made a quick count. Thirty-two young people from all over the area.

Dave's eyes widened and he managed to blurt, "This is a wonderful surprise! Thank you, thank you so much everyone!"

Mrs. Johnson smiled, "Well, I must confess I knew about it, and I have prepared a light meal for everyone!"

Later that night in bed, Dave turned to Melva. "Wow, those gifts are amazing. The young people really sacrificed to give them! God is taking care of us."

"I know. I am grateful beyond words. Johnsons gave us the most beautiful bedspread! And the lunch was amazing! These men and women must really appreciate you a lot, Dave."

September 16, 1940

The floor creaked and Melva turned. "Dave?" she whispered.

"Go back to sleep," he said softly.

"What *are* you doing?" she asked, rubbing her eyes. Dave was on the edge of the bed, pulling up his socks. "I have to study for young peoples."

Melva craned her neck at the desk. The dim moonlight shone on the clock. "At three in the morning?"

Dave sighed as he clicked on the desk lamp. "Melva, I have no other time. As you know, Mr. Johnson has me working from early morning to late, so when can I study and prepare?" He rubbed his forehead. "And I've got a headache." Melva slipped out of bed and gently massaged his neck.

"This last month has been hard on you. Couldn't you ask Mr. Johnson for more time to prepare sermons?"

"Would like to, but that's not how he operates!"

September 28, 1940

Melva felt the blanket next to her. Still empty. She peered at the clock on the dresser. After one in the morning. No Dave. She got up and paced. *"He's working too hard. But what can we do? He can't be a full-time farmer and a pastor at the same time! Impossible!"* Footsteps sounded on the stairs and the bedroom door opened slowly.

"Oh Dave!" Melva approached him and they embraced. "What happened? Why are you so late?" Dave rubbed his unshaven chin and sat on the bed.

"It was Renny! You know that other hired man I've worked with occasionally this month? Well, he and I were told to harvest the oats. After working a while, he complained about how hard the work was and left me by myself! I checked his scythe, and it was dull! Mr. Johnson has told us again and again that the key to a neat cut is a sharp scythe. He also told us to use a smooth slicing motion as we walk down the row cutting, but Renny was hacking his row to bits! I couldn't stop working when he did because when it comes to harvesting oats, timing is everything! Cut them too early, the grain will be wet and mold. Cut them too late, the grain will be too dry and the heads shatter. Mr. Johnson and I have been daily watching the oat field, and today, the oats were perfect. Everyday hereafter, he loses five to eight per cent of the crop." Dave sighed. "Now with the oats ready, I don't know when I'll have time to write my sermon!"

Melva sat on the bed, staring blankly at the slanted ceiling. "Dave, you are just plain overworked. We need to pray about this. Perhaps Mr. Johnson could hire more help. Perhaps he would be okay with you only working nine hours a day instead of—" Deep breathing answered her suggestion and she turned to find Dave stretched across the bed, eyes closed, coveralls on, arms limp at his side. Melva lifted his legs onto the bed and tucked her afghan around him.

October 3, 1940

"Honey? Honey? You coming for supper?" Mrs. Johnson called to her husband in the living room. Dave and Melva, along with Harry Jr. and Barbara waited at the table.

"No, I'm not coming!" his sharp voice sounded.

"Why ever not? Well, for Pete's sake!" Mrs. Johnson marched into the living room. "Your children are waiting for you!"

"I don't care. I'm not coming. And I don't feel like going to prayer meeting tonight. I'm worried about all the money we are losing from my partially harvested oat field!" A rustle of a newspaper sounded, and Mrs. Johnson reappeared.

"Let's eat. Dave, could you please return thanks?"

"Sure. So, who am I taking to prayer meeting?" Dave asked after he prayed.

"We want to go," Harry said as he spooned a mound of potatoes on his plate. Barbara nodded.

"There's orchestra practice after, and I wouldn't miss that for anything," Barbara said.

After the prayer meeting ended, the young people started to play their instruments. Melva giggled. *"That sounds awful. Oh well, that's why it's called practice."* The young people didn't mind the noise and talked and laughed all the louder. It was almost eleven when Dave, Melva, Mrs. Johnson, Harry, and Barbara returned home. Mr. Johnson had gone to bed. They entered the dining room and flicked on the light. The table was just as they had left it—full of dirty dishes. The counter contained unwashed bowls, pots, and other dishes.

"Melva, I want you to clean up," Mrs. Johnson said as she, Harry, and Barbara made their way to their rooms. Melva set her purse and Bible on the table. She looked at Dave and her shoulders sank. As she walked to where the aprons hung, he followed.

"Melva, I plowed all day, and you worked in here all day. I dare say I don't know which of us is more tired." He walked to the stove and with a bucket took warm water out of the reservoir, dumping it into the sink basin.

"Oh Dave, I can do this. You go to bed. Tomorrow you're plowing again, and that's hard work. I'm only cleaning rooms."

Dave wrapped his arms around her. "I vowed for better or for worse. I'll help."

October 7, 1940

Melva pushed a strand of hair from her face. It was unusually warm for an October afternoon. She sighed, walked to the window, and set the basin of wash water on the counter. Outside, Dave was splitting firewood. With each sweep of the ax, firewood landed every which way.

Hours later, Dave entered the kitchen, sweat pouring from his face. Melva watched him wash at the basin while she stirred the soup.

"Melva, the bananas are really overripe, so please make banana bread for dessert," Mrs. Johnson said as she entered the kitchen, tying on an apron.

"Yes ma'am." Melva scurried to collect the ingredients.

"I'm done splitting," Dave said, drying his hands.

"You mean that huge pile?" Melva asked. "All done? Already?"

"Yeah, all done. Neat and tidy. It's a good feeling."

"I'm proud of you, dear."

"I'll grab a quick bath and finish my message for tonight," he whispered in her ear.

Mr. Johnson stepped in the kitchen. "Dave, could I get you to help dig potatoes before you go to young peoples?"

"I need to get ready for tonight, Mr. Johnson. Can it hold off till tomorrow?" Dave asked. Mr. Johnson grunted as he stomped out.

Melva smiled sympathetically at Dave. "What are you speaking on tonight?"

The door burst open, and Harry Jr. raced in, grabbing his gun.

"Dave! Need your help. Skunk in the culvert! Might be a whole family." He ran out.

Dave turned to Melva. "My talk is called, 'Is Life Worth Living?'"

"Is life worth living," she thought as Dave grabbed another gun and ran out. Lately, their relationship was strained, both too busy and tired for romance. A tear slipped down her cheek. She ran upstairs and threw herself on the bed and cried. Minutes later, she sat and glanced at the dresser. Dave's journal lay open. She picked it up and flipped through it. *"Mostly sermon notes,"* she noticed. Wednesday, January 4, 1939, caught her eye. She read, "Guess I'll go down and say goodbye to Melva and Mrs. Smart. Well, that's over—it was not hard to say goodbye to Mrs. Smart in the store. She has been very kind to me while I stay in her home . . . she's given me a standing invitation to her home whenever I'm in town. It was not so easy, however, to say goodbye to Melva. Even an evangelist has thoughts of love—you know—this one is more troubled than others with the disease. I suppose Melva wondered why I waited around so long. I pretended I was interested in the telephone business. However, not a bit. I didn't want to say goodbye. Melva is a swell girl. She is like a ray of sunshine in the morning, bright and cheery, bringing

gladness to an early riser as he looks into its bright refreshing rays..."
Melva pressed the journal to her heart.

October 14, 1940

Melva tied on her apron as she rushed down the stairs. Six-forty.

"Good morning, dear," Mrs. Johnson said, turning from the stove.
"The oven should be warm enough in about fifteen minutes. Today,
the men are threshing the north fields," she said as she stirred a large
pot of oatmeal, "so I need you to make two Thanksgiving dinners, one
for the crew and one for us. You'll find the turkeys in the pantry. And
oh yes, the men like pie, so please bake three, along with a nice cake.
Barbara's home later today, so she can help."

All morning Melva baked. Hours later, in the afternoon, Mrs.
Johnson entered the kitchen. She took the graniteware coffee pot from
the back of the stove and poured a cup.

"Melva, you've been working so hard. Why not take a break? Here,
have some coffee." She opened the cupboard for another cup. Melva
wiped her brow.

"Thank you, Mrs. Johnson." Finder, the family dog, barked and
Mrs. Johnson went to the window. She wiped the moisture off and
peered out.

"Land sakes! It's Mrs. Wilkens and her youngens! Now why in
the world would they come today when it's Thanksgiving! Of all the
nerve!" The thud of knocking sounded. Mrs. Johnson opened the door.
"Well, if it isn't Sarah! Come in, come in! Would you like some coffee?
Melva, could you serve Mrs. Wilkens and her children, please? I'll check
the turkeys." Melva set her coffee down and scurried about to serve Mrs.
Wilkens coffee, as well as giving her children some juice.

Hours later Barbara and Mrs. Johnson took the turkey dinner to
the threshing crew while Melva set the table in the dining room for the
rest of the family. Later, as they ate, Melva got up to pour more coffee.
She entered the kitchen and glanced at the counters. They were piled
high with pots and pans, a rolling pin, bowls laden with sticky dough,
more bowls stained with drying blueberry pie filling, turkey roasters

with drippings pasted on the sides, and more plates, cups, and cutlery than she could care to count. She sighed as she sat and stared at her plate.

"What's wrong, honey. Not hungry?" Mrs. Johnson asked.

"I guess not," Melva said, staring at her coffee cup.

Later that evening Dave entered, straw and chaff clinging to his overalls. Dust covered his hands and face and he kissed Melva as he passed through the kitchen. "The turkey was delicious," he said. Melva's arms were elbow deep in hot soapy water and her fingers were wrinkled and red. She wiped the sweat off her forehead with her arm. Strands of hair stuck out of her kerchief. Melva's once-new apron was stained and dirty.

Hours later, Melva crawled into bed. Dave was already asleep. She lay her head on her hands. A tear landed on her pillow. *"At least Dave got to eat Thanksgiving dinner in the field."*

October 19, 1940

Melva awoke and stared at the white ceiling. *"I hate to get up."* When she arrived in the kitchen, she found a note on the table. "Dear Melva. I am in town. Please scrub all floors. Make a big batch of pudding and lunch for the men and take it to them. They are finishing the oats in the south field. They eat at noon sharp. You have been working hard so take a couple hours off in the afternoon."

"I get a couple hours off this afternoon! What a relief! I can finally have some time to study my Bible school theology books!" She hummed as she worked.

Melva glanced at the kitchen clock. Nearly noon. She wiped her brow and stretched; once again, discouraging thoughts flooded her mind. *"I'm a servant and Dave's a slave. Dear God, please help us and move us somewhere—anywhere—other than here, someplace where Dave can do full-time work for You and have time to study."* Melva slipped on her coat and carried the heavy food crate to the farm truck. Finder jumped into the back and together they drove to the threshing crew in the south field.

The loud rumble of the threshing machine made it impossible to talk, so she approached the men and waved. Dave pulled some levers and the machine slowly rumbled to a stop. As the men filed to the truck, Melva walked to Dave. His face was layered with dirt and his coveralls were covered with a layer of chaff.

Feeling his strong arms surround her, she wilted.

"Melva? What's wrong?"

Melva let the tears fall and could barely talk. "This work, Dave. It's getting in the way of your ministry and I'm tired of all the work I must do. How can I be a proper helpmeet?" Gently, he pulled her closer. Lunch was forgotten as they held each other for what seemed like a long time.

"Melva, Melva, Melva. My sweetheart Melva. How about we go into Olds tonight to get away? Would that help? We could buy you those pretty slippers we saw in the window at W. M. Craig's and Co. last week."

Dave continued to use any available time to write his sermons. The church, realizing how busy he was, relieved him of all pastoral duties except for a sermon every Sunday.

October 25, 1940

Mrs. Johnson and Barbara were working in the garden and Melva was at her usual post, a counter full of dirty dishes. Just as she was about to wash, Dave came into the kitchen.

"Oh good! You're back. I made roast chicken and you're just in time to eat before we head to Raven," Melva said. Dave sighed and collapsed in the corner chair.

"How was your day?" she asked.

"Terrible. Mr. Johnson told me to set up snow fences along the gravel road. I don't know how to describe how much trouble that was. They were all tangled, and the cold wind sure didn't help. My hands felt frozen. It took hours!"

"At least you're home and we won't be late for Bible study," Melva said, fighting doubt. Dave pushed his fingers through his hair. He brought his hand down with a sudden chopping motion.

"Melva, I've tried to be patient, but today was just too much! It's bad enough to untangle snow fences but working with Renny is more than I can handle! What am I supposed to do? And to make matters worse he attends church with us!" He glared across the room and whacked the table with his fist.

CHAPTER SEVENTEEN

VACATION

November 8, 1940

Melva slid across the car seat and snuggled next to Dave. He smiled at her as they drove down the now familiar Johnson driveway.

"I'm so glad for this break, Dave. Aren't you?"

"Yes." Dave heaved a deep sigh of relief. "I've been so down lately, it's like I don't want to go on. Don't know what's wrong with me."

"*I* know what's wrong with you! You're overworked!"

"Maybe. Don't know if that's it. I've just been doing a normal man's job."

"But Dave! You work from sunrise to sunset!"

"Like I said, a normal man's work. Melva, an older man in the Langdon café once told me when he was breaking sod, he started at three-thirty in the morning and didn't get to bed until well after ten! On average, he broke thirty acres a day. No, it's more like I'm resisting giving all my time and energy to farming, because it's not what I really want to do. I've only ever wanted to preach, yet I can hardly find time to study. I'm exhausted!"

Melva patted his knee. "But now we are on our way to the fall conference at Prairie Bible Institute. I'm praying it will be an encouragement to you. It's a miracle Johnsons gave you a six-week break."

"The Johnsons understand and although I am surprised they gave us a six-week break, I guess they felt bad our honeymoon was so short. Mr. Johnson even paid me extra. But harvest is finished, and my parents don't even know you yet. I felt bad they couldn't make it to the wedding, but they'll get to know you well when we stay there. I figure we'll stay in the Prairie dorms for three nights, then stay in Langdon until the twentieth, then head for Moose Jaw. Reckon we'll stay in Moose Jaw at my parents' for about twenty days, come back to Langdon for a week, and then head back to Innisfail. I trust it will be enough of a break so when we get back, we'll both be refreshed and ready to go again. But now? Innisfail here we come. Can't wait to install a heater in this car. Won't *that* be nice, Melva? Imagine driving all the way to Moose Jaw with warm air in the automobile!" Dave said.

"That would be too good to be true!" she giggled.

"How about I drop you off at McKay's so you can visit them while I go to the garage? I'll get it greased while I'm there."

It was nearly two in the afternoon when Dave and Melva pulled out of McKay's yard and headed for Three Hills.

"My, these roads are bad. Too much slushy snow," Dave commented, keeping a tight grip on the wheel.

"Take your time," Melva replied. "We're in no hurry."

Just before suppertime, they drove onto the Prairie campus in Three Hills. After they settled into their dorm room and had supper in the dining room, they entered the Prairie Tabernacle. Stepping into the huge auditorium, Melva's mouth fell open—almost every seat was taken. After they found a place near the front, the congregation stood as a man led them in hymn singing. The pianist's fingers flew up and down the piano and everyone sang wholeheartedly. The music and singing rose to the ceiling in a crescendo, as if all heaven had joined in. The glorious melody saturated right to the heart. Melva smiled and took a deep breath. Already she felt encouraged, as the praise music lifted her spirit. When the audience was seated, a staff member introduced the speaker.

"Good evening, ladies and gentlemen. Tonight, we have Dr. T. Marshall Morsey with us. In 1929, he founded the Harvester Mission, a center designed to lead people to hope through trusting in God. It is going strong today." A middle-aged man approached the pulpit. His frameless spectacles glistened in the light.

"I read about him in the *Prairie Pastor* publication," Dave whispered to Melva.

Dr. Morsey shook hands with the announcer. "My text for today is Habakkuk chapter two, verse one." Although small of stature, Rev. Morsey's voice echoed across the huge room.

"'I will stand upon my watch, and set me upon the tower, and will watch to see what he will say unto me, and what I shall answer...' I have been thinking of the Lord's message to Habakkuk. He lived in a dark time of Israel's history. He found things that challenged his faith, like how God could allow a cruel, terrible nation, to go through the country and destroy people. We are facing that same problem now. It is night and the armies of the two most cruel nations are allowed to slay people by the hundreds of thousands. In a time like that, Habakkuk called, 'Art thou not from everlasting, O Lord my God, mine Holy One? We shall not die. O Lord, thou hast ordained them for judgment; and, O mighty God, thou hast established them for correction. Thou are of purer eyes than to behold evil, and canst not look on iniquity.'

"That is certainly the problem tonight. If you talk to the average person, there is little real faith or trust in God … If you hold a prayer meeting, you will have just a handful, because people are not interested. The Bible has little place in their reading. It is all a strange condition. Then comes Habakkuk's prayer, 'I will stand upon my watch, and set me upon the tower, and will watch to see what he will say unto me, and what I shall answer.' That struck me as a wise suggestion for today. 'I will set me upon the tower.' It doesn't make any difference about what the nations will do. The Bible is plain about that, even though things are dark. I think it will be over before we think. But then there will be a lull, and then back into darkness. What a grand thing it is to stand on our watchtower, when the times are dark, and we don't know just how the news will turn. We don't know what God will do. It is my duty as a preacher to watch for my congregation, and for myself. Stand in your watch tower and watch, keep your eyes open, and look and see what the Lord will do. He spoke to Habakkuk and gave him a vision. It doesn't make any difference how dark things become. We want to stand on our watchtower and hear what God would say to each of us.

"I believe the Lord has been saying things to me these last few months. God never uses or blesses anything but holiness. The first thing Habakkuk sees is the Holy One. The church today has no conception of the holiness of God. Habakkuk looked at the conditions and was in gloom. But then he looked at the Lord, and there was brightness. Habakkuk said, 'I saw the hand of the power of God.' He couldn't see the tanks and machine guns and airplanes. I have been asking God to help me see at this time, to see that this present conflict is not going to be settled by tanks, but by the invisible hand of Almighty God. Eyes off men, eyes off yourself, eyes on the Lord, on that mighty power that goes out of His hand, eyes on His glory. Then Habakkuk says, 'He will make my feet like hind's feet, and he will make me to walk upon high places.' The hind is the most sure-footed of all animals. It is because when he moves forward, he goes with his forefeet and grapples them into a place where he is trying to get up, pulling until his feet strike a solid place. When he springs, he puts his back feet down right where his front feet were. That is a tested track, he has tested it with his front feet. He springs forward and does not slip. The Lord has made us the hind feet and the Lord's feet are the front feet. He steps ahead of us in a sure place, and if we set our feet down where the Lord would have us set them, we will always be safe. That is the only safe spot. Our problem is going to be to keep placing our feet there. Lord, You hold me in that line. Keep me stepping where You would have me step. Then You and I will walk on high places during terrible and dangerous times. The Lord God is my strength, praise His name."

It was late when Dave and Melva slipped under their blankets. "Brrr! I'm cold," Melva whispered.

"Yeah, sure is cold out there," Dave replied, "but that sermon! Amazing. I'm so encouraged that Dr. Morsey has such wisdom for our times."

November 9, 1940

At ten o'clock the next morning, Melva and Dave returned to find the spacious auditorium filling to capacity. A slender man in his forties approached the pulpit, opened his Bible, and read. "Agree with your adversary quickly, while thou art in the way with him."

"That's Mr. Maxwell," Dave whispered. Melva nodded. It felt like only minutes had passed when suddenly, he shut his Bible and went back to his chair behind the podium. Melva glanced at Dave. He sighed a heavy sigh and looked down.

"Are you alright?" she asked. He squeezed Melva's hand.

November 10, 1940

"My sermon today is called, 'The Cross and the Crown.' Dearly beloved," Mr. Maxwell began, "the worst that befalls us often proves to be the best. Crowns are for those who have borne their cross. This law is so inflexible that the call to the cross is truly a call to the crown. The Savior promised, 'To him who overcometh will I grant to sit with me on my throne, even as I also overcame, and am set down with my father on his throne.'

"Joseph was such an overcomer. God's way up for Joseph was down, as it must be for every disciple. His descent climaxed with false accusation and imprisonment. At every point he suffered for no fault of his own, but solely, for righteousness' sake. He had thirteen long years of insult and injury, suspicion and slander, testing and trial and treachery, but all these actually created the king."

Dave whispered, "Melva. I've been looking at my circumstances all wrong." She rested her hand on his as Mr. Maxwell continued.

"So it is with the saints who have humbled themselves under the mighty hand of God. The promise is that He will exalt you in due time. Every downward step, every dying to self, every embracing the cross—whether in the form of denial or degradation, of suffering or separation, of sorrow or vexation, of false accusation or humiliation—all these and a hundred other things we might mention are not a descent but an ascent to the throne. Our call to embrace the cross is a call to reign with Christ!"

Melva leaned toward Dave. "So have I." She wiped away a tear and Dave squeezed her hand.

Mr. Maxwell thumped the pulpit with his fist, and Melva jumped.

"We are commanded, 'Let this mind be in you, which was also in Christ Jesus . . . He humbled himself.' Philippians two, verses five and eight. Thus, Christ embodied all He taught. He summarized the principles of all recompense when He said, 'whosoever shall exalt himself shall be abased; and he that shall humble himself shall be exalted.' Matthew twenty-three, verse twelve. This principle Christ exemplified. From the heights of glory He descended, from the Godhead to manhood. As a man He descended to a servant.

"I'm just a servant and Dave is a slave." Melva bit her lip, deep in thought.

"From life, He descended to death. From a common death, He descended to that of a criminal. And having plumbed the depths, He is highly exalted. His exaltation is measured by His humiliation. His ascent is but His descent reversed, and ours will be the same. These fearful facts must so seize upon us that we begin here and now to shape our lives by this unbreakable law of recompense. Shall we reap what we have never sown? Do we prize seats on the right hand and on the left in His kingdom? The Savior rebuked no one for aspiring to the highest. Someone said, 'God has His best things for the few, who dare to stand the test. His second choice He has for those, who will not have His best.' As we face the cross, we have no option, no alternative. We must descend to the dust in utmost humiliation. But that *must* is never by coercion. We must choose the highest. We have been destined for a crown only if we choose the cross. Amy Carmicheal said, 'If I covet any place on earth but the dust at the foot of the cross, then I know nothing of Calvary love.'"

As Mr. Maxwell continued, his voice rang through the building, piercing hearts, like skillfully launched arrows.

"Come, come to the cross, all those seeking forgiveness and help." A man from the back came forward and knelt at the altar. Many followed. Melva counted.

"Dave! There's more than a hundred up there!" she whispered. "Praise the Lord!"

The meeting ended at noon, followed by lunch and an afternoon meeting that lasted four hours, with many more coming forward. By the time they had finished their evening meal, it was late when they got back to their room. Dave set his Bible and some paper on the night table and immediately began to write.

"What are you doing, dear?"

"Preparing my next sermon for the Baptist Church. And you know what?"

"What?"

"What I got from Mr. Maxwell's sermon is that our pain becomes our podium. No pain, no podium."

Melva ran her hand over the cold iron footboard. "That's a message that desperately needs to be heard today," she said.

November 11, 1940

"Dave, I hate to leave the conference early," Melva said as Dave held the car door open for her.

"Me, too, but we promised your folks we'd be there tonight." He shut her door and she glanced at her watch.

After stopping at Aunt Ada's near Acme for lunch, Dave and Melva headed to Calgary, as they decided to hear Chief White Feather preach at Alahazar Temple. They ate supper at the White Lunch restaurant. It was ten-thirty when they pulled into the farmyard south of Langdon. Dave and Melva entered the house. Everything was quiet.

"Must all be in bed," she whispered to Dave.

"Melva? Dave?" Vera shouted from the top of the stairs. She ran down the stairs, her nightie billowing behind her, followed by Doris, Clara, and Alice. Dave and Melva were smothered with hugs.

"Melva! Dave! You two got married and I knew nothing about it! But at least I saw you both the day before your wedding!" Alice said as she gave them each a hug.

"Alice, thank you for understanding," Melva replied.

"Oh, it's so good to see you both again!" Clara said as she embraced her sister. Just then Donald appeared around the corner from the kitchen.

"Dave, Melva." He hugged them. "Your mother went to bed early. Her hip has been bothering her more with the weather turning cold. Grandma went to Bittles for the week, so you can stay in her room."

"Yes, Melva and Dave," Vera exclaimed. "You get to stay in Grandma's room! She made it all nice for you both! Come, I'll show you!" Vera ran up the stairs with Dave and Melva following her into Grandma's room. It was as beautiful as ever, the soft down pillows and blankets with large roses printed on the cases, and the chenille bedspread was just as white as ever. Melva lifted the afghan on the rocking chair and smelled it. *"Mmm, Grandma's soap."*

Vera interrupted her thoughts. "Come Melva, let's make popcorn and hot chocolate! We all want to hear everything about your new home, your jobs, and your life in general." Melva laughed at her sister's exuberance. Vera took Melva by the elbow and they went downstairs. An hour and a half later, after a good long visit, Dave and Melva headed to bed.

Dave sighed a deep, contented sigh as he climbed into bed. Melva, eyes closed and relaxed, rocked gently in Grandma's chair, hugging the afghan. How good it felt to be home again, with those who loved them. A pang shot through her heart as her mind wandered to Grandpa. *"Grandpa's missing. The last time I was in this room Grandpa was lying in this bed. It feels like he still belongs here. This was his domain. He was the respected patriarch of the family. It feels like there is a gap now."* She sighed. *"Grandpa, how I miss you. Why did you have to leave us? I wish I could tell you about all the farming Dave has done at Innisfail. I know you'd be so interested. You loved to talk about farming at the coffee shop."*

"You coming to bed?" Dave asked as he rolled over.

Melva climbed into bed. "I always wondered what it felt like."

"What what felt like?"

"To sleep in Grandpa and Grandma's bed. All my growing up we weren't allowed in this room without permission. And only special guests got to sleep in this room."

"I guess we're the special guests now."

Melva stared up at the ceiling. "Yes, it's like we've graduated."

Dave sat up. "Hmm. Graduated. That reminds me. I've been thinking about Mr. Maxwell's sermon. He said that Christ's exaltation was measured by His humiliation. It's like we graduate after we pass the test of humiliation. Mr. Maxwell also said Jesus' ascent is but His descent reversed, and ours will be the same. Perhaps it is an unwritten law that before honor is humility, and that is why we have been so humbled, both of us working like slaves. It's training ground for the next season of our life, Melva. Let's take our suffering with joy." He reached over the blankets and squeezed her hand, brought it to his face and kissed it. "In fact, your father has me slated to share at prayer meeting on Wednesday and that is what I'm going to talk about. 'The seed . . . or self . . . must die first before there's a great harvest.'"

Melva smiled. "I think you are right. Even if the exaltation comes much later, I think you are right."

November 14, 1940

The family sat around the breakfast table. Donald passed the hash browns and eggs to Dave.

"Well, Mr. Dye," Dave began as he spooned some hash browns on his plate, "what are your plans for today? Now that I am in the full swing of being a farmer, I'm ready to dig in and help you while we're here."

Donald put down his coffee. "Today, you get the day off to work on sermons," he said with a grin.

"What?" Dave raised an eyebrow. Donald glanced around the table.

"Today, we have a special surprise for Melva. The girls have all taken off work so I can take my five daughters shopping in Calgary."

"Oh Daddy!" Melva clapped her hands. Giggles and laughing erupted.

"It's not too often my girls are all together. The shopping trip is on me, and I'll take you all out for lunch as well. Hazel has offered to stay at home and keep the fires burning." The girls jumped up and one by one, gave their father a hug.

It was evening. Melva and her sisters burst into the house. Melva carried several parcels.

"Look Dave!" she exclaimed. Dave sat at the kitchen table with his Bible open, surrounded by theology books. She opened the boxes. They contained two silk dresses, a slip, purse, gloves, and other matching adornments.

"You will look absolutely stunning in these outfits. In fact, much too good for the wife of a back country preacher!" Dave said. She laughed and kissed him.

The next nine days were spent with Dave helping Vern haul 320 bushels of wheat, visiting friends and neighbors, making ice cream, enjoying popcorn with the Bittles, playing games, singing around the piano, washing clothes, and making meals with Mother.

CHAPTER EIGHTEEN

MEETING THE IN LAWS

November 20, 1940

Dave hit the alarm. "Time to get up!" Melva groaned and rubbed her eyes.

"Three in the morning! I don't think I've ever gotten up this early before," she said. A clatter of dishes sounded from downstairs.

"Your parents must be up," Dave stated as he dressed.

"Today, we leave for Moose Jaw, and I meet Dave's parents," thought Melva as a tingle of nervous excitement pulsed through her. She had seen them once before when they had come to hear Dave speak at the Prophetic Bible Institute, but at the time, Dave and she weren't together. *"I will wear the new silk dress Daddy bought me!"*

Donald, Hazel, and Melva's siblings sat around the breakfast table laughing and talking. Dave enjoyed a lively discussion with Donald and Vern. After breakfast, Doris and Alice made lunches for the travelers and helped pack their suitcases into Dave and Melva's car.

"Goodbye Daddy, and thank you so much for everything," Melva said as she stood on the tip of her toes and kissed him on the cheek. He held her warmly, his unshaven face rough on her forehead.

"Goodbye," he said.

Although Donald was not known to show a lot of affection, Melva could sense the love in his eyes.

After hugging her mother and sisters, Dave and Melva got into the car and waved goodbye. Melva glanced at her watch. Just after four. Still dark. She scraped her window and even though she couldn't see it, she had the driveway memorized—her favorite climbing tree, Vern's favorite tree, the hedge her sisters liked to hide in when they were little.

"Why must things change?" she asked, peering through her tiny space in the frosty window. Dave glanced at her as the headlights picked up the range road.

"So we rely more and more heavily on God. *He* never changes. That's why."

"Just a few more minutes," exclaimed Dave as they entered Moose Jaw. "Won't be long!"

"What a wonderful drive," thought Melva. "I got to see all kinds of new places, especially Medicine hat, Maple Creek, and Swift Current."

They pulled into Dave's parents' driveway. "Finally here. We can thank the Lord for keeping us safe on the roads," Dave said, opening her door. Melva stepped out and stretched. A minute later, Mrs. Stewart approached, with three girls behind her. "Dave! Melva!" she cried as she gave Melva a big hug. "So nice to meet you!"

"And you, Mrs. Stewart!" Melva said.

The three girls stood shyly at their mother's side.

"Melva, this is Jewel, Pauline, and Peggy." Jewel and Pauline smiled, but Peggy, who looked to be about nineteen, did not. She crossed her arms.

"Nice to meet you," Melva said. Jewel and Pauline hugged her and Dave. Peggy stood to the side with a frown.

"Well," Mrs. Stewart said as she cleared her throat, "you've met Dave's family now, all except Kay and Melvin. Kay is working and Melvin's in the war. Well, come on in. You both must be so hungry and tired. Father's still at work. His shift ends at ten," Mrs. Stewart said over her shoulder as they followed her in.

"How's Melvin doing? Heard much?" Dave asked.

"Some. And so far, he's alright. I almost hate opening his letters for fear of bad news from the battlefront."

November 21, 1940

"It's Daddy's birthday today, Dave. I have a card and wondered if you could sign it. Perhaps we could mail it when we go downtown today?" Melva asked the next morning after breakfast. The family sat around the table visiting.

"Sure. I'm going to Eaton's, so we can mail it there." Dave took another sip of coffee.

"Well Dave," his father broke in, "I've booked you to speak in a lot of different places while you're here, as we discussed in our letters."

"Yes Father, I'm glad you did," Dave replied.

"I figure that way family and friends from Moose Jaw don't have to travel all the way to Alberta to hear you, son." He winked. "And … there is a meeting tonight at the Christian Missionary Alliance. Mr. Newman is speaking. Mother and I were so excited about you meeting him that we invited him for supper tonight!"

Hours later, after a lively supper with the evangelist, and attending the meeting, the family returned from church. They had all attended the service, except for Peggy.

Mr. Stewart walked to the fireplace with his coat on and put in a few more logs. Mrs. Stewart glanced around the room. She wrung her hands.

"Where could Peggy be?" she asked her husband. Mr. Stewart blew on the smoldering embers.

"Now dear, I don't think you have anything to worry about. She's been out later than this before," Gordon said.

"Is it because of me?" Melva asked, as she approached. "She doesn't know me. I'm new and I've taken her brother—"

"I don't think it's anything like that," Mr. Stewart replied. "We've been having a bit of trouble with her."

November 22, 1940

"Mr. Newman is giving his testimony at the Alliance Church tonight," Mr. Stewart said next morning after breakfast.

"We'll be sure to attend," Dave said. "I really enjoyed our visit with him last night. Well, I need to go prepare some messages. Thank you for the delicious breakfast." Dave took his plate and left the room. Melva filled the sink and started washing dishes. The girls had already left for their work.

"Honey, I don't think Peggy came home all night, leastwise not that I could tell," Mrs. Stewart said.

"I don't know what to do," her husband replied.

"I never wanted to go through the pain of a wayward child! But here I am … again, suffering away. It was awful when Dave rebelled, but Peggy is worse! It feels like I've just wasted years of my life! I bore these children, nursed them, cared for them, just to have them grow up and stab me in the back! How many times can a mother's heart be broken?"

"Margaret, Margaret, look at Dave now. He's a preacher. Many have been and are being saved by his testimony. Peggy will also turn around; I know she will. Besides, you said you saw her during the day."

"Only for a brief minute—she was in and out so fast. And I don't like the way she dresses and those ridiculous red high heels she wears."

Melva quickly thrust the porridge pot in the soapy water and scrubbed vigorously.

November 23, 1940

The family sat quietly at breakfast. "Pass the milk to Melva, would you, Pauline?" Mrs. Stewart said.

"Yes Mother."

Mr. Stewart cleared his throat. "I heard on the radio there's a funeral today for the two pilots who were killed in a crash. Members of the Royal Air Force are attending."

"Really? I would like to attend," Dave said.

Mrs. Stewart put her hand on her mouth and yawned. "Don't think I'll go."

Mr. Stewart looked across the table at her with concern. "Be sure to get a nap today, dear."

She got up to leave the table.

"Mother, is it Peggy?" Dave asked.

"Oh Dave. She never came home all night again." Mrs. Stewart burst into tears.

"And," Mr. Stewart cut in, "your mother never slept a wink."

"Neither did Melva and I, Father," Dave said. "Maybe we should phone the police."

"Your father did last night, and they've been looking. Oh Dave! Why must I go through this pain all over again? Is God punishing me? I must be such a terrible mother! What did I do wrong? Oh, what did I do wrong?" She buried her face in her apron.

"Mother, Mother," Dave said softly. "I must ask you again to forgive me for my foolishness and how much I hurt you when I was in my teens. I know the pain of a wayward child is one of the most painful and I caused you that torment." His eyes misted. He hung his head. "I heard a message recently, and the preacher said, 'If there is no greater joy than our children walking in the truth, then there is no deeper pain than when they do not.'"

"Now, now," his father cut in. "You've already apologized, Dave. We're all sinners. We all have caused Jesus the most pain, each of us. There is none righteous, no, not one of us."

Mrs. Stewart wiped her eyes with the corner of her apron. "Oh Dave, you know I forgave you a long time ago."

November 24, 1940

It was early evening and a sullen family sat around the supper table. Mrs. Stewart had cried most of the day and had stayed in her room.

"What are you going to speak on at church tonight, Dave?" his father asked.

"Laodicea," he said. The room quieted except for the click of forks on plates. A sharp knock sounded, and Mr. Stewart went to answer it.

"I believe we found your daughter," a police officer said.

Peggy stood behind the officer, head down.

"Thank you, thank you," Mr. Stewart said as he took Peggy by the arm and brought her into the house.

He shut the door. "Jewel! Go tell Mother."

"Yes sir!" Jewel said as she ran out of the room.

Mr. Stewart turned to Peggy. "I'm not even going to ask where you've been. But you've caused your mother an immense amount of grief. I want you to come to church with us tonight. Dave's speaking."

Peggy stared at Dave. "No! I don't want to!" She ran upstairs and slammed her door.

November 25, 1940

Melva slipped on her coat and scarf and tapped on Peggy's bedroom door.

"Come in," Peggy mumbled. Melva pushed open the door. Peggy lay stretched across the bed, staring at the ceiling.

"Hi, Peggy. Dave and I want to take you shopping. Do you want to come?" she asked softly. "It would be nice to get to know you."

"Why? So you can preach at me?"

"No, no, no. Dave thought it would be nice to spend some time with his sister, is all."

Peggy turned. "Well alright. Better than lying around here."

That night as Melva headed to their bedroom, Peggy stopped her. "Thank you for taking me."

"You're welcome," Melva said. "Say, you know those two dresses Dave bought you?

"Yes."

"Well, I heard you tell Dave they were too long on you. I can shorten them." Peggy nodded with a faint smile.

The next few days were filled with Dave's speaking engagements, including a visit to Briercrest Bible Institute, and preaching in front of 106 students. He and Melva also spent time with his Uncle Arch, who lived in Moose Jaw, and who Dave considered one of his spiritual mentors. He loved to glean all the wisdom he could from the older man's knowledge of the Bible.

December 6, 1940

Melva sat at the table and poured more tea. Dave had gone to the Moose Jaw library to study, and she and Jewel were enjoying tea together. Footsteps sounded and both women turned to see Peggy in the door.

"C'mon, join us," Jewel said. Peggy smiled and slid onto a chair while Melva reached for the tea pot.

"How are you doing?" asked Melva.

"Good. Thanks for hemming my dresses."

"You're welcome."

"Didn't the pink one look pretty on her last night at the meeting Dave preached at, Melva?" Jewel asked. Peggy smiled shyly at Melva.

"Yes, it looked beautiful," Melva said.

Later that night Dave and Melva sat on their bed and quietly visited. A soft tap sounded on the bedroom door.

"Who is it?" Dave asked.

"It's me. Peggy." Dave got out of bed and wrapped his bronze-colored housecoat around him. He opened the door. Peggy slipped in and tied her housecoat tighter.

"Have a seat," Melva said as she patted the edge of the bed.

Peggy sat and fidgeted with her ties.

"I . . . I need to tell you something," she said.

Dave sat opposite her on a chair. "Sure. What is it? Go ahead."

"I'm . . . I'm married."

Dave's jaw dropped. "W-what? You're m-married!"

"When I was seventeen. Never told anyone."

"Oh Peggy! You've been married for *two years*?" Dave squeezed her hand. "To carry that secret must be so heavy for you."

Tears coursed down her cheeks. Melva put her arm around her.

"Please, don't tell Mother and Father."

Dave straightened. "Alright. But *you* must tell Mother and Father.

Marriage is not a bad thing, Peggy, but in your case, perhaps the way you did it—"

"I know! I know! Don't you think I know? Half the time I love it and half the time the guilt strangles me!"

"Who is he?" Dave asked.

"He's a nice man, Dave. You'd like him."

Dave sighed. "You might be right. Well, in any case, we will be praying for you."

December 10, 1940

While Dave and Melva said goodbye to the family four days later, Peggy approached.

"Goodbye, and thanks for the everything," she said, giving Melva and Dave warm hugs.

"Goodbye," Melva said, returning her embrace. "We'll miss you."

It was ten-thirty when they left for Alberta. Melva heaved a deep sigh and threw herself back in her seat. "I can tell you, Dave, I didn't know which way it was going to go with your sister, but she's sure softened toward you."

Dave nodded. "I can't judge her, Melva. I know the battle. But let's just pray she tells Father and Mother."

CHAPTER NINETEEN

A NEW IDEA

January 1941

Dave and Melva enjoyed another week at Langdon, then headed back to the Johnsons. That night, Dave sat in the corner chair of their bedroom, reading. He put down his Bible and began to pace.

"You know Melva, I've been thinking a lot about our lives here. We've saved some money and I really want to own something." Melva glanced up from her crocheting.

"Really? Like what?"

"That's what I'm unclear about. At first, I thought of buying a bit of land so I could build a home, but I think, as a circuit preacher, it would be more in keeping with my mission to buy a church. After that, we could put up a small house beside it. That way, ministering to others would be our focus. My only thought against it is the fact that I preach at Innisfail Baptist, but I volunteer there, as well as others, and others could take over that position."

Melva put down her crochet needle. "Buy a church?! I must admit that is a different idea, Dave, but I understand where you're coming from. It is difficult to live with our employers, when our lives and schedules are completely at their beck and call."

Dave stopped pacing to rest his hand on her shoulder. "I'm sorry for putting you through this."

Melva smiled. "Nothing to be sorry about. It's been hard, but we are both paid well, and like you said, we now have some money to venture out on our own." Dave leaned over to give her a warm embrace.

"You know how I have five or six churches and schoolhouses I preach at in the district?"

"Yes."

"Maybe I could buy one of them; it could be ours. Just imagine ministering to the needs of these people full time! Imagine putting up a small manse beside it."

"Oh Dave, that is a noble dream, and I love it, b–but where?"

March 1941

"Well, it's becoming a reality." Dave announced to the Johnsons as they sat around the supper table. All eyes turned to him. Mrs. Johnson scooped mashed potatoes onto her plate.

"What's becoming a reality, Dave?" Mr. Johnson said as he peered over the rim of his glasses.

"I've contacted the head of the Union of Northwest Churches and put money down for their building."

Mrs. Johnson's eyes enlarged. "What building?"

"The one on the corner of Cutline Junction, the one called Faith Mission."

"You *bought* the Faith Mission Church? Land sakes, Dave. *What* are you going to do with a church?" Mrs. Johnson said as she choked.

With a twinkle in his eye, Dave said, "You know how I preach a circuit. Faith Mission doesn't have much, they're a struggling congregation, and they need help. They have never had a full-time pastor. Pastoring a church that I own has been a dream of mine!"

Melva cleared her throat, "The people there really respect Dave. They've been so grateful for a preacher who comes every week. They can't pay anything, but we love ministering to them."

Dave added, "So since I am buying the church, I feel I can take it over full time, whether I get paid to preach or not. Melva and I talked about it. I plan to build a small home beside it, and spend my life there, if God wills. During the week, I could work part time for farmers in the area and take a couple days off to study and write sermons."

Mrs. Johnson cleared her throat. "Well, this is a new thought. Several of my aunts and uncles attend that church, not to mention many friends of mine. Do the members and adherents know you are buying their church?"

"Yes, and so does the church board, and so far, there have been no objections. It will be discussed in more detail in the next board meeting. I've only paid for half and need to keep working until I can pay for the other half."

"Fine, son, that's fine. You may stay and work for me until you can pay the rest," Mr. Johnson said.

Dave looked at Mrs. Johnson. "The Union owns the church, and they are selling it to me."

Later that night, Dave and Melva walked hand in hand down the road. "Oh Melva, I've never been so excited! Except for when I accepted the Lord, and married you, of course!" He laughed as he bent to kiss her.

She squeezed his hand. "I am so happy for you, Dave. This must be the Lord's way of moving us from the Johnsons, so we have more time to minister! I really like the people in that area, don't you?"

"Yes, yes, I do! I've had some of my deepest discussions with the men while fishing with them on the Raven River." Dave grabbed Melva and twirled her around.

"Dave!" she squealed.

April 1941

The creak of the wood stove iron door sounded as an elder from Faith Mission slid another log on the fire. Eight men sat on the first couple of benches. Mr. Thomas, a middle-aged farmer, stood.

"We have really appreciated you preaching here on your circuit, Dave, but some of us didn't want to sell our building. We were too shy to bring this up at first. But the fact is, we've met as a congregation here for eleven years. We built this church, but only signed it over to the Union so they'd supply us with pastors. Didn't think for a minute someone would *buy* it from them."

"But we signed it over to the Northwest Union, so they own it, not us! Dave has every right to buy it," said another.

Mr. Thomas continued, "But we have a say, don't we? We built this building, and we've been meeting here all these years!"

"Not no more we don't," another farmer stated. "Dave here has already paid for half. What's wrong with him buying it anyway? Our church is so far out, no one wants to preach here. Dave's spent his own time and money to conduct our weddings and funerals, not to mention Bible studies and Sunday afternoon services for the last year. Who's more faithful than him? And he hasn't charged us a thing for his services or fuel."

"I just don't want a foreigner owning this property, that's all," Mr. Thomas said as he sat.

Dave stood. "I'm not a foreigner. I want to live here and continue to work among you. I want a more permanent home. Melva and I are grateful for our jobs with the Johnsons, but most of our time goes to serving them, no one else. I'd be a more competent pastor if I lived here, among you, helping you, but I can't do so effectively without living here."

May 1941

Dave came in from seeding and threw his work gloves on the shelf by the door. Birds sang in the tree behind him. Melva sat at the kitchen table cutting seed potatoes.

"Melva, I don't know what to do." She looked at him and raised her brow.

"I've been thinking about it. The church members are still split. Some are glad I'm buying the church, and others are strongly opposed." He tipped back his hat and rubbed his forehead.

Melva sighed. "I didn't think *that* many were opposed." Just then, Mrs. Johnson entered the kitchen and glanced at Melva, then Dave. As she walked away, a cold feeling washed over Melva.

Later that day, Melva responded to a knock at the front door.

"Why, Mrs. Miller. Please come in." Mrs. Miller lifted the netting that came down in front of her stylish hat. She cocked her head to the side.

"Mrs. Stewart." She gave Melva the briefest of polite nods. Mrs. Johnson approached.

"Welcome, Sadie," she said.

"Good day, Nellie."

"Care for some tea?"

Mrs. Miller nodded as she dropped her gloves into her oversized purse.

"Melva, please boil some water and set out the tea service," Mrs. Johnson said crisply.

"Yes, ma'am."

The two women went into the parlor and Melva quickly collected the items.

As she set cookies on a tray, the women talked in low tones. Melva strained to listen, and could just make out their conversation.

"What do you think of Dave buying the church?" Sadie asked, leaning closer to Mrs. Johnson.

Mrs. Johnson cleared her throat. "I-I really don't know what to think."

"As you know, Nellie, Bertha attends there, not to mention Harmon and Nola. They say it's robbery. They've attended for *eleven* years. Their parents built it. Nola said the other day, 'Who does he think he is, just waltzing right in and stealing our church!'"

Sadie peered toward the kitchen as Melva entered the room with the tea tray. She set the teacups in front of the ladies, poured the tea, and returned to the kitchen with the tray.

"And," Sadie continued, "it's causing great division in our church." She sipped her tea. "Lovely tea, Nellie."

"Yes, well, Melva makes the best tea," Mrs. Johnson said.

"Now, where was I?" Sadie whispered. "Oh yes, division in the church. Some, I hear, like Elder Mr. Jacobs, swear by Dave. Says he's a promising young man and of the highest integrity. Thinks Dave buying the church is a grand idea. Do tell me your thoughts, Nellie."

"Well, I'm . . . rather indecisive at this point, Sadie. Harry senior loves him and thinks it's great that Dave is buying the church, but my brother Len does not, and neither does Renny. He works with him some."

"Have a good day today, dear?" Melva said to Dave that night as they slipped into bed.

"Workwise it was fine. I enjoy farming, but I'm getting unsettled about owning the church. It's most disturbing the church is not unified. I talked to the main members before I put down our $250, but it seems some are changing their minds over the whole thing." Dave tucked his hands behind his head and stared at the ceiling. "I feel like I'm in the center of a violent windstorm, with half the wind swirling one way, and the other half swirling the other way. I am in the middle, perplexed."

"Oh Dave." Melva kissed him. "On a lighter note, back home, Vince got engaged! To Blanche. Remember her? Grandma said Dr. Salmon delivered Vince, and four years later, he delivered Blanche!" The two never knew that one day they would marry!"

Dave rubbed his chin. "Yes, you introduced me to Blanche. I remember. A lovely lady and perfect for Vince."

CHAPTER TWENTY

GOODBYE

Fall 1941

Melva turned over in bed when she heard footsteps.

"Dave? What time is it?"

Dave sat on the edge of the bed, taking off his socks.

"It's one o'clock."

"How was the meeting?"

"Terrible." He threw himself back on the bed. Melva sat up.

"Dave! What happened?"

"Oh Melva." He groaned and ran his fingers through his hair. "I resigned."

"You did *what?*" Melva's heart flipped. Dave groaned again and cleared his throat several times before getting up to pace their small room.

"Resigned?" Melva exclaimed. "What *are* you talking about?"

He rubbed the back of his neck. "I can't preach around here anymore, Melva. Too much contention in the Faith Mission Church. Some are for me and some against. The news has spread all over my circuit, with people on both sides. I'm going to have to get my money back and let someone else take over."

"But, but *who?* Dave! Who is there? Mr. Thomas admitted that if you left, they could be without a pastor for months! And what are we supposed to do? Where are we supposed to go?"

"Melva, I'm so sorry to put you through this." He went to the window and pulled back the curtain. He turned to her. "I have no idea what we will do or where we will go, but you know as well as I that we can't stay here. The Johnsons have family and friends in that church, and even *they* don't agree amongst themselves. Sunday's my last sermon."

It was midnight. Tomorrow was Dave's last Sunday. He slept peacefully beside Melva. Melva quietly got up and went to Dave's desk. She lit the lantern and turned down the wick. To one side lay Dave's notes from Bible school and a stack of books. His Bible lay open. Melva picked up a black scribbler of notes and flipped through it. It represented hours of study and note taking. A tear slipped down her cheek. *"To resign would have been the last thing he would have wanted. Dear God, why have You taken his dream away from him? He has only ever had one goal—to glorify You—and You're breaking him. Father, he's broken! I know he has tried to hide it, but I sense it. Everything he was so excited about has been taken away. Why?"*

Melva glanced at Dave. He stirred in his sleep. She peered out the window. Frozen. The whole world was frozen. *"Oh God, please don't let it affect our hearts. Keep them soft. Especially today."* She wiped a tear and looked at Dave again. He lay still, a powerful arm above the quilt. *"How can he look so peaceful when today is his last day?"*

When they arrived at the church, cars and trucks lined the yard under the tall trees. Dave took Melva's hand. "Let's pray, shall we? Dear Lord, give me strength. Help me respond with wisdom and love today, despite everything. Amen." Melva leaned over and kissed him, and a warm smile spread across his face.

"Thank you," he whispered. His eyes misted but he quickly wiped them and took her hand.

As they entered the building, every eye turned on them. Some smiled, others sat stoically. After Mr. Thomas conducted the song service and prayer time, he called Dave to the pulpit.

"Good morning, ladies and gentlemen," Dave said. "My text for today is Acts twenty-eight, verse fifteen. 'And from thence, when the brethren heard of us, they came to meet us as far as Appii forum, and the three taverns; whom when Paul saw, he thanked God, and took courage.'"

Dave looked up. "Paul had just stepped ashore. Behind were many trials. Ahead, the same. Christians from Rome met him. He thanks God and takes courage. This is descriptive of my feelings this morning. I've been with you all these months. I can look into your faces and thank God for each of you. Still a question arises—has my ministry been a success or a failure? To fail is not always dishonorable. As a recent example, look at Sir Neville Henderson. Failure of a mission. He did all possible up to the invasion of Poland. His noble mission hopelessly failed.

"So, this morning—you may be the jury and God the final judge. Have I failed?

"Let me explain what I have tried to do. I came here not to save souls—I came to preach a Christ who could save. I have tried to show that a new birth is necessary to get to heaven. If I have failed to preach any truth about God, heaven, or hell, let me know that I may declare it.

"I've tried to win your confidence and love. Not by consultation of your prejudices—not by taking sides—not by being your yes man, but by preaching a straightforward gospel regardless of where it hit. A minister must have people believing in him, a call to come, a call to go. This flock is small—in the Lord I love each of you. I have always said when, as a shepherd, I lose your confidence, I shall go.

"I have tried to cultivate Christian sociality. There is nothing I like better in a meeting than friendliness. Icebergs are dangerous on the sea. Cold heartedness, jealousies, bitterness, are dangerous on the sea of grace.

"I've tried to preach an everyday religion. Most of you have trials. I have emphasized that Christ is your present help, that He is the Christ of every road, the Christ of every day. Few take this comforting position. They profess to believe it, but in actions they deny it. Sickness comes, and they forget to call on Him. Danger comes, and poverty, and we seek to borrow. We need to get down on our knees and tell Him first. He knows and cares. Remember, when the bottom of your earthly treasure is knocked out, look up, you will find the top of the jewel chest of heaven.

"I have tried to dispel any conventionalities.

"Be it success or failure (you decide) the months have gone, and all chance of recovery with it. What I have not done, will remain undone forever. Let us arise from our knees daily, determined to do better than our best. God Himself—and angels—will defend us. God's people, in God's place, doing God's will, in God's way, to the best of their ability, will have God's blessing."

Every eye followed Dave as took his Bible and sat beside Melva. A deep silence filled the small room until Mr. Johnson made his way to the podium. "Well folks, that was Dave's last message. Let us remember him and his good wife as they venture to new opportunities that the Lord grants them."

Melva turned over in bed and felt beside her. The blankets were flat. "Dave?" she whispered.

"I'm here." He was staring out the window into the depths of a moonless night. The tall spruce tree branches swayed in the wind and scratched on the window.

"I loved this place," he said. "The woods, the churches, fishing with the guys, performing weddings and funerals—" His shoulders shook. Melva approached and put her hand on his shoulder.

"Dave?"

He turned to face her. His eyes were red.

"Oh Dave!" Melva embraced him. He clung to her.

Spring 1942

Harry Johnson Sr. asked Dave and Melva to stay with them until after seeding. Dave and Melva knew they had to move, and so they found an older rental farmhouse near Langdon. Melva went ahead to try to fix it up and plant a garden, while Dave stayed to help the Johnsons with seeding.

Melva entered the post office in Langdon and took her mail. A letter from Dave. It was strange to be home in Langdon without Dave. But she was glad she had some time to think and be away from the constant pressure she felt as a housekeeper. Now, she and Dave would have a place to themselves. The farmhouse wasn't much, but she was relieved it was private and so close to her family. She opened the letter.

"Dear Sweetie. Half past eight and I'm up in our room, not bad, huh? Haven't bathed yet, going to bed as soon as I do.

"Had the tractor going in the field at twenty to nine this morning. Had no trouble driving it on the road except I ran out of gas two miles from Olds. I was very fortunate, got a ride in a truck into town, and then got a ride in a car right back again, lost about twenty minutes. I got the radio going good and loud, but honey-pie, I'm sure lonesome. About tomorrow it will be really terrible. Everything is kind of empty and flat. I hope you get that garden in fast.

"Mother sent me three nice pairs of knitted socks and a couple of hankies. Mother is improving with her needles. Sweetie, I wouldn't work too hard at the house if I were you. Let it go till after spring work then we'll fix it up together. I suppose I'll have to come down to fix papers for fire insurance, etc. I'll be glad when it's all over and we are settled down.

"Hope you're not too all alone down there. Have a good time—if you want me to come and get you in the car, just say so, whenever you are ready. If you come on the train or bus, I will meet it—be sure and let me know in time.

"Well, goodbye my love. Love you more and more, honey. Take good care of yourself. Something's the matter with my eyes, I can't see these keys. God has been very good to me, Melva, in giving me you. I've never been able to tell you all that you mean to me, and I don't suppose I'll ever be able to. Anyway, I love you and will have to say goodnight. Your husband, Dave."

A short while later, Melva finished planting the garden and rejoined Dave at the Johnson's.

It was moving day. They had just finished packing the last of their things in the car. Melva stood by the car door.

"Well, looks like that's it," Dave said, approaching the Johnsons.

"I'm so sorry it had to end this way," Mr. Johnson said, shaking Dave's hand. "Thank you for all your help. Couldn't have done it without you."

Dave nodded.

"And here's your last pay cheque."

"Thank you, Mr. Johnson," Dave said.

Mr. Johnson cleared his throat. "I want you to know I don't agree with the church and Union fighting and not giving back your money. I know they used some of it for legal ramifications but ..."

Dave nodded and put his arm around Melva. "Let's go, dear."

Mrs. Johnson hugged Melva. "Thank you, Melva. Here is your pay."

"Thank you," Melva said. As they drove down the driveway, Melva felt a lump in her throat.

"The Union won't give back our money, Dave. All those hours we worked. For nothing!"

Dave pulled onto the main road. "Knowing God, Melva, He has a plan. Remember Mr. Maxwell's sermon on the crown and the cross? I am interested to find out how our pain will become our podium."

Melva stared blankly ahead. *"Father, I trusted You to heal me from the pain of Earle. And You did. And even though I would not want to go through it again, I feel stronger for it, and able to comfort others. Now Lord, we are walking through intense pain. You helped me last time, You will help us this time. Be our sword and shield, our defense."*

Hours later, they pulled up to the old rental farmhouse just outside of Langdon and stepped out of the car. "I know it's not much, but it's near your family," Dave said as they entered. "Melva, it looks great! You really cleaned things up in here." He took her hands in his. "We'll only live here until we figure out what God wants us to do, and where He wants us to go. In the meantime, your father and other farmers have plenty of work for me, and I can continue to fill in preach."

"Oh Dave," Melva fell into his arms. "I'm so glad to be near my family." She glanced around the kitchen. It was clean, but the paint was mismatched, and the linoleum was faded with a few tears along the edges.

"At least it's private, and you won't have to work nearly so hard, as you won't be feeding four or five other adults," he said as he kissed her forehead.

"Yes. I'm glad that I will only be feeding the three of us."

Dave's mouth dropped, "B-baby? Melva are you—?"

Melva burst into laughter. "Yes. I saw Dr. Hughes last week, but we've been too busy moving to even have a private conversation!"

"Oh Melva!" Dave embraced her. A tear rolled down his cheek. "When?"

"November."

Spring and summer flew by as Dave and Melva fixed the rental and slowly acquired furniture. Melva's family came over often, and both Dave and Melva felt comforted by their love.

August 22, 1942

Dave shook as he held the letter. "What is it? Dave, what is it?" Melva asked as she touched his arm.

"From my sister. He handed her the letter. 'Dear Dave and Melva, Mother asked me to tell you she just received a telegram that Melvin was wounded in the Battle of Dieppe. Mother is all broken up about it, and of course, we all feel badly, and are hoping it's not serious.'" Dave paced. "My little brother. The one who looked up to me." He shook his head. "Oh Melva, I trust he believes. God knows what a poor example I was to him in my teens." Dave sighed and sat.

"But you changed so drastically when God came into your life."
She kissed him. "Don't fret about the past."

October 1942

Dave stood with a letter in his hand and walked to the kitchen window, watching the gold and red leaves flutter to the ground. "Remember Bob Thompson, Melva? He was one of our best encouragers when we lived near Bowden. He wrote me telling me he has been going through a hard time." Melva stopped sweeping and leaned on the broom. Dave continued, "I sure can relate to his pain. God tests us all to see if we will be faithful. I'll write him back."

"Yes," Melva said as she continued sweeping. Dave sat at his desk and after he finished, handed the letter to Melva. "What do you think, dear?"

"Dear Bob. Regarding the darksome road along which you are being lead, don't forget there are precious things brought forth by the light of the moon. It was in the heart of a midnight experience that Paul found some of his greatest spiritual trophies. Surely God delights to try us, to find if there be any wicked way in us. I know from my trials I could be farther along in the life of faith today if I hadn't so miserably failed while undergoing the strain. Now when they come, I simply throw it back on the Lord. He must strengthen me; it is not in me to stand. Not by might, or by power, but by His Spirit. When left to Him, His grace is unfailing, what a sense of relief. Dear brother, if God wants to let your darkness increase, remember this: behind the dim unknown He always stands, keeping silent watch over His own. It is these times of sifting that separates the chaff. We need them. Let us not shirk. God is leading to certain victory. Come what may—we will follow. The burning words in my soul are—blessed is the man who shall not be offended in Me. God forgive me for the many times I have been offended, or mad, at God. I've hurt inside and have been filled with self-pity because the Lord didn't do something just when and how I thought He should. My, what a doubter, what backslidings of heart—I am, day by day, learning that 'though He slay me yet will I trust Him.'

He is working this unflinching trust within me. I praise Him and confess my utter need. I am so glad God has arranged it thus—that everything pertaining to the life of faith must come from Him, so I have crossed myself out. Now, if He lets me sink, well, 'goodbye brother.' I am not going to lift a hand."

CHAPTER TWENTY-ONE

NEW OPPORTUNITY

October 1942

Dave and Melva sat at the kitchen table. "I'm so excited about the baby, Dave," Melva said as she watched her tummy move.

"Won't be long now," Dave said with a wink. The phone rang and he jumped to answer.

"Hello? Why yes, I know who you are. Yes, we listen to you a lot. Oh? What a generous offer. I'll talk to her. Thank you. Really? Okay. Yes! We'll get back to you."

Dave set the phone back on the wall. "That was Chase Sawtell, from CFCN. You know, the one who does the *Heaven and Home Hour*? They live in Calgary but are going on a road trip and they have invited both of us to stay at their home so we can be closer to the hospital when the baby arrives."

Melva's eyes enlarged. "Oh Dave, that would be wonderful! I've been so nervous, with the road's impassable half the time in winter. What a relief! What a generous offer!"

"I'll phone him right back!"

The next day, Dave helped Melva into the car and they headed to Calgary. Melva's feeling of relief increased with each passing mile, knowing she didn't need to worry about snowy, mucky roads while in labor. A while later, they pulled up to a modest home. Melva wiped her forehead. *"Thank You, Jesus, for providing this need from someone we don't really know."*

"By the way, how did Mr. Sawtell know us?" Melva asked as they approached the door.

Dave chuckled. "I guess from the Prophetic. Apparently, he heard me speak."

"Come in, come in!" Chase said, reaching for Melva's luggage. After they were settled in their room, they entered the dining room for supper. Marie Sawtell set a casserole on the table. "Children, come for supper!" she called. Two little ones came running. Chase said grace and passed the casserole dish to Dave.

"Dave," Chase said, "there is something I've been wanting to talk to you about. A ministry opportunity. I think you're ready for it."

Dave's eyes widened. "What is it?" Marie rested her hand on her husband's and smiled.

"It's a radio evangelist. How'd you like to preach the gospel on air?" Melva's mouth opened, and she glanced at Dave. His eyes were wide, and he was speechless.

"It's not near here," Chase said. "It's my old post at Trail, BC. The Lord called me away from there to lead the *Heaven and Home Hour* here in Calgary. It's a great opportunity, Dave, in that it is near the smelter. More than two thousand men work there. The program is called *Back to the Bible*. It is financed entirely by donations. Costs thirty-six dollars a week and right now there's only forty-two dollars in our Trail broadcasting account. I think the position is still available, so if you're interested, I'll let them know and they can write you directly."

Dave stared blankly. "The responsibility," he whispered, "is much more than I've ever had." He turned to Melva. She smiled and nodded, but was thinking, *"Thirty-six dollars a week? How could one ever afford that? Minimum wage is only two dollars and forty cents a day! What if there are no donations?"*

Dave looked around the table. "Let's see if it is the Lord's will, shall we?" he said. "We will pray about it." He picked up his fork and began to eat.

November 7, 1942

Melva sat up in bed and felt her large tummy. "Dave, I think it's time!" Dave switched on the lamp. Two in the morning.

"You sure?"

Melva winced. "I don't know, but that pain was strong."

Minutes later, at the Calgary General Hospital, Dave and a nurse helped Melva to her room. After half an hour, another nurse entered. "How far apart are your pains?"

Melva struggled to sit up. "Haven't had one since coming in."

"How long's that been? About forty minutes?"

Dave nodded.

"I'll get the doctor," she said and a few minutes later, returned with Doctor Hughes.

"Hello, Mrs. Stewart. Been expecting you. Good to see you! Frances says your pains have stopped?" He listened carefully to Melva, took notes on his clipboard, and said, "I'll check back a while later."

The nurse looked at Dave. "Now Mr. Stewart," she said. "I have to ask you to proceed to the waiting room. We'll let you know after the baby comes."

An hour later, Melva groaned. The pain had intensified, yet between pains she had considerable breaks.

A few hours later, a nurse came to check on Melva. "Baby's in no rush," she said as she smiled at Melva. She glanced around the room. "I don't know why they keep these rooms so cold!" she muttered, adjusting Melva's blankets.

"How much longer?" Melva asked.

"Usually it takes at least twelve hours for your first."

Melva whimpered, "I don't think I can last that long. Can't Dave stay with me?"

"Husbands are not allowed. I'll send a nurse to sit with you."

Melva groaned and clung to her pillow. More hours passed. Sweat poured down her face. The nurse dabbed her face with a cool cloth.

"You're doing great, Melva," she said. When Melva gave a loud cry, the nurse rushed her bed into the delivery room. Minutes later, a newborn's cry filled the room. Melva threw her head on the pillow and heaved a deep sigh of relief. She glanced at the large clock: twenty-one hours of labor!

"It's a boy! And a handsome young man at that!" Dr. Hughes announced. Nurses gathered around, talking excitedly. One of them took the baby to the scale and weighed him. "Eight pounds, one ounce!"

Excitement filled Melva. She had a boy! A chubby healthy boy! Dave would be so thrilled! "Can Dave see the baby now?" she asked.

Her nurse smiled. "Yes, when you get to your room. But not for too long. You've had a long and exhausting day and need rest."

Shortly after the nurse had helped Melva into bed in her private room, Dave appeared.

"Oh Dave! It's a boy!" Melva exclaimed as she snuggled the baby next to her. Dave's eyes enlarged as he came near. "Praise the Lord!" He pushed the blanket back. "May I see his toes?

"Why?" Melva asked.

"To see if he has Stewart toes."

"Oh Dave," Melva laughed.

Dave examined the baby's toes. "Nope. He's not a Stewart, that's for sure. He's got the same cute toes as you do. He's a Dye through and through. And I'm glad. I'd rather have him take after his mother than his father any day." Dave bent down and kissed her on the forehead. "God helped you through, dear," he whispered. "I was praying for you, and I phoned your parents. They said they would pray for you, too, and your sisters."

"I know He helped me, Dave, but when I was going through it, I didn't realize it."

"Shall we name him Donald Gordon, like we discussed?" Dave asked. Melva looked down at the chubby-cheeked infant.

"Yes."

A week later, Dave brought Melva and the baby back home to Langdon.

November 21, 1942

"He's two weeks old today," Melva said as she lay little Donnie in his bassinet and tucked blankets around him. Dave walked up behind her, and they embraced.

"What a beautiful boy," Dave said, looking at his child. But as he turned from the bassinet, he clutched his chest and took a deep breath. "I keep having this pain off and on," he said as he tried to straighten.

Melva's mouth dropped, "Dave, are you alright? You never told me about any pain!"

"Because I didn't want to bother you with just having a baby and all."

Melva put her arm around him, holding him firmly as he took several short breaths.

"You should go to the hospital and have it checked."

Dave leaned over a chair for a moment. "Think you're right. I'll have your father drive me in." Minutes later, Donald pulled up to the farmhouse. Melva stood by the car as Donald helped Dave in. Dave turned to Melva. "Please don't worry about me. I'm sure I'll be fine." He kissed her.

Melva returned to the house and, collapsing into a chair, she burst into tears.

November 24, 1942

As she washed dishes, Melva looked at the snow-covered yard. *"I wonder how Dave's doing. Is he all right? It's been three days since he left."* A knock sounded and she jumped. Quickly, she went to the door. "Clara, come in!" Clara hugged her.

"A letter. From Dave. I got your mail."

"Oh, thank you!" Melva took the letter and ripped it open.

"Greetings to my love, my dove, and my dear little wife." Melva's eyes blurred, and she quickly wiped the tears. "Dr. Hughes examined my chest but did not find any trouble. I was glad for that although my pain is still there. But praise the Lord I had a chance to witness to a man and his brother. A blessed thing, how real the gospel is at such a time.

I pray the Lord will water the seed. Neither of them really got it, but a word in season, how good it is!

"Please don't worry about me here. I'm in good hands—the hands that have the marks of the nails. They fashioned the world. They are underneath and round about me, and I fear no evil. My verse for today is, 'Who is among you that feareth the Lord, that obeyeth the voice of his servant, that walketh in darkness, and hath no light? Let him trust in the name of the Lord and stay upon his God.' This is the part that strikes me: 'walketh in darkness'. The last part is my strength. He is the light of the world—my light—my salvation. But He loves to lead us in the dark. I suppose to make us trust Him more.

> Ye fearful saints, fresh courage take;
> The clouds ye so much dread
> Are big with mercy and shall break
> In blessings on your head. (W. Cowper)

"Goodbye my dear wife. Will let you know when I can come home. I'll phone or write.

Love, your husband."

November 26, 1942

Melva stood outside the Langdon post office and ripped open another letter from Dave.

"My Dearest Melva. I'm getting plenty of time to read. But more and more the time is dragging. It seems the hands on the clock never move.

"In a day or two they should know my reactions to different foods. Dr. Hughes allowed me up today, so I jumped into the bathtub. However, I didn't enjoy it too much. Too many distressing things around here—groans, coughs, beds wheeling by, spitting, etc. Very unpleasant. I'm thankful for the health I have—some of these folks are in awful shape, spiritually and physically. I give myself to God as never before to be of some help to them. Wish I was out there to give you a hug—a long one that lasts until morning. Don't let Donnie play you out. They have a way of getting along without too much attention. Much love, your husband, Dave."

Melva held the letter to her chest and slowly got into her car.

November 27, 1942

"Another letter," Clara said as she entered Melva's home. Drying her hands, Melva took the letter.

"Dear Melva, the letter came from the radio station in Trail, BC. CJAT says the opening is there. Let's pray much for God's will and suitable helpers and the right time to start. If we are in His will, He will see us there. If not, may He crash it before we go too far and get disappointed. To me, it's another step of faith and, God helping us, we will take it. I don't know whether to be glad or sad about it. The responsibility will be much more than we've ever had. Let me know your thoughts.

"I used to feel offended in my heart at the hand-to-mouth sort of existence that we as gospel workers have. When I freight-hopped, I felt I was just a bum and a beggar. Hence, in Christian life, I always tried to support myself. The Lord is showing me (although hard on the old man) that living from hand-to-mouth while doing His will is different from what it was while living in the world and following its course. This time, it's God's hand and that's what makes the difference. As we need it, God gives it. Very few have this privilege. I praise Him for all the channels He uses, but whoever the channel is by which the blessing comes, it is always the same blesser. I believe God has ordained it this way to keep us dependant on Him."

November 28, 1942

A car pulled up in the driveway and Melva scurried to the window. *"Dave!?"*

Dave entered their home and set his bag on the floor.

"Oh Dave! I'm so glad you're home again!" Melva said as she embraced him.

"I'm sure glad to be home and to sleep in my own bed again. Oh, I missed you so much!" He held her in a long embrace and kissed her. "But now I am with you again, my favorite place to be, and I can hold you all night." He kissed her again.

"Where's Donnie?" he asked as his eyes scanned the room.

"In the bassinet in the living room," Melva said. Dave approached the baby and lifted him up, cuddling him.

"What is this?" Melva asked as she lifted a smaller bag he had set on the floor.

"Diabetes."

Melva's mouth dropped. "Diabetes? Oh Dave!" She peered in the bag. It contained a weigh scale and other paraphernalia.

"Don't worry, honey. Like your father says, it could always be worse."

"Yes, but diabetes?" A tear trickled down her cheek. He wiped it away and kissed her.

"Please don't fret. I can live with it."

She sighed. "Please Dave, *please* take care of yourself, for my sake, for Donnie's sake." He kissed the baby.

"I missed you both so much when I was in the hospital, dear," Dave said.

"I missed you, too," Melva said. *"I need to trust God with this, too. I guess there'll never be a time when I don't need to trust Him."*

A few hours later, while eating supper, Melva asked, "So they have invited us to Trail for you to fill the position of radio evangelist?"

Dave smiled. "Yes. They did ask me to fill the position." He rubbed his bristly chin. "Well, Melva. Are you sure you are okay with it? It would mean uprooting ourselves from all your family and friends. It's a long way to go, and who knows when, if ever, we'd come back."

"Oh Dave," Melva said as she touched his face. "I have been so fortunate to be near my family for the last six months. I am thankful God put us here for a season. And Dave, before we married, I told the Lord I'd go where He wants me to go and do what He wants me to do. I'm with you. If you believe it's God's will, then I am for it."

Dave kissed her. He walked to the stove and poured himself a cup of coffee.

"Chase said we'd need helpers, a pianist, and some singers." He rubbed his chin. "I'm wondering if your sisters Alice and Doris would want to come. They could sing and play the piano."

"Oh Dave, what a wonderful idea! And, oh, I almost forgot. We got a letter from Vince."

"Really? How is he?"

"It's not easy for him, being in the war and separated from his fiancée, Blanche." Melva took the letter from the desk and read, 'I believe you know Blanche well enough to see what a lucky fellow I am to have a girl like her for my future wife. No one needs think I won't be true to her over here. She is so much a part of my life that no other girl could ever interfere. She keeps me so well supplied with wonderful letters it seems I am close to her always and she is in my thoughts continually.'"

"That's a great letter," commented Dave. "Sounds just like Vince, doesn't it?"

Instead of answering, Melva's mind drifted back to the possibility of separation from her parents and some siblings. "It would be hard," she said, as she let Vince's letter fall back on the desk.

CHAPTER TWENTY-TWO

VENTURING OUT

January 14, 1943

"It is glory just to walk with Him, whose blood has ransomed me; it is rapture for my soul each day. It is joy divine to feel Him near, wherever my path may be. Bless the Lord, it's glory all the way! It is glory just to walk with Him …" The family sang with all their hearts. They were gathered in the Dye living room to say goodbye to Dave, Melva, Donnie, Alice, and Doris. As the hymn ended, Hazel approached her daughters.

"Oh, I shall miss you all!" She embraced them one by one.

"Oh Mother," Melva said as they embraced. The familiar scent of her mother's perfume met her. *"I'm going to miss her. I can't believe we are doing this."*

Hazel took Donnie from Melva. "Dear little boy, when will I see you next?"

Melva looked into her mother's eyes. They were happy, yet tired. *"How hard it must be to be a seasoned mother."* A wave of pity washed over her. Vera and Clara cried softly as they hugged each sister.

"Daddy." Melva kissed her father on the cheek. He wiped away a tear as they embraced. "Dave," he said, "take good care of my daughters." Dave nodded.

"Let's put tears behind us," Hazel said. "It has been such a blessing to have you close this last year. Now, you all are going to do the work of the Lord. He has led you so far and will continue to lead you."

"Amen to that!" Grandma Melvia said from her rocker.

"Did you get the five-gallon drum for gas?" Donald asked.

"Yes," Dave said, "and the two-gallon oil drum. Once they're empty, I'll ship them back."

The family followed the entourage to the waiting car. After final hugs with more tears, Melva waved as they headed down the driveway. Vera, Clara, Vern, Donald, and Hazel waved. They passed the hedge, turned on the dirt road, and drove along the canal, the canal that held so many memories. It was frozen, and an icy mist hovered above it. Melva's window fogged up and she quickly wiped it off and continued staring. Within minutes, they passed Rae's haunted house, where she had helped Clara cook for the threshing crew. It stood like a frozen block against the morning sky. Melva wiped a tear. *"We are headed to somewhere we've never been before, to live, for who knows how long?"* Donnie cooed while Doris held him tightly in the back seat. "At least he's warm enough," Doris said. Melva nodded her approval.

"We'll stop in Calgary to shop and go to the bank," Dave said.

Two hours later, they headed west out of Calgary.

"Dave, the wind is picking up. Think it's safe?" Melva asked as they left the city behind them.

Dave remained focused on driving. "I guess we'll find out," he said, "but we are only going to Stavely tonight. Isn't far."

It was five-thirty when they pulled into Melva's Aunt Nona's driveway in Stavely.

"Thank the Lord, we made it safely so far," Dave said as he leaned back in his seat.

Early the next morning, Dave peered out the window. "It's a howling blizzard!"

Melva rolled over in bed. "What are we going to do?"

"Let's wait until daylight. Might just be local and we can drive through it."

As the sun peeked above the horizon, the group left. Dave squinted through the windshield as they crawled along with snow sweeping across the road. Melva shivered—a cold breeze blew through the cracks around the doors. The fenders shook and even though the heater was on full blast, the cold wind sucked away its warmth. Doris and Alice huddled with Donnie between them in the back seat. Melva turned up her collar.

Dave spoke. "I know you may not agree, ladies, but we're leaving in faith. I believe we can travel through this storm." He glanced in the rear-view mirror. The wind howled and a blast of swirling snow pasted against the windshield.

Hours later, they passed a sign. "Cranbrook 5 miles." A few minutes after that, the car clunked and slid to a stop.

"Something is wrong with the car, but now we are also stuck. Too much snow on the road. Don't look down." Dave tightened his scarf and stepped out. They were perched on the edge of a steep slope. Dave took his shovel out of the trunk and began to clear the snow from the wheels. Within minutes, another car pulled in front of them, and a man jumped out. After a while, Dave re-entered. "I need to get the car checked in Cranbrook, but the man told me we should be able to make it there." Dave tried to drive, but the car spun around until it faced the opposite direction.

"Oh Dave, what are we going to do?" Melva asked. The stranger knocked on the window and Dave rolled it down.

"With these ruts on the road it looks like you will have to back down into Cranbrook," he said. Dave thanked him and began to back along the highway.

"Oh, must we Dave?" Doris asked with a tone of fear.

"Well, it's working." Dave said.

"Yes, but can you see where you're going?" Melva asked.

"Well enough."

Melva looked at her sisters. Alice had shut her eyes and Doris hugged Donnie.

"What time is it?" Melva whispered to Dave as she turned over in bed hours later. Gratefulness filled her as she thought how fortunate they were to be sleeping in a warm hotel. They had stopped at the Byng Hotel in Cranbrook.

"Go back to sleep, honey, it's not even six yet," Dave's voice sounded from a chair in the corner. Melva forced her eyes open and saw Dave at the table holding Donnie. "I tried to keep him quiet; he awoke early."

Melva got up. "I can take over. You need your sleep for driving." She took the baby.

"I had a good sleep. This hotel is nice and warm. I'm hoping the mechanic was able to fix the car at the garage last night." Melva looked at Doris and Alice, who were fast asleep in the other double bed.

"We should get them up if neither of us is going to sleep anymore," Melva said.

Minutes later, the small group sat in the hotel's café. Donnie screamed. Doris walked around with him and talked softly. Dave left them eating while he went to the garage and emptied the barrel of gas into the car. He then went to the train station and shipped the empty gas drum to Donald.

Minutes later, they all piled in the car. Two tire tracks cut through the thick snow ahead of them. Along the roadside and in the ditches great sheets of ice lay every which way, like stacks of broken glass. The mountains rose clear in the azure sky, their tops covered with sparkling snow. As they rounded a bend, a frozen lake glittered in the sun. Melva tightened her scarf and Dave gripped the steering wheel as he fought to keep his tires in the tracks.

"Going to be a long day, ladies," he said. "But a beautiful one."

Later, as they crossed the Kootenay ferry, Dave peered over the railing. Melva stood beside him, clutching Donnie. "When we passed those orchards," he said, "did you notice the fruit hadn't been picked?"

"Yes, I did," she said.

He shook his head. "The harvest truly is plenteous, but the laborers few."

It was eleven-thirty when the little car sighed to a stop in front of a four-story hotel on Bay Avenue in Trail. Dave peered out of the window. "Arlington Hotel. Yup. This is the place." Soft streetlamps shone on the rounded corner of the hotel and a Canadian flag lightly flapped in the cool breeze on top of a conical roof tower. "Ladies, I think we should pray and thank the Lord we made it safely." After a prayer, the group took their luggage to their rooms.

January 17, 1943

It was Sunday. "Stay in bed, Melva. You need your rest," Dave said as he straightened his tie in the mirror. "I phoned Captain Jarrett from the Salvation Army and I'm supposed to meet him soon, so you ladies can eat at the café at your leisure. Pick you up for the eleven o'clock service." Melva nodded. How different it felt for a Sunday. At home, everyone would bustle around getting ready for church, pile into the car—sometimes two or three vehicles—and drive to the church on Main Street. Past the church were wide open fields as far as the eye could see. To the west, the Rockies. Here, lower mountains surrounded the town. It was beautiful but felt more like they were just on vacation. A pang of loneliness shot through her.

True to his word, Dave was back before eleven. "Melva, you'll really like the Jarretts. You ladies ready?" Doris was cuddling Donnie.

"We had breakfast and we're ready," Melva said. Melva breathed in the icy air as they crossed the street to the Crown Point Hotel, headed north past three stores, next to which was the two-story Salvation Army building.

A nervousness came over Melva as they entered.

"And you must be Melva," a kind-looking woman said, approaching her. "I'm Elsie Jarrett."

"Nice to meet you," Melva said as they shook hands. After visiting for several minutes, a man walked to the pulpit. He opened a hymnbook, and they sang several militant hymns.

"Ladies and gentlemen," he began, "today we have with us an evangelist from the Calgary Prophetic Bible Institute, Dave Stewart, and his lovely wife, Melva. He has come to Trail to share the gospel on our radio station CJAT. His wife and her sisters will be bringing the music. Let us welcome them, shall we?" Loud applause filled the room. Dave stepped forward to preach. The congregation was small, but a good spirit filled the air. After, the people gathered around and introduced themselves.

CHAPTER TWENTY-THREE

NEW HOME

January 18, 1943

Melva tucked the thin hotel blanket tighter around her. Dave sat near a small table.

"Dave? Didn't you sleep? Was the bed too hard?"

"Couldn't sleep, honey. Sorry for waking you. I'm just so nervous about being on air. Try to get more sleep, Melva. It's only five-thirty and two hours before I preach. Are you sure you don't want to sing or play the piano today?"

"I'm sure. Doris and Alice have been looking forward to it so much. Take them."

Melva lay back down and stared at the ceiling. Everything was so new and strange. *"Oh well, God brought us safely here. He will take care of Dave's nervousness, money to pay the bills, a home, and everything else."*

When she awoke two hours later, the room was quiet except for the gurgling sounds of Donnie. Seven-thirty. The time Dave was to be on air. Melva said a prayer for him and her sisters. *"Wish I had a radio so I could listen."* She walked over to the crib. Donnie smiled up at her.

An hour later, the door burst open.

"Oh Melva," Dave exclaimed. "I feel so bad! Felt like I just fumbled my way through." Alice and Doris followed him into the room.

"You did fine, Dave," Alice said. "No one would have noticed."

"Well? What happened?" Melva asked.

Dave looked down and sighed. "I was too nervous to announce the time, which I was supposed to do, and I spoke too fast. I ended before my time was up."

"Oh Dave," Melva said, resting her hand on his shoulder. "I'm sure you did fine. You are here to preach the gospel, so don't worry about the details." Dave smiled and embraced her.

"Thanks for the reminder," Dave said, glancing around the room. "Now, let's go house hunting today. Hotel living's expensive! I will trust God to provide a place for us, just like I need to trust Him for boldness to speak on the air every morning." He looked out the window. "It's just so strange, on air. I can't imagine ever getting comfortable with it. Oh, and Melva, I talked to CJAT's manager Walter Dales. He said just what Chase Sawtell told us—the Bible broadcast has forty-two dollars in its account, and we pay thirty-six at the end of each week. This week is covered by the forty-two dollars. That gives us six dollars for fuel, coal, and groceries. Or we could save it to help with next week's broadcast."

Melva sighed. "Oh Dave, I don't know if I'm going to like living this way."

"I know. I know. I can't help but think we would have lots if Faith Mission had paid me back."

"Now Dave, we were not going to talk about that again, remember? The Lord allowed it for a reason we don't understand."

Dave rested his hand on her arm. "I know. Sorry. Shouldn't have said that. I have purposed to never ask for money or go in debt. I believe our God is big enough. And because I want to give all my time and energy to ministry, I have no time to earn money myself, except for odd jobs. We have to pray for funds and live one day at a time."

Melva nodded. *"I don't know if Daddy would understand. He works so hard to provide for his family. He'd think we were lazy or foolish. But Dave is not my daddy. He's following God's call on his life, and I agreed to it. For better or for worse, I must put my greater affections on Dave, and not Daddy, and supporting him in every way I can, even if it's only prayer and loving him."*

"I am thankful the CJAT studio is close. We just walked down Bay Avenue, turned left, and crossed the street," Dave said.

"It has a beautiful piano, too," Alice said.

Dave took Donnie and cuddled him. "Melva, do you want to come house hunting with me?"

"It's too cold for Donnie. You three go ahead," Melva said. "I'll stay and write home. We should let them know we made it safely here."

A couple hours later, the group returned to the hotel. "The temperature is plummeting. Just too cold to look anymore," Dave said as he dropped his gloves on the table. "Besides, Jarrett's have invited us out for supper."

"How have you enjoyed your first day in Trail?" Mr. Jarrett asked that night. Elsie, his wife, and Dave, Melva, and Donnie sat around the table at the Bluebird Café.

"It's a beautiful town here in the mountains, but we didn't have any success finding a place to rent."

Mr. Jarrett perked up and turned to his wife. "Elsie! What about the two empty rooms next to us above the Salvation Army? They're not much, but better than living in the hotel!"

"Yes, of course, Earle. What a great idea. After supper we'll show them to Dave and Melva. Rather small for five people, but adequate. Doris and Alice could stay in one room, and you three in the other. Do you have furniture?"

"Yes," Dave said. "We had it shipped. Tomorrow I'll check at the train station to see if it arrived."

Later, after getting Doris and Alice from the hotel, the group approached the Salvation Army building, headed down the back alley, and went up the narrow stairs that clung to the back of the building.

"Well, here it is," Earle said as he unlocked a dark stained door. It opened to a hallway, which ran along the north wall. As they walked down it, they passed a door. "This is where Elsie and I live," Earle said. They approached another door at the end of the hall. Dave let Melva step into the room first, along with Doris and Alice. It was long and narrow, with a window facing the street. A single door stood in the middle of the south wall. Wooden crates covered in cobwebs jammed the corners and a layer of dust covered the floor. A table stood in the center, and a dirty woodstove stood against the long wall with a few logs in an old wash basin. Not far from it was a counter with a green pump over an enamel sink. Next to that was a hoosier cabinet. Melva opened the cabinet doors. A few plates and bowls, along with two upside-down cups, graced the shelf.

"This will do just fine!" Melva said. She walked to the window. People scurried along the boardwalk; hands deep in their pockets. The Canadian flag fluttered over the Arlington Hotel's conical tower. She glanced at the windowsill. A light layer of frost had collected on it. She ran her finger over it. *"At least it's better than the dust that sat on the sills at home,"* she thought.

Earle Jarrett cleared his throat. "I'm sorry it's so dirty," he said. "I didn't remember it being this way since the last couple moved out. They came to minister here, too. That was more than a year ago and since then, the Salvation Army has used these rooms for storage." Doris turned up her collar and snuggled Donnie closer. Alice tightened her scarf.

"A good fire will warm things up," Dave said. After examining the other room, which only contained one double bed and a single cot, Dave approached Melva and her sisters. "What do you all think?" he asked.

"It will do fine in meeting our needs, Dave," Alice said. Doris nodded.

"Yes, Dave," Melva agreed.

Dave turned to Earle. "Yes, I believe this will do just fine, Earle, thank you. How much do we owe you?" Dave asked.

"As long as you're here as missionaries, nothing. We discussed it as a board when the last couple left. We agreed to use these rooms for fellow missionaries or pastors to stay, free of charge. However, you must supply the wood or coal to heat it yourself, and any other bills you acquire. The outhouse is out back."

"When our furniture comes in, we can use the crates for firewood. Where's the best place to order coal from?" Dave asked. Dave and

Earle continued to discuss coal and wood, while the ladies opened the cupboards and looked around.

"Yes, once we get this place clean, it'll feel like home. It's the cold and dirt that are hard to bear," Melva said.

The next morning, the group brought in buckets and brooms. Earle had given them a pile of wood from his stash. As the fire roared in the woodstove, Melva sat in a chair next to the fire holding Donnie. They all wore winter coats.

As it was nearing supper time, Melva sighed and set down her mop. "We've cleaned all day, and it doesn't look like we've done a thing! And because the floor is cold, the mop just smears the dirt around!"

"But at least the air is warm," Alice said, wiping her forehead, her hair neatly tucked under a kerchief. "But you are right. We've spent the whole day cleaning and it's still a mess!"

"I don't think I've ever seen so much dust on the walls!" Doris said as she dried her hands on her apron.

Melva laughed, "What would Grandma think? I still don't know how she was ever able to keep her living quarters dust free perpetually!"

Two days later, the rooms were clean and warm. Doris and Alice decided to have the second room and they moved the double bed into the first room for Dave and Melva. Now, a fire crackled in the stove and Melva rocked Donnie. Alice bustled about making soup with Doris. Dave had been invited to visit a local pastor who had heard him on the radio.

"One good thing about this place," Alice said. "Everything is within walking distance, not like at home on the farm. Lots easier."

"Yeah, sure will save on fuel. That way we only need fuel for when we do visitation around these mountains," Melva said as she put down Donnie's bottle.

"And for Dave when he wants to go fishing," Doris said with a smile.

The door burst open, and Dave walked in. "Guess what! I've got an invitation to speak at Pastor Hone's church in town, and we've been invited to a nondenominational prayer meeting every Thursday night."

"That's wonderful!" Melva said.

Dave dropped three letters on the table. "Letters concerning the broadcast are starting to come in, Melva. God is working."

January 21, 1943

"Good morning, ladies and gentlemen! This is CJAT, broadcasting from the bowl in the mountains, beautiful Trail, British Columbia! As always, we are the voice of the Kootenays! Joining me again in the studio today is David Stewart, here to bring us the Back to the Bible broadcast. Dave?"

"Yes, and thank you, Walter. I count it a privilege to be here in this studio and have a voice in the beautiful Kootenays. The time is now seven-thirty.

Dave cleared his throat. "Dear friends, my text for this morning is found in John chapter fourteen verse six. 'Jesus saith unto him, I am the way, the truth and the life, no man cometh unto the father but by me.' The Bible says, 'All have sinned and come short of the glory of God.' Not one sin can enter heaven, no not one, and, as we are all guilty of sin, we are all excluded from heaven unless there is a way by which our sins can be forgiven. God has provided a way.

"Paul said Christ died for our sins according to the scriptures and that He was buried and rose again. Second Corinthians chapter five, verse nineteen says, 'God was in Christ, reconciling the world unto himself, not imputing their trespasses unto them.'

"Friends, the whole Bible bears witness that apart from Jesus Christ we have no way to God. Do you believe in the Son of God? Are you trusting Him as your substitute? There is no other way by which we can be saved. Avail yourself, my listening friend, of the substitute. Take Christ as your Savior. Then, rather than being under the condemnation of God, you will be under the love of God. 'Verily, verily, I say unto you, he that heareth my word and believeth on him that sent me hath everlasting life and shall not come into condemnation but is passed from death to life. John chapter five verse twenty-four.' At this time, Doris and Alice Dye are going to sing, '*What can wash away my sins*.'"

After the hymn, Dave continued sharing the gospel.

"In conclusion," he said. "Here is today's thought. If every living person knew what every departed soul discovers, everyone would be saved! This is Dave Stewart, signing off for the Back to the Bible broadcast, CJAT, the voice of the Kootenays."

Dave smiled as he entered their home later. "It was easier today, things went smoother.

"Oh Dave, that's wonderful," Melva said as she kissed him.

Dave wrapped his arms around her. "How would you like to meet more people from this area?" he asked. Melva nodded. "Because tonight, I've been asked to speak at Peoples Church."

January 22, 1943

The next day after coming home from the broadcast, Dave set his Bible and message on the table. "Even though the broadcasts are running smoother, I don't know if I'll ever get accustomed to it," he said. "A man named Gordon Ferguson and his wife Lena, invited Alice and Doris for supper tonight. And Mr. Longden, a man that came to the studio today, is coming over for a visit and prayer with us."

January 23, 1943

Melva answered the phone.

"Hello? Is this Mrs. Stewart?" A voice on the line said.

"Yes. Speaking."

"My name is Mr. Cairn. I'm the pastor at the Apostolic Church in town and I wondered if Dave could preach Sunday night in our church. Is he available for me to talk with right now?

January 23, 1943

"How did the singing go?" Melva asked Doris as she, Dave, and Alice entered the room after that morning's broadcast. Doris approached with a wry smile.

"Terrible. It sounded terrible." She laughed and Dave laughed behind her.

"However," Doris continued, "we have good news. We needed six dollars today, and we received four dollars from someone, two more from Alberta and, Grandma Melvia paid for another day's broadcast!"

"That's wonderful! Hope we'll have funds to keep buying groceries," Melva said. "And Dave," she continued, "the Newshams in the church in Innisfail sent us a letter."

"And?" Dave asked.

"They said they can hear you clearly on the radio over there!"

"That's great!" Dave smiled.

"But they also said your preaching sounded stiff."

Dave groaned. "I know, I know! I feel plumb frozen when I'm on air. I will keep trusting God to help me."

January 26, 1943

A knock sounded and Melva opened the door.

"Just thought you might be in need of some food," a pleasant woman said. She handed Melva a box.

"Thank you, thank you so much!" After she left, Melva unpacked the box to find a bag of frozen peas, four cans of soup, a jug of milk, and a jar of jam.

January 29, 1943

It didn't take long before Dave and Melva and her sisters had acquired many new friends. One couple that became very close to them was Gordon and Lena Ferguson. Gordon conducted a Bible program on air as well, in the evenings.

It was breakfast and Dave put down his cup. "You know, both the coffee and tea taste salty."

Doris took a sip of her tea. "I heard the Salvation Army ladies say it is because of the smelter. After living here a while, they say it leaves a faint taste of sulfur in your mouth."

Dave laughed. "Well, I don't mind that factory. I love watching the smoke rolling out of the chimneys. I would love to tour it one day, but Earle said right now during the war they prohibit visitors, and it is heavily guarded."

Melva sighed. "On another subject, I hope you all don't mind two-day old porridge."

"Tastes fine." Dave took another swallow. "You know, we haven't had any extra funds come in for a couple weeks. I trust you girls don't mind soup and oatmeal, as we still have a lot of that."

"Dave, who said mission work was easy?" Alice said as she heated wash water.

"Well, I've never trusted God this much before. After my time of prayer earlier this morning, God rebuked me for my unbelief," Dave said.

Later that day, when Dave, Melva, and Alice returned from preaching and singing at the Salvation Army meeting below their living accommodations, Doris met them. She held Donnie.

"How did it go?" she asked.

"Gordon Ferguson led the singing. What a beautiful voice," Melva said. "And, a number of people raised their hands, desiring a deeper walk with God!"

"Praise the Lord!" Doris exclaimed. "And here!" She put two letters on the table. Dave opened them. One contained five dollars, the other two.

January 30, 1943

Melva read a letter out loud. "Dear Mr. Stewart. I have been delighted to hear the simple truth of your messages in the morning broadcasts. We do not need denominationalism. That is why I say, thanks for the simple truth." F. L. Truddle

January 31, 1943

"What are your plans for today, Dave?" Melva asked early Sunday morning as she spooned Pablum into Donnie.

"This afternoon, I am preaching at the Apostolic Church, then early evening I speak on Gordon Ferguson's radio program, and then at eight I speak at the Gospel Hall.

Alice spoke up, "Doris and I are teaching the Salvation Army Sunday school downstairs this morning."

"Well, it sounds like a busy Sunday," Melva said. "And add to that, Gordon and Lena, along with Earle and Elsie are coming for lunch."

Several hours later, Dave stood behind the pulpit of the Apostolic Church in Trail. He scanned the audience. The small building was packed with mostly men from the Smelter that kept Trail's economy booming. Dave knew the environment the men worked in. Although the employees were treated well and were well paid, the buildings were hot and dirty, and the men worked long hours. More than two thousand men worked there. A man coughed, bringing Dave's mind back to the present. Dave's heart pained. These men were here to find hope, something richer, deeper, than their present lives contained.

Dave cleared his throat, "The boat was filled with frightened men. They were expecting every wave, each gust of wind, to swamp their vessel. They fain would have cried out for fear, so close were they to death. How thankful and overjoyed they were, when in their darkest hour, when all hope of their salvation was gone, when the waves beat the highest, and the winds blew the hardest, an almighty hand was stretched out to save, and a voice spoke, 'Be not afraid, it is I.' In this story, the condition of my lost soul is portrayed. Beaten about on the sea of life by the waves of sin, with the winds of ungodliness and skepticism threatening to swamp my frail ship, I too, would fain have cried out for aid, but to whom would I cry? In such a dark hour I heard the wonderful story of One who could speak the words of peace and pardon to the guiltiest soul. One who can calm every sin-troubled heart, and in despair, I sought His help. That evening, I met Jesus, and claimed Him as my Lord. Words of peace were spoken to my soul which down through the succeeding years have never left me. From that hour to this, I have never feared death, eternity, or judgment to come because I know that He is able to keep that which I have committed unto Him against that day. Thank God my sins, which were many, were forgiven, simply by taking God at His word, 'Whosoever believeth on Him should not perish but have everlasting life.'"

A young man stood. "Mister, my life is without meaning. I need to be saved," he said. His eyes brimmed with tears, and he strode to the front. One by one, others stood and followed. They knelt by the altar. As more came, Dave's heart rejoiced. He knelt amid them. Weeping ensued.

Dave tightened his scarf as he scurried home that afternoon. The wind nipped at his face, but his heart burst with joy. He skipped up the stairs two at a time.

"Melva! There was a good crowd at the meeting today, and more were saved!"

Melva embraced him. "Praise God, Dave. Praise God! God is saving souls and providing financially for us! Someone just dropped off this letter, and here's what it says, 'Dear brother Stewart, your broadcast fills a great need. Enclosed please find a small offering of one dollar.'"

Letters continued to come in. Some with one-dollar donations, some with two dollars, some just twenty-five cents, some five dollars, and occasionally, ten dollars. As Dave preached the gospel every morning, more and more ministers in the local area were encouraged and invited him to preach in their churches. This, in addition to attending daily Bible studies and prayer meetings, kept Dave, Melva, and her sisters busy daily. Many times, the radio team was invited for meals, and gradually, more and more people came to their door with groceries. Dave also began a ministry with the Doukhobors, preaching the gospel in their meetings, with more than a hundred in attendance.

February 2, 1943

The family had just finished eating supper when there was a knock at the door. Dave opened it.

"Hi, my name is Mr. Friesen. This is for you." He handed Dave a box.

"Thank you, thank you so much," Dave said. It contained a dozen eggs, a pound of butter, and a pint of cream. Later, when they opened the egg carton, they were surprised to find a dollar on top.

February 3, 1943

Dave entered the home and hung up his coat. "Captain Jarrett gave a great testimony today on air. Say, could you come hospital visiting with me today?" he asked, facing Melva.

"Sure," Melva replied, "as long as Doris or Alice don't mind babysitting."

"I thought it would be nice to take Donnie with us for people to see. We could all go."

"Alright. And I hope you don't mind soup again for dinner. But we do have the cream Mr. Friesen gave us yesterday. Maybe I could whip it for our coffee for dessert."

February 5, 1943

As Dave, Melva, Doris and Alice sat at the table, Dave opened a letter. He read it out loud. "Dear sir. Do true believers ever have fears? I have been brought up going to Sunday school and church. I believe in God. Yet ever since I can remember I have had fears."

"You know, ladies," Dave said looking around the table. "It's quite a responsibility to be in the ministry—especially on the radio. I'm beginning to understand what a sacred duty it is. Those on the radio have power to influence multitudes. But preaching the gospel on air? It is a dream come true for me! But—'To whom much is given, much will be required.'"

He took a piece of paper and dipped his pen in ink. "I need to write this lady and while I'm at it, I'll write Mr. Maxwell at Prairie. I never did thank him concerning how much his sermon meant to me three years ago. Guess I'm kind of scared of him."

After he finished writing, he handed Melva the Maxwell letter. She read, "My first acquaintance with the school was when my wife and I attended a conference in 1940. Before then, I had very few chances of listening to other preachers. I had the idea my time was better spent holding meetings somewhere, rather than taking in messages. On that occasion you preached on 'Agree with thine adversary quickly.' I was wonderfully blessed and filled with joy and misery, both at once. I could see on many points where God had an argument with me . . . I have always wanted to burn and glow for my Savior. My conversion from a life of sin was too real to me to be anything else but wholeheartedly His. God, knowing my heart, brought me face to face with your words. The more my self-life dies, the more of His eternal sweetness is mine. The more of His sweetness I get, the more I want to die. It is on the platform of my daily death that the Son of God reveals Himself to me. Yet, the Holy Ghost had to remind me so many times that I was trying by preaching to make a mark in this world, rather than on it. He made it so plain that after all, if I climbed to the top of the world in preaching fame, I'd only be atop a dunghill, and all who are trying to get ahead in the world are going headfirst into the pile of smelly vomit. Even as I write I say, 'O God, what a dog I've been in turning to my vomit.' Israel lusted after the old life. How we must watch! Why is it we find it so hard to die to these things? . . . I thank God for the way of deliverance. The cross. Blessed, glorious cross, when it cuts me off from such a gruesome thing as self, and above all, myself, because I am worse than anybody. A man died alongside me in the Calgary hospital. He had cancer; the smell was killing. I get the same sickening feeling and smell spiritually when God exposes me to myself. Yet, such times are necessary as they magnify His grace and mercy . . . How can we dare expect God to come among us when we are sinning? Yesterday, a minister here in Trail got up from his knees in my living room and confessed he was far from where he once was spiritually. So many are coming to that point that I am getting faith to believe that God might visit us. Different Christians from various denominations are meeting on equal ground. People are actually getting down to shed tears, as they cry to God. Still though, they are finding it hard to have more than two prayer meetings a week. The ground is so parched today. We must go back one hundred years to find a real outpouring. One man told me that God wasn't working today like He did back then. I told him he was right—God wasn't working that way—but not because He didn't want to—but couldn't, because so many of His people were believing that very lie. I have no doubt that when we get lined up with God, we will see such a visitation that we will not have to speak about what happened in Moody's or Finney's day, but what is happening now.

We are beginning to see our sinfulness—surely this is a sign that God is near. Oh, for a union in prayer for all likeminded! Hence, I am all taken up with what I'm sure is God's message for us today: the cross as a death blow to self. When we get it out of the realm of theory and into an everyday experience, the very power of God will be ours with the 'greater works than these.' Weep, blessed Lord Jesus, through me."

As Melva finished reading the letter, Doris answered a knock at the door.

"Another box from Mr. Friesen," she said, peering inside. "A dozen eggs, some bacon, and a pint of cream."

A week later, a letter came in the mail from L.E. Maxwell.

"I read your letter to our board prayer meeting, and we rejoiced greatly for what God is doing for you. I somehow feel God is doing a new thing through this testimony . . . I learned some years ago that we must be resigned to the sovereign wisdom of God relative to how He may choose to manifest His presence. As one reads various accounts of revivals in days past, one is impressed with the different path as to methods and manifestations. In the Wales revival, there was scarcely any human instrumentality that was conspicuous. In Finney's revivals, he was the centre of the whole thing. In Dr. Goforth's meetings, there was a special manifestation in conviction for sin. We must see greater things than these."

Many ministry opportunities began to arise for Alice and Doris as well—teaching Sunday school, holding children's meetings, and working in local Bible camps.

February 7, 1943

Melva and her sisters bustled around collecting the laundry. Piles lay about the floor.

"Ahh . . . wash day, is it?" Dave asked as he came in, holding a bundle of letters. He sat at the table and began to open them. After carefully reading each of them, he announced. "Someone called Prendergast sent ten dollars, the Jensens sent six dollars, Bob Thompson, three dollars, and the Collins family, five. That has just made up the difference and tomorrow I will pay the station thirty-six dollars!" He embraced Melva with a big smile. "God *is* faithful!"

February 10, 1943

"Billy Gates got saved in Sunday school today," Doris said with a smile. "There were thirteen children out."

"Wonderful," exclaimed Melva. "Jarrett's gave Dave two dollars and Mr. Friesen gave us another two dozen eggs!"

February 11, 1943

Doris reached for her diary and dipped her pen in the inkwell. "We were up at five-thirty today. Alice is sick. Melva went downstairs and played the piano for the Salvation Army service. Dave forgot his sermon, so I had to go find it. At two o'clock, Melva spoke at the women's meeting and at four, I taught at the children's meeting. Ten children came. Dave and Melva went to Gordon and Lena's for supper, then prayer meeting after."

February 14, 1943

Cheerful voices rang around the table. Mr. and Mrs. Jarrett sat opposite Dave, Melva, and her sisters. Mrs. Howard, a lady from the Salvation Army, sipped her tea.

"I really feel we need to pray more," Dave said, addressing the group.

Mrs. Howard set her teacup down. "I quite agree." After a few minutes' discussion, it was agreed that each in the group would spend thirty minutes every morning in prayer.

February 18, 1943

"Guess how many children we had out for the Bible class this afternoon?" Doris asked Melva at the supper that night.

"I don't know. Six?"

Doris smiled. "No! *Thirty-five* came to hear the gospel!"

"That's so wonderful!" Melva exclaimed, her eyes wide. "And did I tell you Barbara Walker got saved in the meeting on the twelfth?"

"Yes, that is wonderful!" Alice said. She wiped her hands on her apron as she dried the last supper dish. "I'm exhausted, so I can babysit Donnie tonight while the rest of you go to prayer meeting on Shaver's Bench Street. I heard Gordon is speaking."

"Yes."

"Mrs. Jarrett is sick, so I volunteered to do her ironing tonight," Doris said.

February 26, 1943

Dave wiped his forehead and put down a letter, saying, "War is a cursed thing." Melva looked over from where she was filling a baby bottle. He continued, "This dear lady wants us to pray for her sons." He picked up the letter and read, "You mentioned a while back about boys getting into the wrong crowd. Our third son, a soldier, is just twenty and a swell boy. He was home for Christmas and said, 'Mom, you just can't get out of drinking in the army. The boys say, "Oh come on, don't be a piker."'

"He doesn't like drink but said, 'I have to go and have a few beers.' You can not imagine how I felt. Our boys have never done anything we were ashamed about. Everybody always praised our sons. They were brought up in a Christian home. We had family worship. We knelt every morning, after breakfast, after Father read the Bible, also before we went to bed. Anyways, I've enclosed twenty-five cents for the broadcast. Not much, but we have nothing coming in. I pray for your brother's wounds, that they would heal. Your dear mother has a big worry. Our sons have not been wounded. Sorry I cut the corner off my letter. I got syrup on it and my letter is too long to copy. Sincerely, Mrs. Peterson, Fife, B.C."

February 28, 1943

Melva smiled as she tucked Donnie into bed. "Dave, a lady named Lorraine MacLellan received Christ today after prayer meeting."

March 1, 1943

Gordon and Lena, Harold and Margaret, and a woman named Barbara had just left from enjoying a meal with Dave, Melva, Doris, and Alice.

Dave thumbed through the growing pile of letters. "Couple letters today," he said. "Listen to this. 'Dear Mr. Stewart. Your daily broadcast is just what is needed in Trail.' And here's another nice one," Dave continued. 'Dear Christian friend. I like the plain way you preach the true gospel. Though you may never know the good you are doing, I am sure you must feel you are changing many to think, and I pray, to consider, the state of their lives.'"

"That's true," Melva said as she started doing dishes.

"Let me help you with that, Melva," Doris offered, handing Donnie to Alice. "There are a lot of dishes after company." Doris had a twinkle in her eye. "Besides, right now I'm in a good mood! Daddy sent me enough money to buy new shoes! He must have heard mine had almost worn through."

Dave looked over. "Really thoughtful of him! Another exciting thing: Mr. Cheshire gave me fifteen dollars today!"

CHAPTER TWENTY-FOUR

TESTING

March 3, 1943

Dave sat at the table, staring at the most recent bill from the radio station. "I just don't understand, Melva. The money has always come in. This studio bill is due on the eighth, and we're twenty dollars short."

Melva took a sip of tea. "Oh Dave, finish your breakfast. It will come, don't worry. It's not due until Monday and today's only Wednesday. God will provide." Dave rubbed his chin, deep in thought. He walked to the window and looked out. "Melva, I need to spend time alone. I'm going to cancel my appointments for today."

Melva stood. "Why? Where do you want to go?"

"I will lift up mine eyes unto the hills, from whence cometh my help. I'm going up on a mountain to be alone with God for a few hours."

That evening, Gordon and Lena came for supper.

After supper, Dave said, "When I was on the mountain this morning, I felt God speak to me. 'My house shall be called a house of prayer.' I really feel we must spend more time in prayer." The couples knelt and began to pray. The burden for the lost around Trail grew in their hearts, and they continued to pray for several hours.

March 4, 1943

The next day, Dave showed Melva a letter. It read: "I thank God for your being sent here—the need is so tremendous—I could weep as I think of how little, how very little we do about it. Oh, that God would wake us and make us realize our dreadful lukewarmness! Were it not for His everlasting mercy I would indeed tremble to give an account of my life! I can not see to write more, for tears have blinded me."

That night at prayer meeting, several people broke down and wept.

Tuesday, March 9, 1943

"How'd the broadcast go this morning?" Melva asked as she brushed her hair.

"Fine, fine," Dave said, putting his Bible and notebook on the table. Donnie fussed in his bassinet and Dave picked him up.

"My faith is being tested, Melva. I couldn't pay the studio bill today. First time it's happened."

Melva put down her brush. "Don't forget that the studio said it was alright to be a few days late. They understand."

Dave patted Donnie on the back as he placed him to his shoulder. The baby fussed and squirmed.

"He's hungry," Melva said, handing Dave a bottle. Dave put Donnie down and wrapped him tighter. "He's cold too, poor little guy." As soon as Dave gave Donnie the bottle, he quieted.

"I'd rather pay in advance than on time, and this? I feel it's a bad testimony. Even if we get the money tomorrow, it's still late."

"Dave, let's pray and leave it with the Lord. Maybe the donor is being pressed by the Lord but hasn't yielded. By the way, Dave Friesen is coming over, so let's concentrate on his needs, instead of our troubles."

"You're right," Dave said handing Melva the baby. "It will be nice to thank him again for all the food he has given us."

As the afternoon wound down, a knock sounded. Melva answered the door. "Welcome, welcome. Come in Mr. Friesen." Dave, surrounded by papers and open books, looked up from his studies. He closed his Bible and went to the door.

"Great to see you Dave," exclaimed Mr. Friesen. "How are you?"

After the usual pleasantries, Mr. Friesen explained the reason for his visit. "I wanted to say what you are doing in Trail is amazing. We needed someone to evangelize this area. I know it's expensive being on air every day. How's the giving?"

Melva and Dave glanced at each other. She shook her head slightly.

Dave rubbed his chin. "Well, sometimes things come together perfectly, and other times our faith is tested. Say, it's close to supper time. Would you join us for soup?"

As they ate, Mr. Friesen looked at Melva then Dave. "Yes, there are times when our faith is tested."

After enjoying a pleasant visit, Mr. Friesen got up to go, and at the door said to Dave, "If you're going through a testing time, let me help." He flipped open his wallet and pulled out ten dollars. "Here."

Dave thought for a few seconds then gently and politely pushed it back, shaking his head. "I feel I have failed. I promised God I would never make our needs known, and that I would only pray."

"But you didn't make your needs known," Mr. Friesen exclaimed. "All you said—"

"I said too much. Thank you for your kind thought. So nice of you. And like we've said, we sure do appreciate the food you've given us. Makes a huge difference!"

As Dave closed the door behind their guest, he leaned heavily against it, thinking.

"Was refusing his money right?" Melva asked.

Dave rubbed the back of his neck. "Yes," he said. "We were praying for twenty dollars, and it was almost like I asked him to help. I had promised never to do that."

Wednesday, March 10, 1943

Melva stood to the side in the radio studio. Alice had offered to babysit so Melva could be with Dave in the broadcast. When their guests, the Harrison sisters, finished their duet, Dave stepped to the mic with his Bible open.

"My text this morning is Joshua chapter fifteen, verse nineteen, which says, 'Who answered, give me a blessing; for thou hast given me a south land; give me also springs of water.'" Dave looked at the ceiling. "And he gave her the upper springs, and the nether springs . . .'"

"Very good message, Dave," Melva said later as they walked home. "You sounded so confident."

"How I sound and how I feel are two different things. The bridge that connects them is simply God's promises. We still need twenty dollars."

"Dave!" a man yelled from behind. They turned.

"Why hello, Mr. Bouma."

"Here. For the work of the gospel." He pulled a twenty from his wallet and handed it to Dave. Melva's eyes widened.

"Exactly the amount we were praying for! Oh, thank you. Thank you!" Dave exclaimed. He gave Melva a wink. He turned and headed back to the studio.

The next day Dave came home from an afternoon meeting whistling and slipped a letter on the table. Melva picked it up with a cry of pleasure. "It's from Uncle Ruel and Aunt Winnie!"

"Look," she cried. "Ten dollars! She read: 'We are fine but fed up with the weather. Our roads are blocked continuously. We no sooner get them dug out with much labor when they just drift shut again. We were down home again a couple of weeks ago. It seems funny without a gang of you girls there. It is so nice that they can hear you on the radio as it doesn't seem you are so far away. Dave, you said if Ruel came down, you'd put him on the radio. He says to tell you he is surely going to practice his *Turkey in the Straw* composition in anticipation. Yours, as ever, Ruel and Winnie."

March 12, 1943

Dave stared at the ceiling with his hands tucked behind his head.

"What's the matter? Can't sleep?" Melva asked as she rolled over and adjusted her pillow.

He leaned on his elbow and sighed. "Two things. Firstly, when I was at Gordon's tonight, we gossiped about a certain church. I feel it was unprofitable. I've asked the Lord to forgive me."

"So, why can't you sleep?"

"Well secondly, I'm also burdened for the unsaved at Sand Point, Kelowna, and Penticton. I'm praying we might hear from some of them about the broadcast."

"Well, *I'm* feeling convicted about *my* lack of faith concerning having enough to eat," Melva whispered. "Today, Mr. Reimer gave us a big roast."

March 15, 1943

Dave and Melva walked to the CJAT studio. "I haven't had time to tell you what the Woodrow family dropped off yesterday, Dave."

"Oh?"

"Four cartons of frozen spinach, corn, six pears, a jar of Postum, two tubes of toothpaste, and the cutest little stuffed bunny for Donnie."

"Sure generous of them. And to even think of Donnie!" Dave said.

Minutes later, they entered the studio office. "Here's this week's thirty-six dollars!" Dave smiled, handing the envelope to the station manager. "And look, Melva. We have two dollars left! Let's get a few groceries!'

"Yes, it will be wonderful to shop again!" Melva said.

CHAPTER TWENTY-FIVE

MISSION WORK

March 20, 1943

Dave sorted through a small stack of letters at the table. "Here it is," he said, holding it up. "From someone in Rossland. Melva, listen to this. 'Dear Mr. and Mrs. Stewart. My wife and I are enclosing two dollars for your work in God's service. I am not enclosing my name because we cannot afford the stamp to answer a letter. I cannot reveal our circumstances. But I can tell you I have not had to pay one cent for income tax. My full year's income is less than three hundred dollars, and we are not in debt. Thank God. I hold the love of my dear Lord dearer and more precious than anything on earth, even life itself. We admire your singing and preaching . . . I pray God will bless your work which is the noblest work on earth. I pray that He may urge those who can afford it to help so you can stay on air until He sees fit to take you to His home in glory where I trust through His divine grace to meet you. Amen.'"

March 22, 1943

A pounding on the door interrupted Dave's prayer time. He hurried to respond to the incessant knocking and a voice calling, "Mr. Stewart! Mr. Stewart!"

"Hello? How can I help you? Are you in trouble?"

A middle-aged man, mouth agape and knuckles poised to keep knocking, blurted. "Oh, Mr. Stewart! I need help."

"Come in, come in," Dave urged, beckoning him inside.

"My name is Hugh. Hugh Wilson. I've listened to your program since you started in January." He looked around the tiny apartment and shook. "I-I-I need to get right with God. I was taught the truth, but I've strayed so far—" His eyes misted, and he wiped them with the back of his hand. Dave rested his hand on the man's shoulder.

"Come, sit." Dave and Hugh walked to the chesterfield and Dave explained the gospel. Within half an hour, Mr. Wilson knelt by the couch and prayed to dedicate his life to Christ. As he got up from his knees, his faced beamed. "I-I feel like a new man! On the inside! I now know I was never saved! I feel *clean!*"

"That's because God has put His clean Spirit in you. You are a new man. The Bible calls it being a new creature in Christ. I have an idea. Would you do me a favor?"

"Anything! Oh, Dave. Anything. You name it!"

"Would you be willing to give your testimony, to talk about your salvation on the radio?"

Mr. Wilson's chin dropped. "What? And, and *publicly* testify so all of Trail can hear?"

"Yes," Dave nodded, "that's the idea."

"Yes! Yes! I will! I would *love* to! If only the whole world could feel what I feel right now!"

April 1, 1943

As the weather warmed, Dave and Melva felt the need for larger, more suitable accommodation. Eventually, they found a rental home, #1680, on Bay Avenue for twenty-five dollars a month. It was tall and narrow, and contained a luxury—a radiator for heating, plus two bedrooms, a kitchen, a bathroom, and a living room.

"This will meet our needs much better," he said to Melva as they toured it. Shortly thereafter, they all moved in.

"Look Melva. A letter from Uncle Arch!" Dave said as they made their way home from the post office. He read, "I hope you are physically sufficient for the work before you. As with Paul, there will be many adversaries. Paul's doctrine is the complete frustration of Satan. Victory over death, victory over life. God be praised, hitherto hath the Lord helped us. We will rejoice as the darkness deepens for only so can the morning come, and our daystar arise. How bright, how gladsome will His advent be, before the Son shines forth in majesty. Much love in Christ Jesus, and to the wee family. A.L. Stewart."

April 6, 1943

Dave was looking through a stack of letters and bills.

"What are you doing?' Melva asked as she sat opposite with Donnie on her knee.

"I'm totaling up our broadcast donations. From January 18 to the end of January, just over seventy-four dollars was given. For February, our receipts totaled over two hundred and fifty dollars and in March we received three hundred and twenty-two dollars! And all this without ever mentioning our need of money on air!"

"God is *so* faithful," Melva exclaimed as she kissed Donnie's head.

"You know, Melva," Dave said. "The expenses come in quite heavy, and oft times I wonder if the returns are worth it. But Christians have told me they hear the program blaring through the radios in cafés, so it's a witness." He sighed. "But as far as results go, it's discouraging."

"But there have been souls saved, directly and indirectly, Dave. And many letters stating how the program has been a blessing. Just meeting our bill week by week is a testimony to God's goodness."

He smiled at her and said, "Yes, you're right."

April 7, 1943

Melva read a letter to Alice, Doris, and Dave.

"Dear brother in Christ. Please put my husband's name on your prayer list for salvation. He is so bitter. He calls evangelists *windbags*. We have two boys, one seventeen, one twelve. The boys and I are saved and baptized but our cross has been doubly heavy since being baptized two-and-a-half years ago. Walter, our eldest, has worked morning, noon, and night for four years with his father at our sawmill. His father curses, swears, and calls him all the filth possible (some of which I have heard). He calls him a short version of, 'the son of an indecent woman.' Yesterday, Walter, our son, told me that his dad has raised him up to now, and up to now he had a duty toward his father. But he says he can't stand it much longer. I tried to explain to Walter that if he will only take his troubles to the great burden bearer, who loves him more than we can ever, God will work his life out for him. Our sons live under great difficulties. If they please me, they displease their father, and if they please their father, they displease me. Pray that God will undertake in a definite way for these two lads. Walter never complains or asks for a single thing. Please do not hesitate to write, as my husband cannot read. But his will is law. Everyone must do as he says. His temper is fiery, and he sulks, but he's a splendid provider. Works from seven in the morning to eleven at night."

Dave slowly put the letter on the table. "Amazing," he said. "So hard to believe. She is in pain. I must reply to her right away. Since this is from a woman, will you help me with this letter, Melva?"

"Yes," Melva said.

Dave stood by the mirror getting ready to leave for the studio. "You know, Melva, since God has been providing, I think we should start a broadcast in Nelson. I have heard how spiritually dark Nelson is. I am going to discuss it with Walter. I believe it's CKLN that broadcasts from there." Melva hugged Dave and smiled, running her fingers through his thick hair. "I'll never get over how thick your hair is," she whispered, kissing him. "Do whatever is in your heart, dear. God has always led you and will continue to lead you in the future."

April 10, 1943

"Dear brother Stewart. It is encouraging to hear that expenses have been met and much more encouraging to hear of the ones coming to the Lord. My husband worked with Hugh Wilson for about four years and is certainly happy to hear of his salvation. We met him once since, and *new man* was written all over his face. He was most anxious to tell us all about it.

Mrs. Caroline Dove"

May 3, 1943

Dave rubbed his chin. "Despite everything that happened at Johnsons, I miss the people back there. Tell me, what do you think of this letter to Bob?" Dave handed Melva the letter to proofread. She took it and read: "Dear Bob Thompson. Thank you for your letter. Will Mr. Jacobs be shepherding my dear flock out at Raven? I do hope the Lord will give him much wisdom in his going out and coming in. Diplomacy is the word. Sarah Maclean used to scold me more than enough about being diplomatic or trying to be. However, although she and the Ravenites are at loggerheads, I'm still good friends with both, so it counts for a little. It just doesn't pay to do and say everything all at once. Our Lord didn't. He said, 'I have many things to tell you but ye cannot bear them yet.' Also, it's line upon line, here a little and there a little that ye are brought along.' Take for instance, if Mr. Jacob's, the potential Raven pastor, is against Lutheranism out there, he will blow the mission off the map. The closer he stays to the Lord, the more blessing there will be in the ministry.

"We get lonesome for you all. If we are still here in the summer, load your fishing rod in the car and come down. We made it here on ten or fifteen dollars of fuel and it will be a change for you without much expense. Our house is small, but we can make room. I say *if* we are here.

We live one day at a time. Thus far, God has kept the door open, and I just went down and paid our studio bill for last week, which means we will be here for another week, and so on it goes, week in and week out. All total, we have completed around 150 broadcasts. A testimony to the faithfulness of God, praise Him. Love to all, Dave and Melva."

June 11, 1943

Another one of Dave's dreams came true. The CKLN broadcast station from Nelson contacted him and asked if he would preach every Sunday night from six-thirty to seven and call it Back to the Bible. Dave and Melva, along with Donnie and her sisters enjoyed the trip to Nelson, when they were able to make it. Many times, however, Dave's messages were pre-recorded and broadcast from the CKLN station every Sunday.

One Friday, Dave entered the studio at Trail.

"Good morning, Dave," Walter, the radio manager, said as he adjusted the mic.

"Good morning," Dave smiled.

"I received a letter from a pastor at Nelson. He said that at their business meeting it was unanimously decided to write to the CKLN radio station and express their appreciation to the Back to the Bible broadcast. Here," he handed Dave the letter.

Dave read. "There are many in the Nelson district who do not have the opportunity to attend church and the broadcast reaches them, and all who wish to listen, as it does not conflict with any church service in the city. On behalf of the evangelical church of Nelson, we thank you and hope it will be possible for this program to stay on the air. Yours truly, Pastor Erickson."

Dave looked up. "Praise the Lord for what He is doing."

The radio manager smiled. "So, I wrote Pastor Erickson back. This is what I said." He read from another letter. "Dear Mr. Erickson. Thank you very much for your letter regarding the Back to the Bible broadcasts, written on behalf of the members of your church. It is greatly appreciated, I assure you. I have sent a copy of the letter to Mr. Stewart, director of the broadcasts, who is responsible for Back to the Bible being on the air. As to keeping the programs on the air, that rests entirely with Mr. Stewart, and I am sure that while Canadian Broadcasting Corporation regulations do not permit him to ask for contributions (without special permission from the Corporation) it depends to a large extent on the financial support he is able to enlist. We, on our part, have extended to Mr. Stewart the privilege of our non-commercial rates, and shall do all we can to help him continue the broadcasts. With many thanks to yourself and your congregation, I am, yours very truly, Manager, CJAT."

June 1943

"What do you think?" Dave asked as he handed Melva a letter he had been working on. "This month's prayer letter." Melva took the letter.

"Dear Christian helpers,

"We wish to take this opportunity to thank all our friends who have been praying and so faithfully giving. We have undertaken the additional broadcast over CKLN Nelson, each Sunday evening from six-thirty to seven. We ask for your earnest prayers that God will establish the work there. We will do our best to keep you informed. In regard to sharing the gospel on CJAT, we give God all the glory for what has been accomplished since the program started January 18. Our policy has been to put the broadcasting fund before everything else. We are determined to not go in debt. We thank God for your enthusiastic response. Except for once, we have always met our responsibilities on the first of every week. It has been constantly on my heart, and I feel would be to God's glory, if rather than paying one week behind all the time, we could keep the account paid one week in advance. This is not a plea for money, but for prayer—so join us to this end. God has His mysterious ways of working and can (and has) provided the means for His work. However, God has ordained prayer as the way to get His provision. Yours sincerely, in broadcasting the gospel, A.D. Stewart."

Fathers' Day, Sunday, June 20, 1943

Melva found a parcel left on the step and handed it to Dave. "Look what it says," she smiled. "To my boy, from Mrs. Wilson." Dave opened it and lifted out a man's brand-new silk dress shirt, with a matching tie and two tie pins. One was engraved A.D.S.

"Oh Melva. This is good. The fruit of the gospel is incredibly good. It is indescribable how I feel every time a soul is saved. Mrs. Wilson is giving me a costly gift, like the woman in the Bible who poured ointment on Jesus. She is so grateful, but what can I say? It wasn't me who saved her husband, Hugh, but God! And He has done an amazing work in his life."

July 10, 1943

"I heard the program, Dave. The children did great!" Melva said. "It was a good idea to get children to sing on air!"

Dave kissed her. "I think they did great as well. Added something special to the program." Minutes later, the phone rang. "Hello? Yes, Dave Stewart here. Oh, I'm sorry you feel that way.

Goodbye." Dave hung up and shrugged. "Some woman complaining about us using expensive broadcast time for children."

Melva rested her hand on his shoulder. "Dave, Jesus said to let the little children come to Him and forbid them not."

Letters continued to pour in. Dave and Melva were delighted to get one like the following. "It was through Dave's understanding and patient explanation that I found Christ." Miriam Hollands

"Dear Dave, I was led through your sermon to give up tobacco. What a blessing I have received since." Henry Wood

July 11, 1943

A knock at the door sounded as the family sat at the table after supper. Melva answered it and greeted a young man holding a box of fruit.

"Hi, my name is Bill. Bill Shoemaker. I brought Alice some fruit." He smiled. "Of course, she can share it with the rest of you."

Melva smiled. "How nice of you. Won't you come in?" He nodded and set the box on the counter. It was full of apricots.

"I have cherries and plums in the car, too," he said. Dave held out his hand. "Thank you, Bill, I'm Dave." Bill shook his hand and glanced around the room. His eyes rested on Alice.

"Hi Alice," he said.

Alice smiled. "Hi."

"Well, won't you sit for a while?" Dave offered.

After bringing in another box of fruit and visiting for a couple of hours, Bill left. Alice stood by the window and watched him drive away.

"That was awkward. Glad he's gone," she said.

A week later, a parcel came in the mail for Alice from Bill. "What am I going to do with all of this?" Alice asked as she examined six yards of material. She looked at the tag. "It's from Scotland!" It was a heavy black and white checkered velvet. Included in the parcel was bright red lining, balls of cotton and wool, aprons, embroidery work, and yarn. "I know! If there's enough of this red yarn, I'll crochet a sweater for Donnie."

July 19, 1943

Doris stood at the door. "Sure you have everything?" Melva asked.

"Yes, I'm sure," Doris said as she gave her sister a quick hug. She was leaving to work at a Bible camp on Upper Arrow Lake.

"I've decided if I like teaching at the first ten-day girls camp, I might stay for the next two camps."

"Oh Doris! We might not see you for a whole month! Well, let the will of God be so," Alice said as they hugged.

"Are you sure you haven't changed your mind about coming with me?" Doris smiled at Alice.

"Love to, Doris, but Melva can't always play the piano, so this is where I need to be."

CHAPTER TWENTY-SIX

VICTORIOUS ONE

Monday, August 2, 1943

"Dear folks,

Gordon and Lena's wee one is due the first week of September. He and Dave are planning on going to Nelson on Saturday morning or Friday night and taking a tent and camping out till after our broadcast Sunday evening—of course that means us all—it might be nice, but I have my doubts about the camping excursion."

"Who are you writing?" Dave asked, leaning over Melva's shoulder.

"My parents," Melva said as she dipped her pen into the ink bottle.

"You may have to change those last lines. Gordon and I have decided to rent two cabins for the weekend at Kootenay Lake. That way you ladies have it a bit nicer."

Melva put her pen down. "Cabins? How lovely!"

Dave ran his hand through his hair. "But I hate to miss communion on Sunday."

"You have been working so hard, running to all the prayer meetings, and preaching all over Trail and Nelson, not to mention doing the daily broadcasts. You need a break, and a fishing trip is just the thing. Gordon has also worked hard in the ministry; it will be nice for him to have a break, too."

Dave smiled. "I hate to argue with you," he said, giving her a warm hug and a kiss.

August 6, 1943

"Ready?" Dave called to Melva. She grabbed Donnie's hat and a few last items and hurried to the car.

"Sure you don't want to come?" Melva asked Alice.

"No, but thanks anyway. I have things that I want to do here."

As they headed out of Trail, they sang a few familiar hymns.

"Isn't it beautiful today?" Dave said as they wound their way through the mountains. The sun shone between the clouds and Dave rolled down his window to take in the fresh mountain air. They headed north and after driving through Castlegar and Nelson, they arrived at Belfour Bay. As soon as Dave parked by the rental cabins, Melva took Donnie to the sandy beach. He grabbed handfuls of sand and giggled. Dave went to the lodge to pay and get the key.

Melva stood at the lake. *"This is so beautiful and peaceful, just the kind of break we all need, away from the constant calls and demands of the ministry."* She could see across the lake, which was long and narrow, much like an inlet. It looked like it was only a mile across. Minutes later, Dave returned with a key. The fresh smell of pine from the surrounding trees enveloped them. They entered the cabin. A table stood in the middle of the room with four chairs around it. In the corner stood a double bed and nightstand. The front room had a large window overlooking the path to the beach. A small kitchen occupied one corner and a chesterfield sat under the front picture window.

"This will do just wonderfully!" Melva proclaimed as she slipped baby bottles into the ice box.

Dave set his fishing gear on the floor. "Can't wait until Gordon gets here!"

"There'll be time for you two to go fishing tonight!" Melva replied.

"I'm going to see about the boat rental. I'll try to get one with an outboard motor," he said.

Melva put Donnie on a blanket and as she was putting her things away, Gordon and Lena pulled up to the cabin next door. A small path through the trees joined the cabins. Melva stepped out and took a deep breath of the fresh aroma. A breeze whistled through the trees and as she looked up, the swaying tops almost made her dizzy.

After a barbeque, the men climbed into the boat. Lena and Melva stood on the shore and watched.

"Bye, dear!" Dave yelled as he waved, a big smile on his face.

"Bye! Have fun and be careful!" Melva waved back.

"How about we sit on the lawn chairs by the shore?" Lena suggested.

"Great idea!" While they relaxed in the chairs, Donnie played on his blanket at their feet.

"How have you been feeling?" Melva asked.

Lena rested her hand on her large belly. "Pretty good. Can't complain. The baby is due the first week of September, so I've only a month left. Gordon and I are so excited. We watch the way you and Dave are with Donnie, and how cute he is, and that makes us very excited to have our own little one."

"Donnie is a blessing," Melva said as she scanned the rippling blue water. In the distance, they could see the small silhouette of the fishing boat.

A few hours later, the men pulled up and disembarked.

"Catch anything?" Lena asked, looking up from her knitting.

"Nope! Maybe tomorrow we'll have better luck," Gordon said.

"I was hoping for at least a trout, or even a largemouth bass or a Kokanee salmon, but not tonight," Dave said.

"Even perch or mountain whitefish would be fun to catch," Gordon said.

The families spent a pleasant evening roasting marshmallows around a campfire.

August 7, 1943

The next morning after a hearty breakfast, Dave put down his Bible and grabbed his tackle box. He stood at the cabin door.

"Goodbye, Melva," he called. Melva turned from clearing the table. She approached him.

"Goodbye, Dave. Have a good day fishing!" She kissed him. "Thank you for taking me on this trip, Dave. It is a break for me."

Dave smiled. "Yes, for me as well. All I can say is thanks be to God for His many mercies."

A few minutes later, Lena came over. The two women carried their lawn chairs outside and Melva put Donnie on a blanket. After an hour, it began to cloud over.

"Looks like rain," Lena said as she picked up her knitting and folded her lawn chair.

Melva looked at the sky. "Think you're right." She took Donnie from his blanket and invited Lena to her cabin. "We can visit there," Melva said, and within a few minutes, they were enjoying tea just as the first drops of rain splattered on the front window.

"Hope they come back soon. It's looking dark," Lena said, peering out the window.

An hour later heavy rain pelted the thin glass window. Melva looked up from feeding her chubby nine-month-old.

"It's getting worse. Wish they'd come back," Lena said, pacing the small cabin.

"Lena, we must be patient."

"But they've been gone two hours and it's been raining for at least one hour."

Melva's heart sank. *"I must release Dave to God, if the worst has happened."* She glanced at her rustic surroundings. The small cabin which was such a delight yesterday suddenly seemed cold and uninviting. Donnie whimpered and Melva's mind flipped back to the present.

"Time for your nap, my little man," she said, kissing his chubby cheek. She lifted him out of his highchair and laid him in his pram. Thunder crashed, and a sense of alarm hit Melva.

An hour later, Lena continued to worry. "I don't understand why they're not back," she said, her voice tight with strain. "Who would want to fish in a storm? Oh Melva! Something must have happened to them! What are we going to do?" Looking out the rain-drenched window, Melva could barely see the large waves crashing on the shore.

"Perhaps we should run to the lodge and talk to someone," Melva said.

"I'll go. You have to watch Donnie." Lena slipped on her coat and ran outside. Several minutes later, she returned, wet and shivering. "There were some people in the lodge," she said as she hung up her coat. "The manager said he would phone the police, and a man named Mr. Groutage offered to search for them. He owns a big boat with a motor and thinks he can make it through this storm. Says men from the prairies aren't used to the mountain squalls that appear out of the blue. I told him they left from here, Belfour Bay, around ten-thirty this morning. He figures, judging by the wind, and if they had any trouble with their motor, their boat probably drifted toward Queens or Pilot Bay. He is going out right now to look."

Melva breathed a sigh of relief, "Oh, thank You God."

"Both men belong to God, Lena. Let us rest in that fact, and that someone is searching for them. Besides praying, there's not much else we can do."

Two hours later the storm started to abate and Melva could see the beach from where only five-and-a-half hours ago their husbands had left. Had Dave taken his insulin before leaving? Did he have it in the boat? She looked in his travel bag and found a small glass bottle. Tears threatened to overwhelm her, but she wiped them away. *"I don't think he took it this morning. Maybe. He was just so excited. It's my fault, for not being stricter with him."*

It was four-fifteen in the afternoon. A knock rang through the cabin and Lena jumped to answer. A police officer stood there with a solemn expression.

"Gordon, my Gordon! Where is he?" Lena shouted. The officer pointed to a group of people on the beach.

"I just talked to Howard Groutage. He managed to rescue Gordon Ferguson from an upturned boat, and they just pulled up minutes before I got here," the police officer stated. Lena clapped her hands to her face and shrieked. She ran out the door.

"Mrs. Melva Stewart, I presume?" the officer said, turning to her.
"Yes?"

He pulled a card out of his wallet. "My name is Constable Hugh Lindsay from the Nelson detachment." He sighed and was momentarily speechless. "Is your husband Dave Stewart?"

"Yes."

"Ma'am, it is with my deepest sympathy that I regret to inform you that your husband drown today on the Kootenay."

Melva's mouth dropped. Instantly, a heaviness pierced her, numbing her arms and legs. Her heart pound. She peered at the lake. A small group huddled around the shore. Lena held her husband. Another police officer was wrapping a blanket around Gordon. Waves slapped against the sand and thin bands of sunlight pierced the clouds. The wind, so loud only minutes before, had quieted to a breeze. Donnie cooed.

"Oh Donnie," Melva cried, "your daddy has gone to heaven." Melva lifted Donnie and held him in a tight embrace, weeping. Dave's open Bible sat on the table. She clutched Donnie tighter and ran past the officer toward the beach. Tears blinded her. Her mind fought to remember Dave's words, his last words, any words, anything about him to hang on to. *"Melva, I need a supportive wife in ministry, won't be easy ... All I know for certain is that God's call on me is to preach the gospel... though He slay me, yet will I trust Him ... He is working this unflinching trust in me ..."* and his last words, *"Thanks be to God for His many mercies."* Melva sniffed. *"Mercies? Mercies? Is this what mercy looks like? What about me now?"* She wiped her tears. *"But God WAS merciful to Dave through out his life, and He WILL be merciful to me now, and everyday, the rest of my life."* Then, a realization dawned on her. *"Dave had a real sense of urgency; his whole life and message were centered on eternity."*

"Melva! Melva! Dave . . . is gone!" Lena blurted as she ran to Melva.
"I know."

"How could this happen! Oh Melva, where was God in this? Why didn't He save him? This can't be true! No! No! It just can't be! How could He allow His servant to die? Who will carry on the work?! Oh Melva . . . Donnie . . . is fatherless ..." Lena threw her arms around Melva and wept.

"Lena, Lena," Melva said. "Dave sang about heaven, talked about heaven, and now he is in heaven. I can not wish him back."

Lena covered her mouth and gasped. "Oh!" She ran wildly in a circle, and then to Gordon again, weeping uncontrollably.

As Melva watched wave after wave, a deep peace—a surreal peace—filled her. *"He has finished the work God had for him, … I… have not."* Her dress and hair blew in the breeze. *"Somewhere under that deep expanse is Dave. But not really. The real him I will see again."* She wiped her tears and stared across the water for how long, she did not know. Time lost all significance. Melva hardly knew that others had now surrounded her, embracing her, crying. Her mind focused on desperately trying to make sense of her new reality, to accept it as from God, and to sort through the life-changing ramifications. A searing pain and weight crushed her heart, seeking to sever her from her life-long faith. But the Savior stood by her, saturating her soul with wave after wave of comfort, soothing her broken heart with a healing balm that penetrated deeper than the tragedy. A thought stuck in her mind, *"Although I do not understand, one thing I have learned: God makes no mistakes."*

EPILOGUE

Melva was two months into her second pregnancy when the accident occurred. Her parents arrived in Trail on Monday, August 9, and the family left Trail for good Thursday morning, August 12, 1943. As noted in a letter from Mr. and Mrs. Woodrow: "We did hate to see you drive off from Bay Avenue Thursday morning. Of all those we have met in the past years of missionary work, we know of none who has become so dear to us as you."

At the end of October, Gordon Ferguson, who partially took Dave's place, held a studio presentation to honor Dave. People from all over Trail attended the meeting. The audience sat through one hour of Dave's recordings. The place was so packed that one girl fainted.

Melva lived with her family in Alberta and worked for a time at the phone office again. The Faith Mission finally paid her back three hundred dollars for the church. Records suggest Dave had made two payments of two hundred and fifty.

Melva delivered a healthy baby girl on March 30, 1944, in Calgary. She named her Ardith Darlene, not only because she liked the name, but because it had the same initials as her husband, A.D. Stewart. In 1949, Donald sold the farm by Langdon and bought another large farmhouse west of Olds, Alberta.

Although other men were interested in her, Melva never remarried, but put all her energy into raising Donnie and Ardith and helping her parents on their farm. Melva passed away quietly on November 17, 1974.

Melva and Dave's descendants and their spouses

Two children and spouses, five grandchildren and spouses, thirty-seven great grandchildren and ten spouses, fifteen great, great grandchildren and counting. "The LORD will destroy the house of the proud: but He will establish the border of the widow" (Proverbs 15:25).

Dave and Melva's children

Don (Donnie) Stewart married Dolores Fehr on October 16, 1965. They have five children.
Ardith Stewart married Ervin Wagner on May 22, 1980. He passed away on March 24, 1993. She married Bryon Seeley on November 9, 2012, and he passed away on June 27, 2013.

Melva's parents and siblings

Donald, father (1892–1977)
Hazel, mother (1891–1969)
Alice (1914-2009)—married Keith Lonie, a pastor in Alberta
Clara (1917-1975)—married Donald Rae; they farmed near Langdon
Doris (1919-1983)—never married and became a missionary in Nigeria with S.I.M.
Vera (1921-1983)—married Vince Newton, a professional painter from Calgary
Vern (1924-2017)—married Ruth Nafziger; they farmed west of Olds, Alberta

On September 8, 1943, Gordon Ferguson wrote the following to be read over CJAT:

Most of you have heard of the passing of brother Arthur David Stewart, and the rescue of myself from the icy waters of Kootenay Lake. Brother Stewart and I had each been carrying on radio work for the Lord over station CJAT in Trail. We felt the need of a well-earned rest over the weekend for ourselves and our wives. So we went to Kootenay Lake to spend a couple of days together. In everything God so marvelously worked, that not for one minute did we think His hand was not in it or that His frown of disapproval was upon us. On the other hand, I can see so clearly now that God had a purpose in it all. One of His servants had finished his ministry, had spent his all, giving even his health in his zeal for Christ. Like Enoch, he had this testimony, that he pleased God. So, God prepared to take him home. The other servant had need of some lessons, and how could the heavenly Father better teach that child, than to take him out upon the swelling boisterous waves of a turbulent mountain lake, with the elements raging above and around and 300 to 400 feet of icy water beneath chilling to the bone, until no strength remained and utter dependence upon God's infinite and loving mercy was not an alternative, but an only hope?

Thus, we look back and see how God led us out there, gave us a very happy time on Friday evening, and on Saturday morning especially blessing our hearts in times of reading and prayer. And then how He led brother Stewart and myself to go out in a boat at 10:30 on Saturday morning to try and catch some fish. How it was the wisdom and will of God that allowed one of those unpredictable mountain lake squalls to arise in a matter of minutes, resulting in the capsizing of our boat. Oh, the blessing of the divine presence from the very minute the waves began rising! Oh, the nearness of Jesus as earnest prayers ascended in His mighty name! Then the glory and thrill when the assurance came, even before the boat capsized, that I would be rescued. This assurance was as definite as the assurance of my salvation, and all through that ordeal it remained with me. Brother Stewart, on the other hand, seemed only to have an assurance of being in God's great hands! [Later, it was recorded that Dave had said, "My work is finished, but you will be rescued."] Not once did he say amen to my exclamations of our certain rescue. It was this that made me finally realize that he knew he was going home. Oh, how wondrous and complete was his confidence in God! No word of complaint or fear escaped his lips. He was practicing what he preached. We prayed and sang hymns together as we had often done in meetings and on the air. Brother Stewart would come out of each of those tossing waves singing. Had God taught this child of His nothing else, it would have been a profitable experience just to witness this glorified display of practical sanctification.

Each time the boat was tossed and turned over by the wind and the waves, more of our strength was lost until, after two hours in those icy waters it seemed we were completely exhausted. Then a huge ten-foot wave swept brother Stewart from the boat. Ordinarily, a man in this position would have struggled and cried out. This was not the case. For an unnatural period of time God held dear brother Dave up on the waters that I might catch a fleeting but glorious glimpse of his home going. His face bore a faint smile, but most of all, a look of serenity, blessing, and perfect peace. No words were spoken. One could feel the very presence of God and eternity. Finally, another great wave came over and dear brother Stewart was lost to sight but found to heaven! Now I found myself alone with God on the upturned boat. I was completely exhausted, so I just told my heavenly Father that I would surely go down if the boat went over once more. Faithful to His assurance, He kept the boat from turning over again. For three more hours, I clung to the boat. During that time, God spoke many things to my heart. He showed me how helpless and completely dependent on God is man. He showed how His power so far transcends the powers of all His creation. He showed me how trivial are things of earth and how looming and magnitudinous and near are those of eternity.

God has been burdening me to get out and give out and burn out for Him. My only desire is to win precious souls for Him. The poem says, "If thou wouldst work for God it must be now!"

A letter from Lena Ferguson, December 17, 1943

Dearest Melva,

I have never told you how sorry I am for the way I acted at the lake that Saturday. I realize I didn't make things any easier for you by breaking down the way I did and I've been sorry ever since that I didn't control myself. Not that I didn't try. I don't know what was wrong with me. May I blame it on my condition? At first I was afraid we had gotten out of the will of God by going out there in the first place and then when Gordon told us how gloriously Dave went home and seemed so sure that it was God's will, I felt bitter toward God for taking him. May He forgive me. I saw afterwards, though, how everything worked out for His glory.

In a article written by Earle Jarrett

When I was a younger, I was greatly impressed by a radio evangelist who was fully committed to the Lord's work. I was only to share his friendship for a short while as he lost his life in a tragic happening on Kootenay Lake. While fishing with a minister friend, a squall came up and their boat overturned. For several hours the two men clung to the boat and together they sang hymns to stimulate each other's faith. My friend, Dave, finally could hold on no longer and went down to a watery grave. The other minister was rescued and was therefore able to tell Dave's wife of her husband's last moments. She manifested great self-control and I heard her say, "Dave sang about heaven, talked about heaven, and now he is in heaven. I cannot wish him back." You might say that she was super-human, as she cheerfully went about caring for her two- year-old son and making little garments for another new life that shortly was to come into the world. I think if we believe God's promises and experience a daily walk with God, we can meet life's knocks with fortitude and courage.

George Robinson

George Robinson, who recommitted his life under Dave Stewart's ministry, married Inez, Melva's friend. He spoke on the *Sunrise Gospel Hour*, CFCN, from 1949–1953. He travelled with Youth for Christ and preached to thousands. In Taiwan, he was privileged to have an extensive audience with Madame and President Chiang Kai-Shek. He pastored churches in the United States and Canada and became a licensed alcohol and drug therapist. He received awards for outstanding services. (Source: George Robinson's obituary)

-A pamphlet of Dave Stewart's testimony is located on the Calgary Prophetic Bible Institute website, Early Students and Staff (aberhartfoundation.ca) Also, www.biblebillfoundation.ca

Permissions

Sermons excerpts, with permission from the Aberhart Foundation (www.aberhartfoundation.ca)

Dr. Marshall Morsey, sermon excerpts, *The Tower of Vision*, used by permission of The Harvester Mission

L. E. Maxwell's sermon excerpt, "The Cross and the Crown" (*Born Crucified*. L.E. Maxwell, 1945, Moody Press)

Some history taken from *Langdon through the Years*, 1880-987 (Langdon History Book Committee, 1987)

Other sources—six years of Melva's diaries, Dave's 1943 journal, Alice's 1943 diary, and many letters written to Dave and Melva

As Dave and Melva's granddaughter, I echo
the old familiar hymn with them:

Must I be carried to the skies
On flowery beds of ease
While others fought to win the prize
And sailed through bloody seas?

-Isaac Watts
Am I a Soldier of the Cross, Isaac Watts (1674-1748) public domain

Front row from left to right: Donald Dye, Alice, Clara, Vern, Hazel. Top row from left to right: Vera, Melva, Doris.

Verne and Melvia Dye

Donald and Hazel Dye

Dave and Melva Stewart

BACK TO THE BIBLE
CAMPAIGN
BY　　　　RADIO

OUTSTANDING	BIBLE LECTURER
CANADIAN	AND
FUNDAMENTALIST	GOSPEL SINGER

EVANGELIST A. D. STEWART

PLACE **CJAT - TRAIL, B.C.**

Commencing - - -

DATE **JAN. 18th and Each Week Day Morning**

7:30 to 8:00 a.m.　-　-　610 Kilo's

SLOGAN

"The Bible for Canada - Canada for the Bible"

It Will Do You Good, Be Sure To ▬▬▬

Tell Your Loved Ones

LARRY DODGE   A. D. STEWART

✦

EVANGELISTS

Christ Died for Our Sins . . . .

According to the Scriptures
1 Cor. 15

By Him all that believe
are justified from
ALL THINGS.

Acts 13: 38-39

• • • • •

Share with us in this work
of spreading the gospel
of Christ.

. *Evangelists* .

Larry Dodge

—AND—

Dave Stewart

2

*Outstanding
Fundamentalists*

INVITE YOU

To attend the
Gospel Meetings

*

now being held in

Delia.

EACH NIGHT

Old School House,

at 8 O'clock.

Come & Bring a Friend

An interesting program
in store for those
who attend,
with lively congregational
singing and special
vocal and instrumental
numbers.

* * *

Spend the evening with us

The Fellowship of Gospel Churches
Incorporated

God is faithful, by whom ye were
called unto the fellowship of His
Son Jesus Christ our Lord.
1 Cor. 1:9

Mr. K. Jardine
Chairman

Evangelist A. D. Stewart
Field Secretary

Rev. A. H. Muddle
Councillor

Dr. R. N. Thompson
General Secretary

A. D. STEWART
EVANGELIST

Dave Stewart

The Dye family in Iowa in front of their home, approx. 1908. Front row from left to right: Aunt Ruth, Uncle Lynn, Uncle Ruel, Aunt Muriel. Back row, left to right: Aunt Dorothy, Grandma Melvia, Aunt Nona, Grandpa Verne, Uncle Roger, Donald, (Melva's father)

Dave farming, preaching on CJAT, and with some friends

Melva Dye

Melva with Ardith and Donnie

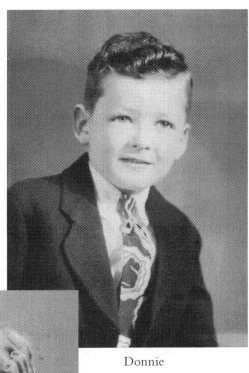

Donnie

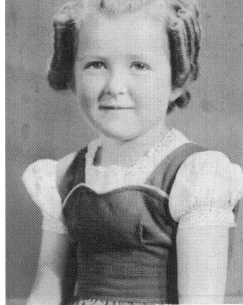

Ardith

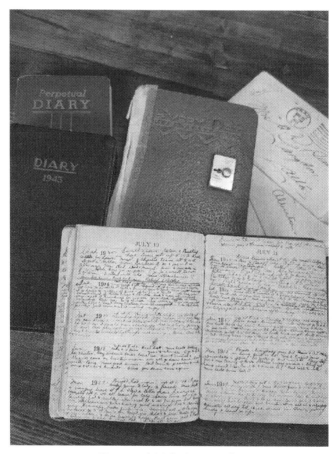

Dave and Melva's journals

Melva's wedding ring

The heirloom- Melvia's 137 year old perfume bottle
mentioned in the chapter, "Rob Williams."

Printed in the United States
by Baker & Taylor Publisher Services